CW01561655

THE RITUAL YEAR

Also by Kiera Chapman, Lulah Ellender,
Rebecca Warren and Rowan Jaines
from Granta Books:

Nature's Calendar: The British Year in 72 Seasons

THE RITUAL YEAR

A New Calendar of British Feasts, Festivals and Folklore

Kiera Chapman, Lulah Ellender
and Rebecca Warren

With line drawings by Rebecca Warren

GRANTA

Granta Publications, 12 Addison Avenue, London W11 4QR

First published in Great Britain by Granta Books, 2026

A CIP catalogue record for this book is
available from the British Library.

2 4 6 8 9 7 5 3 1

ISBN 978 1 80351 286 0 (hardback)
ISBN 978 1 80351 287 7 (ebook)

Typeset in Miller by Patty Rennie

Printed and bound by CPI Group (UK) Ltd,
Croydon, CR0 4YY

The manufacturer's authorised representative in the EU for product safety is BGC Sustainability & Compliance, 7 avenue du Général Leclerc, 75014 Paris, France (gpsr@baldwinglobalconsulting.com)

www.granta.com

[dedication]

Contents

APRIL

MAY

JUNE

JULY

NOVEMBER

DECEMBER

Note on Illustrations

It has been a privilege and a pleasure to illustrate this book, and I am grateful to my co-authors for allowing me the freedom to choose subjects which have seemed the most appropriate. Customs are, almost always, communal activities. Some involve hundreds or even thousands of people, while others require only a few, but they are all, by their very nature, 'activities'. From the outset, it was clear that to try to draw these events in their entirety would exceed the space available. I have, instead, focused upon a single item that seems to me to sum up, or to be the central focus of, each custom, to give a sense of what makes these traditions unusual and distinctive. In order to draw something, one has to observe it closely, and in doing so, I have been impressed by the sheer effort and attention to detail that people put into the celebration of their customs.

In illustrating the seventy-two entries, I was struck by how many of our customs involve food – usually bread or biscuits – or fire. Yet, the more I have thought about it, the more understandable this has seemed, for the sharing of food, warmth and light are perhaps at the heart of what it means to live in a communal society. I hope the drawings impart something of the flavour and feel of each of the fascinating traditions that make up this eclectic calendar of customs.

REBECCA WARREN

Ritual Locations

1 **Boys' Ploughing Match**
St Margaret's Hope
South Ronaldsay, Orkney
Mid-August

2 **Burning of the Clavie**
Burghead, Moray
11th January

3 **Years'end Oddfellow's Parade**
Newburgh, Fife
31 December

4 **Burry Man and Ferry Fair**
South Queensferry, Lothian
Second Friday of August

5 **Whuppity Scoorie Day**
Lanark, South Lanarkshire
1st March

6 **Selkirk Common Riding**
Selkirk, Scotland
Mid-June

7 **Appleby Horse Fair**
Appleby, Cumbria
Early June

8 **Egremont Crab Fair**
Egremont, Cumbria
Mid September

9 **Bradford Mela**
Bradford,West Yorkshire
Mid-July

10 **Pace-egg Plays**
Calder Valley, West Yorkshire
Good Friday

11 **Whitworth Rushcart**
Whitworth,Lancashire
Early September

12 **Haxey Hood Game**
Haxey, Lincolnshire
6th January

13 **Sheffield Carols**
Sheffield, Yorkshire
Mid-November– December

14 **Bawming the Thorn**
Appleton Thorn, Cheshire
Third Saturday in June

15 **Cheshire Soul-caking**
Antrobus, Cheshire
2nd November

16 **Laxton Jury Day**
Laxton, Nottinghamshire
25th November

17 **Bonsall Hen Races**
Bonsall, Derbyshire
First Saturday in August

18 **Penny Loaf Day**
Newark, Nottinghamshire
Sundat nearest 11th March

19 **Hare Pie Scramble and Bottle Kicking**
Hallaton, Leicestershire
Easter Monday

20 **Whittlesea Straw Bear**
Whittlesea, Cambridgeshire
First Saturday after Plough Sunday

21 **Hinckley Plough Bullockers**
Around Hinckley, Leicestershire
Monday after6th January

22 **Broughton Tin Can Band**
Broughton, Northamptonshire
Third Sunday in December

23 **Wroth Silver Ceremony**
Knightlow Hill, Ryton-on-Dunsmore, Warwickshire
11th November

24 **St Nicholas Night**
Alcester, Warwickshire
6th December

25 **Ras Beca**
Preseli Hills, Pembrokeshire
Mid-August

26 **Cheese Rolling**
Brockworth, Gloucestershire
Late May Bank Holiday

27 **LlansteffanMock Mayor**
Llansteffan, Camarthenshire
2nd August

28 **Election of the Deputy of the Cinque Port Liberty of Brightlingsea**
Brightingsea, Essex
Early December

29 **Levellers' Day**
Burford, Oxfordshire
17th May

30 **Knollys Rose Cerem**
All Hallows by the Tower
and Mansion House, Lon
Early June

31 **Hop Hoodening**
Canterbury, Kent
Mid-September

32 **Chulkhurst Dole**
Biddenden, Kent
Easter Monday

33 **Christmas Horse Pub Crossing**
Bucks Green, East Sussex

34 **Ebernoe Horn Fair**
Ebernoe, West Sussex
25th July

35 **Jack in the Green**
Hastings, East Sussex
1st May

36 **Lewes Bonfire Night**
Lewes, East Sussex

37 **Hunting of the Earl of Rone**
Combe Martin, Devon
Late May Bank Holiday

38 **Turning the Devil's S**
Shebbear, Devon
5th November

39 **Holsworthy Pretty M**
Holsworthy, Devon
Early July

40 **Honiton Hot Pennies**
Honiton, Devon
Tuesday after 19th July

41 **Bolster Day**
St Agnes, Cornwall
Early May

42 **Midsummer Eve Bon**
Redruth, Cornwall

SCOTLAND

ENGLAND

WALES

1 2 3 4 5 6 7 8 9 10 11 12 13 14 15 16 17 18 19 20 21 22 23 24 25 26 27 28 29 30 31 32 33 34 35 36 37 38 39 40 41 42

Introduction

It is a scene from the apocalypse: against the pitch-black winter's night a spectacular glow illuminates the sky above the unlit houses. Roofs and chimneys are silhouetted against billowing clouds of orange smoke, and fire appears to fill the crowded streets. For a time, it seems the town might be engulfed, but eventually the blaze resolves into a snake of flaming torches, uncoiling itself slowly to move between the buildings. And somewhere in the centre, between the flickering lines of fire and smoke, the dark shape of a Viking longship can be made out. Surrounded by people, it is being dragged to its destruction, its dragon-headed prow rearing high above the watchers below. A thousand marching figures, their faces lit up by flame, walk beside the ship until, reaching the open space where the climax of the festival will take place, it comes to a halt. For a moment, the longship is surrounded by a moving, wheeling mass of people, flames and fire, and then the first torch is thrown into its open hull. Others follow, sparks flying through the air, landing on the timber deck until the rigging catches light. Within minutes the boat is a conflagration, a firestorm, a blazing pyre. Fire is everywhere in Lerwick tonight, torches in the streets, flames in the sky – the town has become a festival of flickering light and heat.

Here, in the joyous exuberance of Shetland's Up Helly Aa celebrations, is traditional custom at its most raw and its most dynamic, bringing the town to a stop, filling the streets with people. It feels at once both ancient and modern, an annual gathering that draws a community together, welcomes strangers in, and faces outward into the darkness of the night, dazzling and proud.

The Ritual Year offers a chronological exploration of the British calendar year through a wealth of old and new customs that mark the changing seasons. The British Isles have a rich and intriguing calendar of traditional customs, feasts and festivals, and contemporary Britain is witnessing something of a renaissance of interest in these celebrations. Many of these appear to provide a reassuring connection with our deep past, a time often perceived, albeit erroneously, as stable and unchanging; one might say that the 'Merrie England' of the imagination has its apogee in pancake-tossing and cheese-rolling. Some of our customs do, indeed, have roots stretching far back in time, but many others have died out at some point in the past, only to be revived much later in forms that reflect current ideas and needs. In fact, the customary year has always been far more dynamic than we might imagine, reflecting not an unchanging version of British history, but one of gradual evolution, with interesting and unexpected links to the world beyond our shores. This process of change and assimilation has been reinforced by the widening of multicultural British society, which has introduced a range of vibrant new celebrations that light up and reshape our national calendar. So the calendar of British customs and traditions that we offer here, incorporating new celebrations alongside the old, is intended to reflect our contemporary society, demonstrating that the customs that we practise today can teach us not only about the past but also about our future.

In drawing up this collection of customs and festivals, we have had to grapple with the problem of defining a 'custom'. Traditional practices can range from the simple fashioning of a small cross out of rowan twigs to hang beside a door to the vast scale of a carnival parade or a fire festival, and this range in scale and form has defied simplistic definitions. In consequence, we have settled upon four loose rules in considering what constitutes a custom, concluding that the event or activity must have been in near-continuous practice for at least a generation – usually taken to be thirty years – and that it must have a more than purely commercial or legislative basis. Customs must also be linked to a particular location, be it a single site, town, region or even country. Of course, some of the customs we cover here are found in other settings too, but each entry focuses on the way in which something is practised in a particular place. And finally, customs require the repetition of actions and words, not necessarily exactly as they have been done before, but sufficiently closely to be identifiably 'the same' as previous iterations.

The long history of the British Isles means that many of our customs and traditions come out of the Christian tradition, and this influence will, necessarily, be seen throughout the book. Yet although we have intentionally avoided the major ceremonies of any religion, which are beyond the intention of this book, we have deliberately included a wide range of cultural beliefs and practices. Inevitably, the decision to include one culture's customs but to omit others may seem perfunctory or tokenistic, but we have tried to achieve a balance that allows us to include at least some of the many types of custom, whether large or small, ancient or modern, or based in different cultures or religions. And we hope that the entries on some of the customs that are local to specific areas will surprise readers by revealing links to a much wider world.

Geographically, we have included customs from across the British Isles, but we have excluded Northern Ireland, which has a unique culture that deserves more thorough treatment than space here allows. And we have sought to reflect the diversity of the British Isles as it is today, discarding any sense of cosy nationalism. We want to reclaim ideas of what it means to be 'British', rejecting the influence of jingoistic movements, and offering an alternative: a forward-thinking, inclusive interrogation of our traditions past and present.

Many of our customs have shared roots and themes – the celebratory use of fire and the presentation of folk or 'mumming' plays being particularly widespread. And many have drawn in other elements of 'folk celebration', such as Morris and Molly dancing, which have not, historically, been part of their practice, but which have become an important part of the festive atmosphere. This inclusivity, this openness to new influences, is perhaps what gives our traditional customs their resilience and attraction in a changing world.

Moreover, the ritual year, when seen in its entirety, reveals a cycle of traditional practices that still reflects the ancient rhythm of the solar year. And perhaps there is something in the seasonality of some of these events, in their connection to the cycle of the natural and agrarian year, that feels increasingly precious in an era of climate change. Many of the customs of January and February feature traditions associated with the start of the agricultural calendar, including new-year celebrations and plough blessings. These are followed by others that welcome the burgeoning of spring, or that impose dietary restrictions associated with Lent, concluding at Easter. May Day is celebrated across the country with a host of carnival traditions, and with revivals of the 'Celtic' festival of Beltane to mark the transition from spring to summer. May also witnesses Levellers Day, the first of several customs championing the rights and struggles of working people, before festivals renewing rushes in churches and dressing public wells with floral decorations take the year towards the midsummer solstice. There are numerous carnivals and fairs during the summer months, after which celebrations of the agricultural harvest lead us through the autumn. In October and November, the approach to winter is marked with bonfires and revelry, and perhaps an attempt to connect with the imagined world of spirits and lost souls. Christmas traditions, including carols, mumming plays and sword-dancing, dominate the end of the year, as people come together over the darkest days.

One of the striking developments in our modern ritual year has been a resurgence of interest in reimagined pre-Christian festivals. Linked to the movement of the Earth around the sun, the solstices of midsummer (21 June) and midwinter (21 December) and the equinoxes of autumn (around 23 September) and spring (around 21 March) have reappeared in the customary calendar through a variety of celebrations, including, most famously, the midsummer festival at Stonehenge in Wiltshire. To these have been added the older 'Gaelic' festivals of Samhuinn (around 31 October), Imbolc (around 1 February), Beltane (around 1 May) and Lughnasadh (around 1 August), which are today celebrated in such customs as Edinburgh's Samhuinn Fire Festival.

Many of the customs featured in this book are the descendants of practices that fell into abeyance and were later revived. The later nineteenth century, in particular, experienced a reawakening of interest in these vanishing traditions, especially those linked to the agricultural landscape. At a time of rapid industrialisation and urbanisation, this may have reflected a nostalgic desire for the imagined stability of the pre-industrial rural world. This period also saw the rise of early 'folklorists', who gathered barely remembered words and rituals from those who used to participate in them, before they were forgotten forever. In the twentieth century, the social dislocation that accompanied the two world wars further weakened the practice of traditional customs. And yet it seems that we have an abiding and unquenchable need for our rituals and traditions. Over the last sixty years many that had been abandoned have been resuscitated again, albeit often encouraged with a hefty dose of commercialisation.

Yet the popularity of many of today's customs, revived or otherwise, is curious. Why *do* we enjoy hurling ourselves down a steep hill in pursuit of a cheese? Or standing in the rain to watch a play involving St George, a knight and a devil? Much ink has been spilt analysing the role of custom and tradition in today's society, but for the purposes of this calendar it is worth simply saying that, despite the endless forms of entertainment now available to us electronically, it seems that participating in a shared experience, one that roots us to a place, that speaks of our past or gives us a sense of who we are and where we belong, is something that many people still value. The fact that many customs involve an element of the absurd also seems to appeal to us. So perhaps we just welcome the opportunity to laugh and be silly in company, when much in our lives is otherwise serious and consequential.

Of course, this should not blind us to the pressures facing our traditional customs. There are many that have ceased altogether, particularly following the arrival of the COVID-19 pandemic in 2020. Equally, widespread concerns about legal responsibility, health-and-safety legislation and the financial and social costs of public disorder have forced some customs to change. For example, in Edinburgh, the Samhuinn Fire Festival has been obliged to register as an official 'event' for which tickets must be sold and entry restricted, turning it from a vibrant custom into something more commercial. Meanwhile, the Gloucestershire Cheese Rolling was declared unsafe in 2009, although its popularity remains such that it has taken place 'unofficially' ever since.

In fact, traditional customs sometimes find themselves on the front line in the battle between our mutual responsibility for each other's welfare and our desire to indulge in practices that involve both fun and a measure of risk. In some cases, the stripping out of elements of mischief and misrule results in the sanitising of the experience, when perhaps part of the role of some traditions is that they push boundaries, ask questions of us, and force us to confront difficult ideas, either squarely or obliquely. Yet in other cases, the need for modification feels essential to avoid giving offence to groups of people who, in the past, were the target of discrimination or abuse. One such example is the now-unacceptable practice of 'blacking up' white faces in folk plays or on Morris sides. The great strength of our traditional customs is that they can and do change to suit the times.

As the calendar of our ritual year evolves, we also have to face up to the inevitable spectre of 'authenticity'. One line of argument suggests that changing certain aspects of some customs to suit our modern sensibilities risks losing the historical validity of the custom itself. And yet a closer examination of most 'ancient' customs often reveals a history of minor changes and adaptations. In fact, a search for 'authenticity' immediately begs the question of what we're trying to be authentic to, especially since detailed records of *how* customs were practised in the past rarely exist. We suggest that a custom is 'authentic' if it contains the essential components that identify it with its practice in the past. Beyond that, it is in the very nature of a practice that has been handed down through the generations that some elements will already have been adapted to suit the changing times and that they will adapt again to suit those to come. Our heritage of customs and rituals has already welcomed new cultures, new traditions and new standards of behaviour, some of which reflect our global, postcolonial status, while others show our increased awareness of the value of those communities that have been victimised or overlooked, as well as of their contributions to society. It is a tribute to our customs that they continue to evolve, mutate and survive.

In *The Ritual Year*, we invite you to join us on a joyous romp through an eclectic selection of intriguing, fascinating and downright bizarre traditional practices. Along the way we offer some thoughts on the deeper historical and religious influences that underpin the rhythm of the year. What emerges is a captivating story, full of insight into local communities and regional differences, while recognising the wider celebrations that bind us together as a society. It is a collection of traditions that encourages us all to reflect and to participate, honouring the past and welcoming in the future.

A Note on Dates

It might be thought that drawing up a calendar of customs would involve the creation of a simple list of dates and events. Not so! While some customs are indeed reliable and predictable, remaining loyal to a specific date, others are more slippery, sliding around from one date to another. Some of these peripatetic occasions, such as Easter and the Lunar New Year, rely on the moon to fix their timings, but others have been forced by the five-day working week to move to the weekend nearest their original date. And for yet others, it is the day and month which determine their date; at Honiton in Devon, for example, the town fair traditionally takes place on the first Tuesday after 19 July, whichever date that Tuesday falls upon.

To complicate the calendar further, many customs have no fixed date at all, occurring at different times depending on where they are being celebrated. The tradition of 'well dressing' at Tissington in Derbyshire, for example, takes place on Ascension Day (itself a movable date), but other villages dress their wells on dates throughout the summer.

Finally, some customs have stubbornly remained faithful to their original date, only to find themselves cut adrift from the event which gave birth to them. One such is the Burning of the Clavie at Burghead in Morayshire, which celebrates the arrival of the new year – but it does so on 11 January. The reason for this oddity is that the custom of clavie burning came into being before 1752. In that year, Britain adopted the Gregorian calendar in place of the older Julian calendar. The Gregorian calendar was eleven days ahead of the Julian, so the British calendar had to 'lose' eleven days in order to align itself with other countries that had long since adopted the Gregorian calendar, facilitating easier trade and travel and, perhaps most importantly, bringing the practice of its Christian festivals into line with those of the wider western Church.

To accommodate such complexities, we have chosen to 'fix' our customs *either* on the exact date when they take place (for example, the Christmas Horse Pub Crossing always takes place on 25 December) *or* in the middle of a longer period when they occur (for example, the Mari Lwyd takes place any time between early November and mid-January, so we've plumped for December). Perhaps most fluid of all, however, are the dates of those customs that are tied to the movable date of Easter, which can occur in the months of March, April or May. For these, we have had to place them in a plausible order relative to each other, although in some years, they will take place in a different month to that given here.

JANUARY

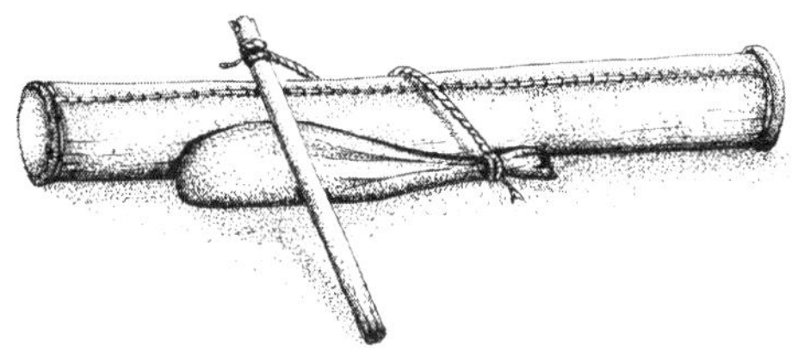

Haxey Hood Game

Haxey, Lincolnshire

6 JANUARY

Even the non-rugby fans among us feel the hairs on our arms stand up or a lump in the throat when we watch the New Zealand All Blacks' haka. This stirring pre-match ritual honours the country's indigenous Maori roots, telling the world, 'This is who we are. This is where we are from.' It connects the team's identity to a larger national story and allows players to psych themselves up for the game, to challenge and acknowledge their opponents and to prime their bodies for battle. Teams from Tonga, Fiji and Samoa perform similar ceremonial dances and chants before a match. These displays of strength, unity and aggression improve competitiveness and focus, but are also powerful ways of binding a team – and the wider community – in a shared endeavour.

While the Haxey Hood custom doesn't start with a war dance, we find similar elements of rousing song, physicality and a sense of belonging. Occurring on 6 January

(Old Christmas Day, or Epiphany), it is one of the most important days of the year for the Lincolnshire village of Haxey. The build-up starts on New Year's Eve, when a two-foot-long leather cylinder called the Sway Hood is taken from its display in one of the village pubs and carried around the area by a group of ten men in red jumpers known as the Boggans. As the hood makes its way round the local pubs, the group sing the traditional songs, 'Drink Old England Dry', 'John Barleycorn' and 'Farmer's Boy' as they collect donations for community causes.

Five days later, on 'Hood's Eve', the leader of the event, known as the Lord of the Hood, makes his wand – a staff made from thirteen willow withies, bound thirteen times. The Boggans make twelve canvas hoods. Around midday on 6 January, the Lord leads the Boggans and the Fool – a man dressed in colourful rags and patchwork trousers – to the Mowbray Stone, the remains of a medieval cross near the village church. Here, the Fool makes a speech to a large crowd of onlookers, explaining the rules of the game (no throwing or kicking the hood, and no running with it), and then leads the following chant:

Hoos agen hoos
Toon agen toon
If thou meets a man, knock 'im doon
But doan't 'ot 'im

House against house
Town against town
If you meet a man, knock him down
But don't hurt him
[this qualifying line is a later addition]

A pile of damp straw is lit behind the Fool, creating choking black smoke, before he leads the crowd to the field for the game. Suitably roused and energised by this shared chant (and plenty of ale), hundreds of men try to catch the hoods as the Lord throws them high into the air. The Boggans take up fielding positions, and if one of them gets a hood it has to be thrown back into the crowd. When all twelve canvas hoods have been caught, the Lord cries, 'Sway!' and launches the Sway Hood into the crowd. There are no formal teams or identifying kits, creating a chaotic mêlée, with rivalries based on proximity to one of the four village pubs. Like a vast rugby scrum, the 'sway' has to push the Hood to its chosen pub, where it's placed on the bar by the landlord or landlady to close the game. As the sway staggers and pushes, its members bellow out songs and have been known to knock down walls with the strength of their efforts. It is a boisterous performance of camaraderie and masculinity. It is anarchic and dangerous – and the locals love it.

The most common origin story for the game dates back to the fourteenth century. It goes like this. Lady de Mowbray was riding in a Haxey field on Old Christmas Day when a sudden gust of wind blew off her silk hood. A group of local farm workers raced to catch the hood, stumbling and competing with each other to be the heroic rescuer. One man managed to catch it but was too shy to give it to the Lady, so another man did the honour. The tale goes that she was so amused by the sight of them scrabbling and fighting that she decreed there should be an annual game to commemorate the event, in return for her donating thirteen strips of land to the village. The Fool represented the shy man, while the Boggans were the other peasant men.

The custom has evolved over the centuries. The Fool was traditionally 'smoked' by being suspended and swung over a large pile of burning straw, but, as one account rather nonchalantly describes it, this practice ended in the eighteenth century because 'the boggans had nearly suffocated a fool at Westwoodside, and had some difficulty in restoring him, [so] that part of the performance was dispensed with'.

Other accounts describe the Boggans singing for 'hot furmety' (a kind of boiled wheat or barley porridge) as well as money. Local families have long associations with the specific roles, but it is not only villagers who take part – unsuspecting visitors have also been known to be bundled into the sway, like a travelling salesman in the 1940s who was forced out of his car and had his keys thrown into the middle of the scrum.

Some offer a different origin story for this custom, taking James George Frazer's theory that many customs are relics of ancient ritual, and claiming it was a continuation of a magical practice related to sun worship. They argue that throwing the Sway Hood mimics the sun's arc as it passes through the sky; and there are similar folk practices recorded in France where people attempted to secure good weather for the coming year. According to this theory, the smoking of the Fool could be seen as the sacrifice of the past year's fertility in order to generate new growth.

But there are more persuasive explanations. Similar games took place in nearby Epworth and Belton, indicating a wider local practice unrelated to Lady de Mowbray's windswept hood. To understand this custom more deeply, we need to look at the geography and history of the area. This region, known as the 'Isle of Axholme', was fenland until Dutch engineers brought over by wealthy British landlords in the seventeenth century drained the marshes and began intensive farming. Suddenly, the places where people had just about been able to survive by shooting and fishing, and where they had gathered and played, were disappearing, leading to protests, physical attacks and even arson.

Folklorist Venetia Newall argues that the Haxey Hood game was 'a ritual perpetuation of the habitual disorder in the area', revealing how the troubled history of the place could have prompted a reassertion of the villagers' claim to the land and to their identity. 'Folk-football' games were not uncommon in pre-industrial England, often providing working-class and agrarian populations with an outlet for their anger at the enclosure of common land and an opportunity to express solidarity and pride in their local place, even if just for a day.

As historian Catriona Parratt notes, the centrality of Haxey's pubs, as well as the importance of the fields, the Mowbray Stone and songs sung during the game, demonstrates its local specificity. But the songs serve a more fundamental purpose too. Singing brings about changes in our respiration, hormones and circulation, releasing endorphins and engendering a sense of well-being. Music is an evolutionary adaptation that humans have developed over thousands of years to bond with each other and create a collective identity. Research shows that group singing is a fast way to create social bonds, even among large numbers of people. This is why the songs and anthems crowds bellow out before football or rugby matches and the stamping, grimacing and chanting of the haka are so effective. We are hard-wired to raise our voices together in a shared cause. Ultimately, the Haxey Hood custom is about the profoundly human need to stand together and mark time and place. No doubt the levels of testosterone in the village return to normal on 7 January, but the sense of community and uniqueness will remain.

LULAH ELLENDER

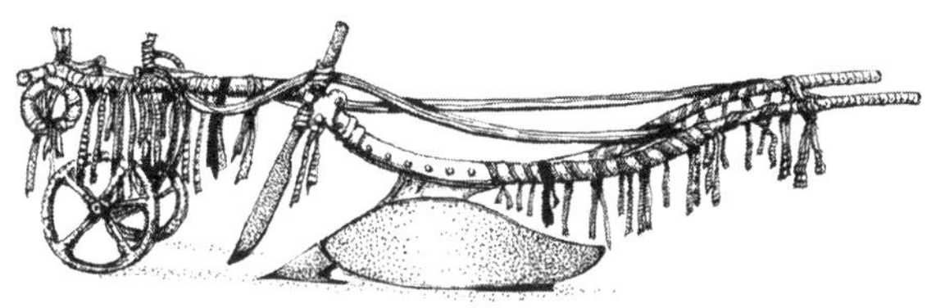

Hinckley Plough Bullockers

Leicestershire

MONDAY AFTER 6 JANUARY (PLOUGH MONDAY)

Hands up if you've ever ploughed a field. No? Well, don't worry – nor have the majority of the people who celebrate Plough Monday, including most of the residents of Sapcote, Stoney Stanton and Sharnford in south Leicestershire. But then, that's part of the charm of so many of our revived customs – they require neither in-depth knowledge nor personal experience of what is being celebrated. All that's needed is a willingness to step outside the norms of everyday life, to get involved, to muck in and, quite often, to briefly lay aside one's dignity. And the Plough Bullockers of Hinckley, a small settlement halfway between Leicester and Coventry, have certainly grasped these requirements with enthusiasm. In very early January, they dress up in black clothes decorated with coloured ribbons, sashes and handkerchiefs, to wheel an old horse plough, also festooned with ribbons, along the road from the little village of Sharnford on to Sapcote, and then on again to Stoney

Stanton. Along the way, they stop to dance outside several houses and pubs where, in customary tradition, they also 'partake of liquid refreshments'. To the untrained eye, the Bullockers look like traditional Morris men, but not so! They do not wear the usual jingling bells – or ruggles – of Morris sides, and their dances are more closely aligned to those of Molly dancers, a distinct if subtle difference seen again at the Whittlesea Straw Bear festival. that is seen again at the Whittlesea Straw Bear festival. Anyway, it's all in a good cause, for the Bullockers are out and about in the chill January air to celebrate Plough Monday, the traditional start of the agricultural year.

Plough Monday is the first Monday after Epiphany, or Twelfth Night, which is usually taken to be 6 January. In times gone by, Twelfth Night was often celebrated more boisterously than Christmas itself, marking the last of the twelve days of Christmas, when seasonal festivities came to an end and the cycle of back-breaking work on the land recommenced. Before returning to the fields, however, it was traditional for young plough boys, who led the horses or oxen up and down the fields, to take a decorated plough from house to house begging for money or small gifts. If nothing was offered, the unfortunate householder faced the prospect of having part of their property ploughed over in retribution. It was for this reason that the plough boys masked their faces with some kind of 'paint', to prevent recognition by future employers. The Hinckley Plough Bullockers keep up this custom, wearing scarlet face paint as a modern version of the red dye – or raddle – used by their predecessors to mark those sheep that were in lamb.

Plough Monday was firmly situated in the religious calendar of medieval parishes, although some scholars have suggested it may incorporate whispers of earlier pagan fertility customs that were brought into the Christian calendar during the conversion of Britain. We first catch sight of it in the written record in the early 1400s, a century before the Protestant Reformation, when parish churches were still filled with the smell of incense and beeswax, and lit by candles placed before numerous saints' altars. Many of these candles were funded by local guilds – groups of parishioners who shared a common interest. In some parishes, ploughmen formed their own guild to provide spiritual and financial services for each other at critical moments, and the income generated by the plough boys' antics may have helped to fund the not-inconsiderable cost of burning their guild's candle throughout the year.

After the Protestant Reformation, candles and guilds were abolished and the Plough Monday custom became more heavily focused on sociability. Some communities put on mumming plays, while others simply used it as an excuse to further overindulge in food and drink. In the nineteenth century, the Victorians helped to revive some of the Plough Monday traditions that were falling away, and memories of mumming plays were captured before being lost for good. One such example is the mumming play at Brattleby in Lincolnshire, during which the cast sing:

Good Master and Good Mistress, you sit around
the fire,
Remember us good plough boys that go through
muss and mire.
The mire is so very deep, the water is so clear,
Put what you like into our box, and a jug of your
best beer.

Today we have largely forgotten the importance of the plough, but for most of our history it was fundamental to the survival of communities, so much so that our traditional measure of land – the acre – derived from the Old English word *æcre*, meaning the amount of land an average yoke of oxen could plough in one day. Ploughmen were respected and valued members of society whose skills could mean the difference between feast and famine, but on their shoulders lay the responsibility for caring for the soil that went beyond its mere preparation for seed-sowing. Over winter, especially in the wetter areas of the country, ploughmen would turn the soil into high ridges to preserve it from seasonal saturation. Where summer drought was likely, especially in the eastern counties, these ridges had to be ploughed down again in spring to create wider, lower ridges less likely to dry out, while still allowing excess water to drain away on either side. Ploughing also reduced the spread of annual and perennial weeds, some land requiring almost constant cultivation before each year's crop was planted in order to give the germinating seed a chance to grow. Every three or four years, fields were left unplanted to regain their fertility – but this did not mean they were left entirely unworked during that fallow year. The plough could be busy then, too, helping to prevent excessive weed growth and spreading animal manure to enrich the exhausted soil. When the time came to bring these fallow fields back into cultivation, the plough was used yet again to bury grass and weeds, to return the soil to a usable, well-drained tilth and, in many cases, to re-form the necessary ridges.

In the later nineteenth century, farming became more mechanised. Underground land drainage was slowly introduced and larger machines were employed that were incompatible with the old, narrow ridge-and-furrow ploughing of previous centuries. Even so, the skills and competence of ploughmen remained an economic necessity. The cultivation processes that followed ploughing, especially the use of the new horse-drawn seed drill, relied upon the regularity and consistency of the furrows created by the plough. If these furrows were not exact, the mechanically sown seeds being dropped into them would miss their target and be eaten by birds. Moreover, cereals growing in irregular or uneven rows would remain on public view until after the crop had been harvested, a humiliating and lasting advertisement of a ploughman's weaknesses. It is hardly surprising that these men took pride in their work.

The custom of celebrating Plough Monday was most popular in the arable lands of the East Midlands and East Anglia, where some villages maintained a communal plough for use by those who did not possess their own. More recently, the celebrations have spread to other areas, and some parishes have revived the Victorian tradition of 'Plough Sunday', when tractors and ploughs are blessed – although these ceremonies often take place, understandably, *outside* the church. In one parish at least, buckets of soil are brought into the church for blessing, perhaps picking up on early medieval rituals for blessing the earth, and linking to Rogationtide processions, which blessed the land as they passed along parish boundaries around Easter.

Back in south-west Leicestershire, the Hinckley Plough Bullockers resuscitated the Plough Monday tradition in 1986, after an absence of roughly eighty years. Braving whatever weather the winter is throwing at them, they drag their brightly decorated plough along the lanes from Sharnford to Sapcote and on to Stoney Stanton, dodging the cars and cheerfully disobeying the road signs. Periodically, in time-honoured tradition, they sing out, 'Higham on the hill, Stoke in the vale, Wyken for buttermilk, Hinckley for ale!' and 'God speed the plough!'

The procession is a convivial affair, and a cheerful one, on a dark January day. And perhaps, in this age of internet-enabled, multi-horsepower tractors, it is good to be reminded that with or without sophisticated technology, we still depend upon the age-old practice of cultivating the soil to provide us with our daily bread.

REBECCA WARREN

Whittlesea Straw Bear

Whittlesea, Cambridgeshire

FIRST SATURDAY AFTER PLOUGH MONDAY

Humans first settled down to farm the land sometime between the late Neolithic and the early Bronze Age, around 4500 bce to 2500 bce. With this development, a shared early language may have emerged, which linguistic historians call 'Proto-Indo-European', or pie for short. Many modern European words are derived from pie. For example, the pie word for 'bear' was something like *rktho* (pronounced 'uktho'). This is the origin of a group of words for bears that survive today: the French word *ours*, the Latin *ursus*, the ancient Greek *arktos*, and our English word, 'ursine'. But what attitudes towards the bear did *rktho* signify? We can glean a clue from its relationship to a related Sanskrit word, *rakshas*, which means 'harm'. This creature was, after all, a destructive force, capable of lethal violence – so its name signals danger.

Some northern European languages, however, use a very different group of words for the same creature: in English we have 'bear'; in German, *bär*. Another painstaking linguistic reconstruction suggests that these derive from a very different PIE word: *bher*, meaning 'brown'. So while one group of languages stuck with words for the bear derived from *rktho*, another switched to *bher*. What lay behind this change? Some scholars think that in the cold north, encounters with these animals were more common. They hypothesise that this led to a prohibition against naming this creature, so that the word *rktho* became taboo. The bear became the animal-that-could-not-be-named, and a euphemism was born: 'bear', meaning 'the brown one'.

If this theory is correct, then bears may have had a special role in the belief systems of our ancestors. They may well have been creatures that were both revered and feared, making them a repository of folk beliefs. This significance may echo down to the present day, in the shape of one of our oldest and strangest rituals: the straw bear.

Today, on a cold Saturday in January, a dancing figure dressed in a straw costume that somewhat resembles a bear forms the heart of a motley procession of musicians and dancers who parade around the streets of Whittlesea, a small Fenland market town in East Anglia. On the Sunday after the parade, the bear is ritually burned. Crowds of onlookers will gather to watch as the effigy is mounted on a straw frame, its dry stems kindling quickly to the flame. The ritual fell into abeyance in the early twentieth century. It was originally a Plough Monday festival (see 'Hinkley Plough Bullockers'), but when it was revived, like so many other customs, it was moved to the weekend.

Similar customs survive across Germany, the Czech Republic and Poland. Folklorist Roslyn Frank is convinced that they have a shared and unimaginably early origin, reflecting the 'pan-European cosmogeny' of a hunter-gatherer society that feared bears, but also believed that humans were descended from these animals. Frank links straw-bear customs both to the bear taboo and to a figure called the 'the Bear's Son', who was half-man, half-bear, and gave rise to a host of ceremonial performances, including ritualised bear hunts and 'good-luck visits'. A representative of the Bear's Son, she explains, would stop by houses in the winter to help get rid of physical or spiritual sickness, or in response to an outbreak of disease. The custom, she thinks, later developed into a parade in which a bear figure covered in straw was accompanied around a small town or village by a number of people playing music and wearing bells – which is very like what happens in Whittlesea today.

The performers around the bear include 'Molly' sides, who represent a distinctive style of folk dancing from the east of England. The Molly style of dancing was often described as rough, wild, and even slightly intimidating, with those who refused to give a donation to the performers sometimes subjected to humiliating punishments. Performers wore outlandishcostumes designed to conceal the identity of the wearer: hunch-backed outfits, colourful clothing and animal masks abounded. One 1851 account records people 'dressed and beribboned in a most grotesque fashion to represent various beings, human or otherwise'. If Morris was an airy, leaping, summer dance form, Molly was its dark, mad and drunken winter twin.

At the heart of Molly dancing is the practice of cross-dressing: at least one of the all-male party, and sometimes several members, dress up as women and mimic female behaviour. This opens an intriguing possibility: that Molly may have been frowned upon not simply because it was a 'cadging' custom, but because it reflects a distinctly 'queer' folk tradition. We started this piece with the prohibition surrounding the old pie word for bears, and we here reach a second act of linguistic euphemism: the word 'Molly' was an eighteenth-century word for 'gay', and 'Molly houses' were meeting places for a gay male subculture centring on gender-subversive activities. In 1726, Margaret Clap was tried at the Old Bailey for keeping one such establishment, with an informant providing a colourful account of what went on there:

> Sometimes they would sit on one another's Laps, kissing in a lewd Manner, and using their Hands indecently. Then they would get up, Dance, and make Curtsies and mimick the voices of Women – O, Fie, Sir! – Pray, Sir! – Dear Sir! Lord how can you serve me so? – I swear I'll cry out. – You're a wicked Devil. – And you're a bold Face. – Eh ye little dear Toad! Come, buss! – Then they'd hug, and play, and toy, and go out by Couples into another Room on the same Floor, to be marry'd, as they call'd it.

The word 'Molly' was not applied to folk dance until the 1860s, but the associations of the word may suggest something subversive about the play with gender conventions in this performance. Recent folk performers, musicians and scholars have begun to draw attention to a buried LGBTQ history in popular songs and rituals. Bristol's Molly No-Mates troupe dance as drag kings, extending and revivifying this dance tradition in a way that celebrates non-cis participation. The 'Queer Folk' project, run by Sophie Crawford and George Sansome, draws attention to gay lyrics in folk songs that have hitherto been ignored, while new musical collectives such as Scotland's Bogha-frois are gathering gay and non-binary performers to play this music. There is a growing awareness, then, that folk culture has long contained representations of a historical LGBTQ community.

The old tradition of blackening the face during Molly dancing raises questions of racial inclusivity, too. (For a more detailed discussion, see the entry 'Adderbury Morris Men Day of Dance'.) Defenders of the practice argue that it is a form of disguise against human and supernatural beings, or even a symbol of good luck and fertility rather than a signifier of dark, demonic forces. But another etymological slide might give us reason to pause. The word 'Morris' may itself derive from the terms 'Moorish' and 'Morisco', both of which refer to the Muslim culture of North Africa that ruled much of the Iberian Peninsula during the Middle Ages. Of course, this linguistic chain of equivalence may have been a later development, reflecting the reinterpretation through a racialised lens of an earlier tradition that had nothing to do with race. After all, the way that race is interpreted is not set in stone, but changes over time, so the link between 'Morris' and 'Moorish' might not have had negative connotations before the early modern period.

However, it is undeniably the case that from the 1600s onwards, racism *was* used to justify and develop a system of chattel slavery and colonialism, leading to denigratory representations of the black community, including black-faced 'entertainments' like minstrel shows. While this may all have happened after the origins of Morris, the historical trauma it involved inevitably inflects the ways that face-blackening is interpreted by audiences in our own era. Fortunately, many dance sides are adapting the tradition creatively: instead of blacking up, Fenland side Pig Dyke Molly, who perform at the Whittlesea custom, wear striking black-and-white makeup.

The straw bear is surrounded by a sense not only of the power of words, but also of their euphemistic ability to navigate taboo. Whether it's the shift from *rktho* to 'bear', the use of the word 'Molly' to signify an illegal eighteenth-century gay subculture, or the slippage between 'Morris', 'Moorish' and 'Morisco' that calls attention to the racialised history of this dance, this festival reminds us that diversity is a long-standing element in our living, ever-evolving popular history.

As the straw figure dances its way through Whittlesea's streets, this potentially ancient festival thumbs its nose at an understanding of folklore that is white and heteronormative. Perhaps, then, it's time for this restricted understanding of our popular past to exit the scene – pursued, of course, by a bear.

KIERA CHAPMAN

Burning of the Clavie

Burghead, Moray

11 JANUARY

There's something about a fire that brings people together; it creates an intimacy, drawing us into a world of light and warmth. Firelight in the darkness encourages affinity; feelings are shared and connections made more easily than in the daylight. Yet even in the day, fire creates a focus around which we gather; we add material to a bonfire, stamp out escaping sparks, or just move in close to enjoy the heat. Despite its obvious danger, fire attracts.

It's not surprising, then, that so many customs, especially in the cold months of winter, involve fire – and that's certainly the case in Burghead on the north-east coast of Scotland, where the new year is greeted with the annual custom of Burning the Clavie.

Burghead lies on a small promontory overlooking the Moray Firth. The current town was constructed after 1805, but it was built over an early-medieval Pictish fort, or broch, much of which was unfortunately destroyed during the later building work. Some of the original ramparts remain, however, including a high point named Doorie Hill.

On 11 January, many of the inhabitants of Burghead, known locally as Brochers, celebrate the new year by carrying a burning half-barrel, or clavie, on a pole through the streets of the town. On the way, a few important residents, including the local publicans, are given a piece of still-smoking clavie wood to bring them good luck throughout the year. Once the procession has reached the summit of Doorie Hill, extra fuel is thrown up onto the clavie to produce a spectacular blaze, before the whole thing bursts apart, collapsing onto the hilltop and spreading flames and sparks across the grass.

It's easy to see the attraction of the event: in the dark days of January, it brings the town together for a convivial and sometimes riotous evening of company and entertainment. Once the blazing clavie has reached the hill, the uncontrolled fire that erupts from it imparts a palpable feeling of excitement and danger, and as the flames lick across the grass, dark figures can be seen haunting their edges, defying the intense heat to secure fragments of burnt-out wood.

But why are they doing this on 11 January? Well, back in the eighteenth century, the Brochers chose to continue to welcome in the new year on the day after 31 December, regardless of the fact that with the change to the Gregorian calendar, that day had been re-dated as 11 January. And, showing a commendable adherence to ancient tradition, they have continued to burn the clavie in Burghead on 11 January ever since.

REBECCA WARREN

Burns Night

Scotland and beyond

25 JANUARY

Comedian Craig Ferguson calls haggis 'a hotdog with a bad publicist'. He's not wrong: grabbing a bundle of sheep innards, mixing them with suet and spices and boiling the whole thing inside a stomach might sound deeply unappetising, but it's not that different to the more familiar sausage. Whether you're repulsed or intrigued by this most Scottish of foodstuffs, however, it is undeniably the centrepiece of Burns Night, the 25 January celebration to honour Scotland's national bard, Robert Burns.

Burns Night suppers began in 1801, five years after the death of the poet. Burns was known for his love of dinners with recitations of verse and light-hearted toasts, so his friend, the Reverend Hamilton Paul, decided to commemorate his birthday with a meal at the house where he had been born. The format Paul established proved contagiously convivial, drawing on wider traditions of formal masonic celebration and the more fluid culture of the gentlemen's clubs, which allowed sociability to be extended across class and political divides. Today, it is celebrated around the world: the University of Glasgow keeps a global map of contemporary Burns suppers, listing festivities not only across Europe but as far afield as Sierra Leone, Riyadh and Hawaii. In 2009, on the 250th anniversary of Burns's birth, some nine million people worldwide celebrated Burns Night.

Traditionally, guests arrive at a Burns Supper accompanied by the sound of Scottish music – more up-market events may hire a live piper for the occasion. Once they have been seated and welcomed by their host for the evening, they say the simple 'Selkirk Grace'. Like much of Burns's poetry, it is written in a light form of Scots, one of Scotland's regional languages:

> Some hae meat an canna eat,
> And some wad eat that want it;
> But we hae meat, and we can eat,
> And sae the Lord be thankit.

After a soup course comes the main event: the haggis, which should ideally arrive to the sound of bagpipes. Before it can be eaten, however, the knife that will cut it must be sharpened and Burns's 'Address to a Haggis' recited, eulogising this 'Great Chieftain o' the Puddin-race!' The Address criticises those who eat fancier food, like fricassees and French ragouts, contrasting them unfavourably with the hale and hearty demeanour of the haggis-fed rustic.

Dessert is followed by a mixture of entertainment – often a singer or a musician – and a series of speeches with toasts, including one to Burns's immortal memory. Later comes the 'Toast to the Lassies', a speech on the state of women that praises those present. But this is no one-way conversation: the women get a chance to respond in the 'Reply to the Laddies', firmly rebutting any libels that might have been uttered against their sex. Songs and poetry recitals then follow, until the evening closes with the singing of 'Auld Lang Syne', the words to which are by Burns, though the tune is an older Scottish folk song.

While the format has remained largely the same, the organisation and politics of the Burns Night supper have changed over time. By the early twentieth century, there were complaints that the dinners had become a stultifyingly respectable establishment ritual, a kind of Scottish 'kitsch' that missed the point of Burns's earthy poetry. Leading the detractors was fellow poet Hugh MacDiarmid, whose long poem *A Drunk Man Looks at the Thistle* (1926) voices appalled disapproval at what he saw as an ignorant, sentimental reverence for a poet whom few of those attending had either read or understood. Modern readers may be troubled by MacDiarmid's attitude to race: the poem's narrator criticises what he perceives as the 'inauthenticity' of communities holding Burns suppers in Timbuktu and Baghdad, and, still worse, ridicules the accent of an imaginary Chinese participant, who is depicted praising the haggis in a horrible caricature of pidgin English.

Yet those who lay claim to this custom to promote an exclusionary concept of Scottish identity and culture have a tendency to come to grief on the rocks of history. As Clark McGinn has commented, Burns Night was celebrated in

Sunderland before it was commemorated in Paisley, in Oxford before Kilmarnock, and in Tasmania before Irvine. At its core, the Burns Supper enacts an anti-puritanical commitment to conviviality, sociability and wit in a manner that is politically, socially and geographically flexible. After all, while Burns's voice consistently speaks from the margins in class terms, he was surprisingly promiscuous in his political associations. At times, he could espouse a Tory loyalism, but on other occasions, he supported a radical republicanism; in 1792, the year of the French Revolution, he got into trouble with his employers for singing the *sans-culottes* anthem '*Ça Ira*' in a Dumfries theatre. There is legitimate evidence, then, for both the political left and the political right to claim the Scottish bard as their own.

Consequently, from its inception onwards, Burns Night has been celebrated in politically contradictory ways. In the 1820s, one group of weavers expressed their dislike of the government by refusing to drink any alcohol and eating only bread and cheese during their Burns Supper, refusing to swell the coffers of the Treasury by consuming anything that was taxed, while also emphasising the poet's working-class credentials. At the opposite end of the spectrum, the Burns Festival of 1844 in Ayr was sponsored by aristocratic Scottish Tories and was intended to display the loyalty of the working classes and the military to the British government, while also advertising the greatness of the British Empire. It incorporated a large procession, in which tens of thousands of people marched under the flag of the Union Jack. In more recent years, Burns has been celebrated by both independence-seeking Scottish nationalists and by unionists who want to retain close ties with the rest of the UK. In 2018, in the wake of Brexit, the

British Prime Minister Theresa May held a Burns Night supper to demonstrate her commitment to the union, though the effect was somewhat diminished by a social media post that misspelled the names of five of the Scottish guests and the Scottish Whisky Association. Meanwhile, the Scottish National Party (SNP) holds annual celebrations that portray Burns as a figure who supported an independent Scotland.

This mercurial political quality also allows the custom to become a scene of creative cultural reinvention. The charity Glasgow Afghan United organises a celebration in which Burns is honoured alongside Molānā Jalāl ad-Dīn Muḥammad Rūmī, the Afghan poet better known as Rumi. By establishing a multicultural dialogue between these two powerful literary figures, the event recognises both the importance of Scottish heritage and the enriching presence of new communities. Speeches about the messages and meanings of the two poets intersect, highlighting resonances between their work, with Scottish folk songs followed by renditions of Rumi's 'Listen to the Reed'. The food, too, is multicultural: guests at this multicultural Burns supper enjoy a hot and fragrant biryani alongside the much-maligned haggis.

KIERA CHAPMAN

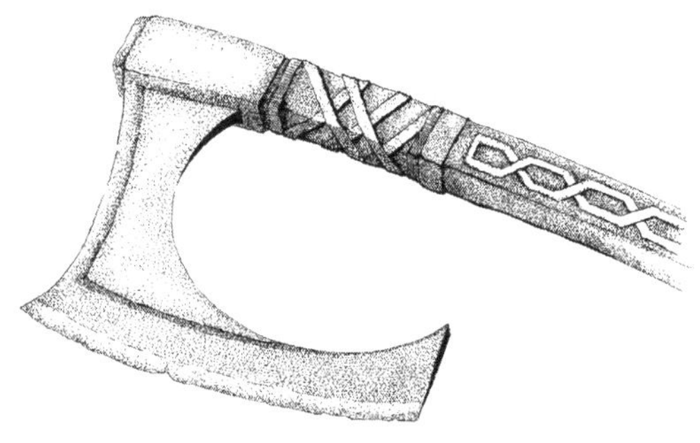

Up Helly Aa

Lerwick, Shetland

LAST TUESDAY OF JANUARY

My son recently took a DNA test, curious to trace his roots as far back as possible. He was disappointed when the results showed scant Norse heritage. Of all the diverse peoples he could have been connected to, it was the Vikings who held the most allure. It is not surprising – this culture is vividly depicted in blockbuster TV shows, Lego sets, fancy dress and video games. We can all conjure images of horned helmets and hairy men setting sail over strange seas. And its powerful narrative is at the heart of the Up Helly Aa fire festival in Lerwick, Shetland.

Held on the last Tuesday in January, Up Helly Aa is the largest of the Shetland Isles' twelve fire festivals. The festival itself lasts for twenty-four hours, but the preparations take months, with locals creating their costumes, making torches and building the Viking galley (longship) that forms the centrepiece of the event. The day starts with the Jarl Squad (a group of Vikings led by the leader, known as Guizer Jarl) wolfing down a hearty breakfast and then marching around the town, visiting the town hall, two primary schools, the hospital and the museum. They stop to view the Bill, a large decree displaying instructions, satirical jokes and artwork that have been kept secret until the big day. The children's Junior procession marches next, with its 'peerie galley', a smaller ship the youngsters then burn. Finally, at around 7 p.m., the blast of a maroon (a loud firework) summons the other forty-six squads made up of people in various non-Viking costumes and carrying 900 flaming torches. With the Guizer Jarl and his Jarls at the helm, the galley is led past thousands of spectators to the burning site. No members of the public or press are allowed into this part of the event.

For the festival finale, the squads process in circles around the galley before throwing their burning torches on to it, creating a huge blaze that lights up the town. When the burning is done, the squads make their way to various halls and venues where they put on shows, drink and make merry with friends, family and visitors. The next morning, tired, fuzzy-headed and soot-blackened, they make their way home.

Up Helly Aa is an important day for Lerwick, not just for the tourist revenue it generates, but because it brings the community together at the end of winter. The fire is a defiant marker of survival after the long, hard, dark season, and a roar of relief that the days are getting lighter. But today's ritual has surprising origins that have less to do with Vikings than we might think.

The fire festivals in Lerwick date back to the 1820s, when soldiers returning from the Napoleonic Wars with a taste for gunpowder began a rowdy annual Yuletide celebration that involved drinking, smashing windows and leaving dynamite on people's doorsteps. Later, they pulled burning tar barrels through the streets, often fighting among themselves and clashing with the police. These unruly celebrations gradually became more organised, featuring processions, disguises and performances. In 1874 the tar barrels were banned, and from 1881 people began carrying torches. These first iterations of the Up Helly Aa festival didn't involve Vikings at all. The Viking element, which came to define the custom, was largely introduced in the late nineteenth century by Shetland poet and teacher J. J. Haldane Burgess, who had a particular penchant for the Vikings. He was also a Marxist and saw the Vikings as freedom fighters – a characteristic that appealed to local people who wanted to rebel against British imperial culture and create their own distinct identity.

Haldane wrote the 'Up Helly Aa' song that now kicks off the celebrations, developed the role of Guizer Jarl and the Viking costumes, and invoked a Norse warrior history to give the festival a unifying spirit of resistance and the reclamation of public spaces. The first squads of Vikings began marching in the 1920s, and the pageantry remained unchanged until 2023, when women were allowed into the Jarl Squad for the first time. In 2015, a smaller South Mainland Up Helly Aa festival had appointed a female Guizer Jarl, but it took longer for Lerwick to accept the demands for equality.

*

Viking societies were predicated upon exploration and seafaring. The did not comprise a coherent race or nation, but were united by the shared Norse language (albeit with different dialects) as well as common customs. Their way of life defined their collective name, which probably comes from a verb, *vikingr*, meaning to go on a raid or expedition. It has been argued that Vikings were no more violent than other contemporaneous groups, and accounts of barbaric ritual torture have been dismissed by many historians. They fought well in small groups (like Lerwick's squads), where they could surprise their targets and make use of their nautical prowess, but they were less successful in large-scale conflicts. They also had a proto-democratic system known as the *Althing*, through which disputes were resolved and in which women could take part in consensus-based decision-making.

Haldane Burgess's personal interest in the Vikings may account for some of the later details of the fire festival, but the gusto with which the Shetlanders embraced these elements (and continue to celebrate them) suggests a more widespread identification with the Norse warriors. The islands are only 200 miles from the western coast of Norway, so there is a clear geographical connection. Viking settlers displaced the Picts in Shetland from the ninth century up until 1469, when the islands were sold to Scotland by a Scandinavian king to settle a debt. DNA tests on Shetlanders show they have only around 20 per cent Norwegian ancestry, with most of the rest being Scottish. But it is easy to see why this remote, hardy community would look to a warrior elite for inspiration. The Up Helly Aa fire festival is as much about who gets to write and perform the narrative of identity as it is about shared heritage.

Perhaps the historical facts are not what matters here; it is more about the symbolism and story we tell ourselves to construct our identity, drawing on elements of the past to make sense of our present.

LULAH ELLENDER

FEBRUARY

Candlemas and the Blessing of the Throats

St Etheldreda's Church, London

2 AND 3 FEBRUARY

If Candlemas Day be fair and bright,
Winter will have another flight.
If Candlemas Day brings cloud and rain,
Winter will not come again.

There was an old belief that on 2 February, at Candlemas, hibernating animals woke up to check the weather. If it was fine and clear, they would roll over and go back to sleep, knowing that winter was not yet over. If, however, the day was dreary and wet, they would (somewhat reluctantly, one might imagine) get up and head outside, assured that spring had finally arrived. And so, in weather lore, it is a date which looks both back to the past and forward to the future.

The same might be said, too, of Candlemas in the Christian calendar, where it looked back to the day of Christ's birth in December by marking the day of Mary's purification forty days later, but also forward to the future, by celebrating the public presentation of Jesus at the Temple in Jerusalem. In the medieval church, this presentation was widely observed by the blessing of candles, which symbolised Christ bringing light into the world. In many communities, these candles were carried in procession through the parish, before being brought back into the church to be used for prayer and for decoration. Eventually, they would be taken home by parishioners, where they were especially valued at times of illness or even when approaching death, as symbols of divine blessing.

The Reformation stripped away many of the old religious festivals, including the celebration of Candlemas in parish churches. Yet the desire for marking this point in the year with light and warmth did not entirely vanish, and candles continued to be displayed in people's homes. In some parts of Wales, this used to be accompanied by carols, a practice that lasted in some areas until the late eighteenth century. Why these communities clung on to the tradition of Candlemas later than others is unclear, but it may have been due to its near conjunction with St Brigid's day on 1 February, bringing together two popular traditions of early spring festivals centred around the 'mother' figures of Mary and Saint Brigid.

Yet Candlemas had an important role in the secular calendar too. By early February the days seem to be lengthening appreciably, and so Candlemas marked the date when employers across the textile and leather industries deemed that sufficient daylight had returned to make it unnecessary to provide expensive candlelight for their indoor workers.

By the nineteenth century, Candlemas had largely fallen out of our national calendar, yet more recently it has begun to re-emerge as a festival within the Church of England. On 1 February at Ripon in Yorkshire, for example, the cathedral is lit up by thousands of candles, and a candle-lit procession takes place within the building during the Eucharist.

In the Catholic church, Candlemas has always been a day of celebration, and at St Etheldreda's Catholic church in London, a further use is found for the candles that accompany the festival. On 3 February – St Blaise's Day – an intriguing custom known as the Blessing of the Throats takes place. This brief ceremony draws on the tradition of St Blaise, a fourth-century bishop from what is now Turkey. Blaise became the patron saint of carders, or wool-combers, and also of those with sore throats, after he miraculously saved a child from choking on a fishbone. At St Etheldreda's, the two festivals of candle-blessing – Candlemas on 2 February and St Blaise the next day – have been brought together symbolically in the tying together of two candles into a cross. They are then held by the priest against the throats of those in pain in a bid to effect a cure, or perhaps simply to ensure good health. A tiny ritual now, left over from what was once a widespread and joyous day of light-filled celebration.

REBECCA WARREN

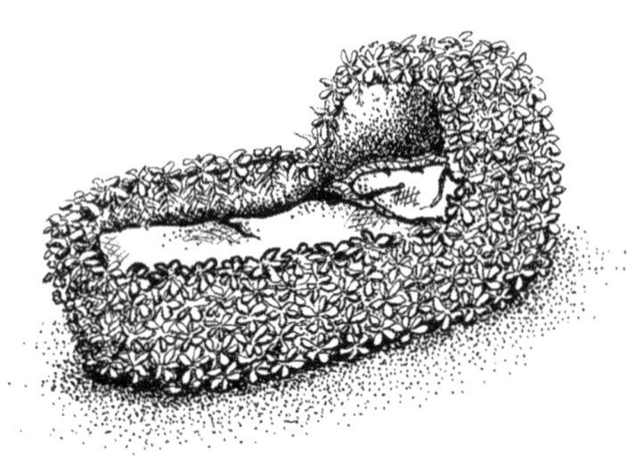

Blidworth Cradle Rocking

Blidworth, Nottinghamshire

SUNDAY NEAREST CANDLEMAS

Like many English towns and villages, the centre of Blidworth in Nottinghamshire is marked by a statue. Rather than commemorating a local aristocrat, soldier, or public figure, however, this piece of public art depicts a metal cradle festooned with flowers. It pays permanent homage to a custom that dates back over 400 years: on the Sunday nearest to Candlemas, the local baby born closest to Christmas day is baptised and then rocked in a specially decorated cradle at the Church of St Mary of the Purification.

The present ritual has been practised continuously since 1922, when the custom was revived by the vicar of the day, the Reverend J. Lowndes. A newsreel from 1952 shows a rather serious occasion: a tiny baby is brought to the altar by well-dressed parents and handed to the vicar, who gives a blessing before gently placing it into the cradle, which is then rocked while the congregation gives thanks. In the footage, apparently awestruck villagers look on, silently huddled in their winter coats, to the accompaniment of a solemn organ.

Older historical accounts, however, suggest that the rockings used to be a much livelier affair, complete with games and drunken revelry. Look at the walls of St Mary's and you will see an inscription decorated with horns, hunting knives, bows and a hound chasing a deer. It commemorates the 'verderer' (forest ranger) Thomas Leake, who was killed in a brawl on the day of the cradle rocking in 1598. Local legend has it that Leake was courting the daughter of the landlady at Archer's Water, an alehouse on the road from Edinburgh to London. Not best pleased at the idea of Leake as a son-in-law, the landlady waited until he was extremely drunk and then fomented a row between him and two soldiers. In the ensuing fight, Leake was fatally stabbed. That's one way for a mother to protect a daughter from a dubious marriage.

The cradle-rocking ceremony itself, of course, relates to the story of Mary's purification and the presentation of the young baby Jesus at the Temple (see 'Candlemas and the Blessing of the Throats'). As a result, questions about the role of mothers have often been raised in the sermons that accompany the event. Preaching in 1935, the Reverend Lowndes concluded that the custom celebrated a traditional vision of the family where women stayed at home. In his view, urban children who were left in day nurseries while their mothers worked in the factories were 'deprived of much of what motherhood meant'. Rural places, by contrast, moved by a very different rhythm, one that was centred on the importance of 'family life'. This view must have rankled with anyone in the congregation who had little choice but to seek paid employment, and raises a dilemma about the balance to be struck between waged work and motherhood that remains laced with guilt for many women even today. Yet the Church has changed a great deal since Lowndes's day – the current vicar of Blidworth is a woman, as is the recently appointed Archbishop of Canterbury.

Today's ceremony is an uplifting affair. The twin aspects of Candlemas unite beautifully in the symbolism of the cradle – and the spring flowers that decorate it provide a welcome sense of renewal and a reminder that warmer, lighter days are just around the corner.

KIERA CHAPMAN

Lunar New Year in Soho

Soho, London

SECOND NEW MOON AFTER THE WINTER SOLSTICE, BETWEEN 21 JANUARY AND 20 FEBRUARY

Lunar New Year is celebrated by people across East and Southeast Asia and their diaspora communities all over the world. The Chinese celebration of this festival that takes place in the Soho district of London each year is now the largest event of its kind outside Asia, involving some 700,000 participants. Yet, as we shall see, it is not without controversy, with critics levelling accusations of demeaning orientalism, inauthenticity, and capture by the Chinese state.

There has been a Chinese community in London since the eighteenth century. At first, transient groups of

Chinese sailors employed within colonial trade networks would stay in boarding houses in the London Docklands, especially around Limehouse. Gradually, they put down roots, and by the 1910s, a distinctive multicultural area had emerged, centred on some thirty Chinese shops and restaurants along two roads: Limehouse Causeway and Pennyfields.

By the 1930s, however, this diaspora was dwindling in size. The shipping trade had been hit by a combination of the economic depression and technological changes that made the old docks unsuitable for modern boats. Heavy bombing during the Blitz then accelerated the area's decline. But running alongside this economic and industrial impact, the British Chinese community was also caught up in a racialised culture war. Their part of Limehouse became a byword for criminality: in the short story 'The Man with the Twisted Lip' (1891), Sir Arthur Conan Doyle's fictional detective Sherlock Holmes visits the area to glean clues about a man's disappearance in an opium den; and in Sax Rohmer's series of popular novels featuring Dr Fu Manchu, published from 1913 to 1959, the criminal mastermind has his headquarters here. These stigmatising portrayals fuelled a backlash against the Chinese community, which took the shape of legislation against gambling and narcotics and disproportionately heavy policing of these East End streets. Hand in hand with this came the British government's active discouragement of Chinese settlement in the UK, fanned by fears of a 'Yellow Peril' that threatened white British wages and cultural identity.

Everything changed, however, in 1949, when the Communist takeover in mainland China resulted in mass migration to the British colony of Hong Kong. Subsequent overcrowding led to tighter immigration regulations there, and many families consequently decided to emigrate to the UK, particularly after the 1948 British Nationality Act had given Commonwealth citizens the right to settle. A new Chinese community emerged in London, but its geographical centre now shifted from the Docklands, which had become the focus of slum-clearance schemes, to the Gerrard Street area of Soho. For many people, food remained a powerful source of cultural connection to their earlier lives, with many new immigrants opening restaurants that quickly became popular with white British customers.

One of the earliest full accounts of London's Chinese Lunar New Year celebrations was written by folklorists Roy and Monica Vickery, who witnessed what they believed to be the first public celebration of the event in Soho in 1971, though other accounts suggest that festivals had been happening there from the 1960s. They describe a relatively small-scale 'dragon dance':

> The dragon consisted of a large multi-coloured, garishly decorated mask with a young man inside. To the back of the mask was attached a decorated cloth tail under which a small number of youths moved in an attempt at unison with the occupant of the mask. As these dancers became exhausted they were replaced by others from a group who, aided by long bamboo poles, usually succeeded in preparing a way for, and keeping the crowd from, the dragon. Music was provided by a small gang of percussionists and the party was completed by a teaser whose main function seemed to be leading the dragon from one offering

> to the next. These offerings consisted of bank notes – both unwrapped and enclosed in red packets – lettuce and other vegetables, tied to long pieces of string which hung, like fishing-lines, from the windows of Chinese shops and restaurants.

Yet this description raises as many questions as it answers: while the group of people bearing a head and a train does suggest a dragon dance, the traditional dragon does not usually eat lettuce. Rather, this behaviour is normally associated with the lion and its dance, but the lion costume only involves two people. It's possible, of course, that the Vickerys got some of the details wrong – but it may well be that this event had a certain looseness to its treatment of folk tradition right from the start.

The Vickerys state that the custom was not repeated in 1972, but that the 1973 festivities were well attended. At this point, the Gerrard Street area was under threat of redevelopment, and the local community made use of the new year festival to publicise the distinctiveness of this place and fend off the planners. This time, the Vickerys note, it was a bright pink lion (definitely a two-person costume this time) that danced through lantern-decorated streets, while tourists and European observers showered the performers with rice. The event proved so lucrative for restaurateurs in the area that it quickly became an annual venture: by the mid-1980s, the London Chinatown Chinese Association was actively promoting an expanded festival. Simultaneously, the Chinese community worked with Westminster Council to revamp the area into a deliberately ethnicised urban space, with exaggerated Chinese-style architectural flourishes, such as elaborate gates, stone lions and bilingual signs with oriental-style fonts. London's Chinatown was born.

Critics of this version of the Lunar New Year, and of the wider spatial redevelopment of Chinatown, are understandably troubled by this appeal to European orientalism. They accuse London's version of this event, which draws on the customs of the Cantonese-speaking community from Hong Kong, of bearing little relationship to celebrations in the Mandarin-speaking areas of China, and of reinforcing stereotypical depictions of Chinese culture as colourful, mysterious and 'other'. But another group disagrees, contending that the festival represents a new custom, a British–Chinese hybrid that is interesting in its own right. In their view, the Soho celebration of Lunar New Year offers an opportunity for canny businesses to defend the literal and cultural space of the Chinese migrant community in the capital with an entrepreneurial, consumption-driven reinvention of a calendar custom to suit new circumstances and needs. However, this argument is somewhat undermined by the fact that many of the properties rented by Chinese food outlets are owned not by this community, but by a firm called Shaftesbury Capital, which began to buy up property in Chinatown in the late 1980s, and now owns 80 per cent of the real estate in the area.

As this particular Lunar New Year festival has grown larger and more complex, its politics have also shifted, as has the governance of Hong Kong, which ceased to be a British colony in 1997, and is now a special administrative region of China. The Gerrard Street area remains the centre for the food-based elements of the festival, but the parade has moved to Charing Cross Road, and a large stage show now takes place in Trafalgar Square. The Chinese government, keen to use the festival to emphasise cultural links to the diaspora across the world, sends top artists to perform, including singers, musicians, dancers, martial artists and acrobats. However, Lunar New Year is also celebrated by people whose heritage lies in areas of East and Southeast Asia outside Mainland China, such as South Korea and Singapore, along with a new wave of emigrants who have come to the UK in response to the handover of Hong Kong. These groups are not always enthused by this display of soft power by the Chinese state, despite the fact that performers often emphasise harmony among different races and nations. In recent years, too, a new tradition has been born: the growth of international travel now means that many wealthy Chinese tourists are choosing to spend this holiday in the UK, though their visits mostly centre on attractions and shopping, rather than on the British–Chinese celebrations of the season.

Of course, Lunar New Year is celebrated privately too, focusing on rituals of renewal that welcome in abundance. Homes are cleaned and then decorated with red and gold to welcome the gods of prosperity. On New Year's Eve, people bathe (often with tea leaves added to the water), dress up in new clothes, and come together with friends and family for 'reunion' dinners. These meals are redolent with symbolism. Fish is served whole – but be careful not to eat it all, because the Chinese word for 'fish' sounds like the word for 'abundance', so a surplus must be left to welcome in plenty. Noodles signal longevity, so the longer they are, the better, while spherical sticky sweet rice balls make for family harmony and cohesion. Incense is burned to pay respect to the ancestors, candles are lit for luck, and fireworks are set off, while young people receive red envelopes stuffed with pocket money for good fortune. On New Year's Day, the theme of welcoming in wealth continues: it is considered bad luck to clean, to remove anything from the house, to leave through the back door, or even to wash or cut your hair, since this could cause ill fortune for the coming year (the Chinese character for 'hair' is similar to that for 'prosperity', so shampooing could symbolically wash away your fortune).

What, then, are we to make of this version of Lunar New Year, with its different public and private faces? Is the former a spectacle of demeaning orientalism? Or does it assert a distinctive British-Chinese identity that has diverged from the mainstream Chinese ways of celebrating the occasion? Is this an example of an entrepreneurial migrant community using customs to defend their space in the city, or a carefully curated exercise in orientalism governed by the strategic desire of global capital to extract high retail rents? Has the festival been co-opted by the Chinese government, or are there many different celebrations, with varying political tendencies? Wherever you fall on these debates, Soho's Lunar New Year is likely to remain a deeply contested custom – and one that will continue to change in the future. There is so much more to it than a colourful dance.

KIERA CHAPMAN

MARCH

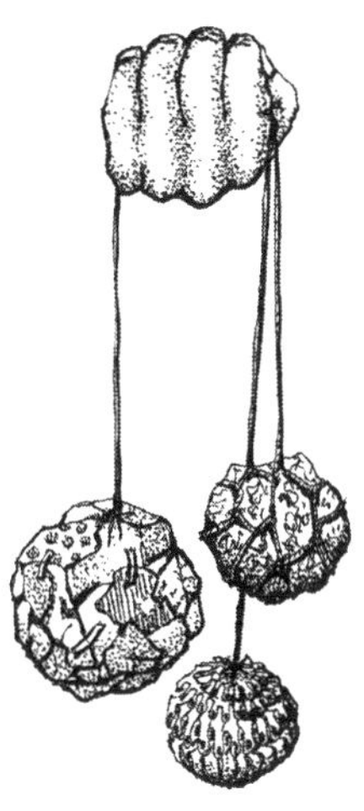

Whuppity Scoorie Day

Lanark, South Lanarkshire

1 MARCH

There is a magic to church bells – it's not just that you can hear them for miles around, their low-frequency sound also resonates in your body. Before watches and digital technologies existed, church bells marked the rhythm of the day, telling you when to wake, pray, eat and sleep, celebrating happy events and alerting people to danger. Some argue that they were even used to reinforce authority, the Church owning and controlling the right to make a noise. Others see the sound as purely practical or devotional. Today, the majestic, nostalgic sound of bells adds to the drama of Lanark's Whuppity Scoorie Day.

There is much about Whuppity Scoorie Day that is mysterious – and it is carefully kept that way by Lanark Community Council to preserve the event's air of magic. The one thing we know for certain about Whuppity Scoorie is that it always starts at 6 p.m. on the dot on 1 March.

At 5.45 p.m., children (plus some parents and dogs) assemble at St Nicholas Parish Kirk holding paper balls on pieces of string, representing bonnets or caps. When the bells chime six o'clock, the children run clockwise three times round the kirk, swinging their paper balls above their heads. There is much shrieking and laughing, and cheers from onlookers. After the race they gather for a coin scramble – a custom that has replaced the older tradition of finding rivals from New Lanark and beating them with your cap.

But beyond this, little is known about when or why Whuppity Scoorie began. Some believe the name of this custom comes from 'whup', meaning 'whip', with 'scoorie' denoting the scurrying of the participants, possibly connected to the punishing of criminals. It is also claimed that the custom's clamour was intended to scare away evil spirits. The name is recorded in the *Hamilton Advertiser* newspaper in 1890, but there are no solid records of the first time it took place or of the reason for its existence. When you are a young child racing round the streets and then scrambling for coins, the origin is irrelevant. It is just great fun – and a rite of passage for local people.

The kirk bell plays a significant role, not only as the instigator of the race, but also as an instrument to awaken the town from the slumber of winter. Historically, St Nicholas's bells are silent between October and February, so Whuppity Scoorie announces the arrival of spring.

As the town comes to life in a riot of joyful ebullience, this custom celebrates life's unstoppable renewal. The children go home tired and happy, and a few pennies richer, knowing longer daylight hours and the endless summer holidays will soon be here.

LULAH ELLENDER

Penny Loaf Day

Newark, Nottinghamshire

SUNDAY NEAREST 11 MARCH

On 11 December 1644, Hercules Clay, the mayor of Newark, wrote his will. Newark was then at the centre of some of the worst fighting of the Civil Wars and, recognising the danger that swirled around him and his community, Clay began by leaving £100 to successive vicars of the town to preach an annual sermon to 'exhort the people not to sett their affections upon things of this world but by their good works to lay a good foundation for themselves that so they may lay on eternal life'. This was followed by a further £100 to 'be paid upon the 11th March yearly to the poor in the church in Newark, either in bread or money at the discretion of the vicar and churchwardens'. The date of 11 March was chosen with care, for it was a very significant date in Clay's life. On this day, exactly nine months before he wrote his will, he and his family had miraculously survived a direct hit by a 'granado', or firebomb, on his house in the centre of Newark.

During the early years of the Civil Wars, Newark had been an important town in the fighting between royalists and parliamentarians. Garrisoned by the royalists for its critical position on the Great North Road and its bridge over the river Trent, it successfully withstood a parliamentarian attack in 1643. By 1644, however, a stronger, better organised parliamentarian force had returned and was laying siege to the town again. In early March that year, Clay, in his house in central Newark, was woken by dreams that his home would be burned down, so he promptly evacuated his family to a safer location. His action was well timed, as the building was hit by enemy cannon shortly afterwards and then destroyed by fire. Despite extensive damage, the town itself withstood this second siege too, and was still in royalist hands when Clay made his will in December. Clay died the following year and, perhaps fortunately, did not live to see Newark finally surrender to the parliamentarians after a third siege in the winter and spring of 1645–6. Shortly afterwards, the king conceded defeat and the first phase of the Civil Wars came to an end.

Clay's donation of £100 for bread for the town's poor was notably generous in its amount, but it was by no means unusual as a bequest. The post-mortem donation of money or food to the less fortunate has a very long history, and even today many of us continue this tradition by leaving money to charities in our wills. Before the Protestant Reformation of the mid-sixteenth century, however, the specific provision of food for the hungry and clothing for the naked were part of the Catholic Church's 'seven works of corporeal mercy'. These charitable acts were required of obedient Christians as symbols of God's grace, but they were also, literally, 'good for the soul'. Those who left such bequests could expect their generosity to be remembered by those benefiting from it, who, in return, would include the giver's name in their prayers. It was believed that the more prayers that were said for someone's soul after their death, the quicker that soul might pass through the waiting room of purgatory and ascend into heaven.

The Reformation swept away the concept of the 'seven works of corporeal mercy', along with the belief in purgatory and the idea that good works done on earth would lead to the saving of a soul in heaven. Yet the Protestant Church continued to encourage charity, especially to the poor, regarding it as a welcome sign of God's grace in devout Protestants, as well as being an important social good – this was, after all, a world without a welfare state. So Hercules Clay, as a Protestant of considerable social standing in Newark, was leaving a legacy which would, at the very least, benefit others in his community, besides, no doubt, being a very sincere sign of his heartfelt gratitude for the divine providence that had so recently saved his life.

In the centuries since his death, Hercules Clay's legacy has continued to provide the poor of Newark with money for bread. On the Sunday nearest 11 March each year, , carrying Clay's personal Bible, the current mayor and dignitaries process from the town hall, which is still adjacent to the site of Clay's house, to St Mary's Church, where what is known as the 'Bombshell Sermon' is given. At the end of the service, bread buns are handed out to the assembled gathering and the remainder of the bequest is given to the poor through charities that provide food and shelter for the homeless.

REBECCA WARREN

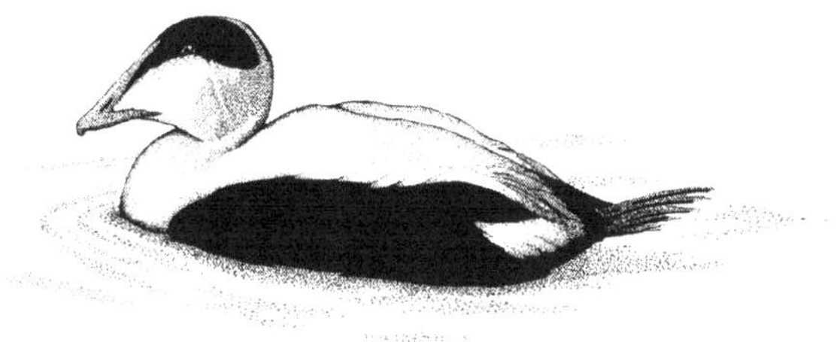

St Cuthbert's Day

North-east England

20 MARCH

St Cuthbert is the patron saint of Northumbria and, arguably, of the wider north. A monk who lived from 634–87 AD, he resided for a time at the monasteries of Melrose and Lindisfarne, but also spent periods of his life on the remote island of Inner Farne, off the coast of Northumberland. His was a time of great religious change. Christianity was still relatively new, and two strands of the early religion were battling for supremacy, one Roman in origin, the other Irish. Part of their disagreement was over the way they calculated the dates for Easter. This led to a geographical split, with northern and western Britain, where the Irish system dominated, celebrating one day, and southern Britain, where the Roman method prevailed, another. In Cuthbert's Northumbria, both systems had powerful adherents, creating chaos around this important religious festival. Since the dates could differ by as much as four weeks, some converts were still in their austere

Lenten fast while others were merrily feasting to celebrate its end. The situation was finally resolved at the Synod of Whitby in the year 664, when the Roman way of calculating the date won out.

However, some ordinary people remained resistant to the arrival of the new religion. We see a glimmer of this distrust in a posthumous history of the saint written by the Anglo-Saxon historian Bede. The chronicler recounts Cuthbert witnessing a near-disaster at sea: his monastic brethren were trying to land five timber-laden rafts on a river, when violent winds started to blow them off course, until they were 'like five tiny birds riding on the waves'. A large group standing nearby on the shore began to laugh and mock those on board, and when St Cuthbert upbraided them for their callousness, they replied with bitter asperity. 'Let no man pray for them and may God have no mercy on any one of them,' said one, 'for they have robbed men of their old ways of worship, and how the new way of worship is to be conducted, nobody knows.' Cuthbert, however, knelt down to pray, and quickly calmed the wind, his mastery of the weather converting some of the sceptics in the watching crowd.

This tiny snippet hints at the sense of loss and disorientation that many people may have felt at the arrival of the new religion, but it also shows how the early Christian Church countered this dislocation by presenting leading religious figures as powerfully connected to the natural world. A literary tradition of tales sprang up around the relationship of saints to more-than-human beings, beginning in Egypt in the fourth and fifth centuries ad, spreading into Europe by the fifth and sixth centuries, and becoming a fully fledged popular genre between the seventh and thirteenth centuries. The stories tell of holy figures who were able to influence or control the normally indifferent natural world, signalling their goodness through this privileged relationship with the divine.

In one of Bede's two accounts of Cuthbert's life, for example, the saint decides that he must farm the land to survive. However, his endeavours to grow wheat prove fruitless, meaning that he is instead forced to sow a crop of barley. Despite the fact that it is now far too late in the season to begin planting seed, the grain springs up in great abundance. However, before it ripens, a flock of birds start to devour the harvest. Cuthbert approaches the interlopers and gently asks them whether they have permission from God to eat a crop that they haven't themselves produced. Chastised, the flock departs, never more to return.

In a similar story, two ravens pull thatch from the hut that Cuthbert has built on his island, taking it for their own nests. The saint implores them to stop, but they ignore his pleas, until he is forced to dispel them by a command to leave in the name of Christ. The birds obey, but one returns three days later in a forlorn state, feathers ruffled and head drooping, begging for forgiveness. Cuthbert understands that it is soliciting his permission to come back to the island, and, on receiving his blessing, both of the ravens return. They bring with them a peace offering, in the shape of a lump of pig fat, which Cuthbert uses to preserve his shoes. Thereafter, the saint and the corvids live in harmony, with the birds providing an exemplary lesson on the virtue of humility.

However, the bird most famously associated with Cuthbert nowadays is probably the eider, *Somateria mollissima*, known in Northumbria as 'Cuddy ducks' ('Cuddy' being an affectionate nickname for 'Cuthbert'). While living on Inner Farne, Cuthbert is said to have established a rule that forbade his brethren to kill or eat these large black-and-white seafaring birds. In return, the ducks became tame and tractable, nesting all over the island, even next to the altar in church (today, eiders are well known for being gregarious and confiding birds). However, this tale feels slightly different, perhaps because it originated later, in a twelfth-century retelling of Cuthbert's story by the monk Reginald of Durham. Here, the relationship of the saint to nature is more reciprocal than in the stories of the ravens and the barley-thieving birds: Cuthbert does not simply dominate the natural world, he protects and cares for it. No wonder, then, that when the modern conservation movement emerged in the nineteenth century, Cuthbert became its patron saint.

Cuthbert was buried in AD 687 on Lindisfarne, but his rest was far from undisturbed. His coffin was first opened eleven years after his death, by monks who intended to transfer his bones into a beautiful reliquary that had been specially constructed to house them. However, they found his corpse in a state of such miraculous preservation that they were forced to build a new wooden coffin instead. Its remains, which look somewhat hastily constructed, can still be seen at the Durham Cathedral museum.

In 875, the growing threat of Viking invasion led the monastic community of Lindisfarne to flee, accompanied by Cuthbert's relics and other treasured possessions, including the stunning illuminated manuscript known as the *Lindisfarne Gospels*, which was produced in the saint's honour. On their travels, they found refuge in a number of places, including Chester-le-Street and Ripon, before finally returning to Durham in the year 995. Cuthbert's remains are buried today in Durham Cathedral: as you climb up the hill and pass through the enormous wooden door with its lion-headed sanctuary ring, stepping into the cool, Norman-arched nave with its broad geometric piers, the saint's shrine is at the east end. The modern grave is simple, marked by a slab of dark stone and surrounded by four dully glinting metal candlesticks, but in the medieval period, Cuthbert's relics were stored in an ornate metal and wooden box, covered in gold, silver and precious gems, which sat atop a painted marble base surrounded by niches to allow the devout to kneel next to it in prayer. The casket was protected by a gilded wooden cover that could be raised with pulleys that rang six tinkling silver bells to signal that it was open to view. The sight must have been magnificent, and such was the devotion of the surrounding population to their saint that they demanded that the bishop allow them constant access to pray.

Today, on or around 20 March, Saint Cuthbert's feast day, this holy man of the north-east is remembered with a procession in his honour. It follows part of a longer pilgrim's route, proceeding from the church at Chester-le-Street, six miles north of Durham, down to Finchale Priory, and then on to Durham Cathedral, a distance of some eight miles. The walk offers a chance to connect with 1300 years of history, taking in places that Cuthbert would personally have known, as well as those associated with his posthumous travels. But it is also an opportunity to traverse the Northumbrian landscape and marvel at its beautiful landscapes. It feels like a fitting celebration of this saint's life and legacy: taking time out to appreciate the natural world is surely an activity of which St Cuthbert himself would have approved.

KIERA CHAPMAN

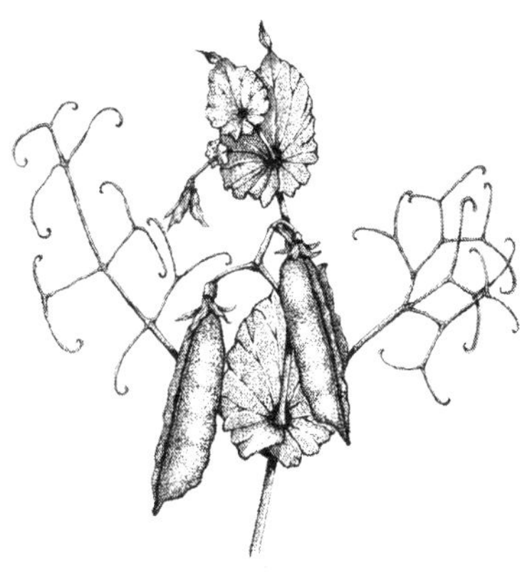

Carlin Sunday

North-west England

FIFTH SUNDAY OF LENT

For many of us, the most obvious sign that Lent is drawing to a close is the ubiquitous presence of chocolate eggs on the supermarket shelves. But for many people across the north of England, the harbinger of Easter is a pea – the Carlin pea, to be exact – so called because it is traditionally eaten on Carlin Sunday, the fifth and penultimate Sunday of Lent.

According to Christian tradition, Lent is a period of forty days of abstinence and denial before the celebration of Easter. In the past, people were expected to eschew rich foods, including meat, eggs and milk products, as well as sensory pleasures, including sex. Well, the Carlin pea has its fans, but no one would claim that it is high on the list of epicurean or sensory delights, so it is hardly surprising that it was allowed to remain on the menu during this period, providing much-needed sustenance during the long Lenten fast. In fact, dried peas and beans have been a staple of the British diet since time immemorial, playing a critical role in tiding hungry families over the long winter and spring months, until the new season's produce became available. For reasons that remain unclear, however, the eating of this one particular pea became associated with this one particular day in the north-east of England, where it clings on as a regional custom even now.

Yet the Carlin pea itself is subject to much confusion. Which pea is it? Why is it associated with the north-east? And how did it acquire the name 'Carlin'? As ever, where fact is missing, imagination has filled in the gaps, and several versions of an origin story are widely recounted. During the Civil Wars of the 1640s, it is said, when royalist Newcastle was under siege from an invading Scottish army, a ship reached the starving city with a cargo of dried peas, thus saving the embattled population from a slow and grim death. Sometimes the Scottish invasion story is pushed back by three hundred years to the invasion by Robert the Bruce in 1327, and, in other versions, the peas reach the starving inhabitants unintentionally, as a result of shipwreck, when they float to the shore and are scooped up off the beach – presumably rather 'well-seasoned' by then.

There is no definitive evidence for any of these accounts, and yet there may be something behind the tales. Dried peas and beans were often used as food on sea voyages, and no doubt some of these cargoes *did* come to grief, if the ships they were carried in foundered. Moreover, the seventeenth century saw a rapid expansion in maritime trade networks, enabling many new foods and crops to be imported. In 1640, the eminent Jacobean botanist and apothecary John Parkinson entered a large array of pea and bean species in his botanical encyclopaedia *The Theatre of Plants*, including fourteen kinds of 'kidney beans', various 'French beans', lentils and numerous peas, adding, 'There hath come likewise unto us and others, both from *Africa, Brasill*, the *East* and *West Indies, Virginia, etc* sundry other sorts and varieties which were endlesse to recite . . .' So the account of the Carlin pea's arrival in north-east England by ship, either in cargo unloaded in the Tyneside docks, or as wreckage washed up on the coast, is by no means implausible.

Dried peas and beans would have been eaten by the poor throughout the year, but the Carlin's prominence in the calendar of the north of England is reflected in the traditional local rhyme 'Tid, mid, misere, Carlin, Palm, Pace-Egg Day', which listed out the Sundays in Lent: the second Sunday – *tid* – was when the *Te Deum Laudamus* was sung; the third – *mid* – featured the *Mi Deus*; the fourth – *misere* – referred to the Miserere psalm; and the fifth was Carlin Sunday. The sixth and final Sunday of Lent was, of course, Palm Sunday, and Pace Egg Day referred to Easter Sunday, Pace being a corruption of Pasch, the old term for Easter. It is unclear why the eating of Carlin peas was commemorated in this otherwise religious rhyme, but perhaps it was a wry comment on the dwindling food supplies of mid-spring, combined with the rigorous restrictions of Lent.

To add to the Carlin pea's complex history, there is widespread confusion over its identification. Frequently – but erroneously – reported as *Cajanus cajan*, the Carlin peas eaten today are actually maple peas, a form of field pea (*Pisum sativum*). *Cajanus cajan* is a tropical pea, called the pigeon pea, which cannot grow in Britain, although it may, in the past, have been imported. The situation is further complicated by the fact that Carlins are referred to locally as 'pigeon peas', as they are commonly fed to homing pigeons, which are still widely kept in the north-east. And if that is not confusing enough, maple peas are also eaten in both Lancashire and the Midlands, where they are referred to as black, grey, parching or – of course – pigeon peas; when it comes to pea-eating, every region has its local tradition, each with its own strongly held views. It seems likely, however, that different pea varieties have been consumed changeably across time and region, according to what was available and when.

As for the origin of the name 'Carlin', many theories abound, but the most romantic is that 'carling' was a northern dialect term for an old woman, or sometimes a witch. When the pea crop had been gathered in, the last dried stalks were fashioned into a corn dolly or witch figure, to be burned at the end of the harvest. Perhaps the peas shaken from these last plants were cooked and eaten in celebration, before the rest of the crop was stored away, to be finally consumed in the hungry days of Lent.

All the traditions are in agreement, however, that after long soaking, these mealy peas are best when boiled and eaten with salt and vinegar, or, for those with a sweet tooth, with sugar, butter and rum.

REBECCA WARREN

APRIL

Pace-egging Plays

Calder Valley, West Yorkshire

GOOD FRIDAY

'Pace-egging' sounds alarmingly athletic – perhaps a high-speed version of the egg-and-spoon race at a school sports day? Rest assured, it's not. As we have seen in 'Carlin Sunday', the 'pace' of pace-egging comes from its connection with Easter, which was commonly called 'Pasch' in the Middle Ages. The 'egging' refers to the age-old association between eggs and Easter for, in its early days, pace-egging took place either on Good Friday or on Easter Sunday, after the Lent restrictions on eating meat and eggs had ended. Eggs, of course, are at their most abundant around Easter and have therefore long been regarded as symbols of springtime renewal and rebirth.

The gift of eggs as a dole for the poor or an offering to the church was once widespread across the whole of Britain, but in the early nineteenth century a distinctive strand of this tradition emerged in the north-west of England. Here, young men and boys would dress up in costumes to beg for eggs, sometimes in return for a song or two, a custom that was similar to the well-known tradition of children begging for 'a penny for the guy' in the run-up to Bonfire Night in November. In parts of Cumbria, Lancashire and West Yorkshire, however, the pace-eggers' use of costume and song developed into the production of a full-blown play, using similar themes, figures and language to the medieval folk-plays once performed at Christmas. And although many of the pace-egging plays died out in the early twentieth century, a handful continue to be performed today.

Despite the name, 'pace-egging' plays nowadays have little to do with eggs. Instead, they fall into the typical 'hero-combat' form of traditional mumming plays identified in a study by Eddie Cass. The two best-known and most long-standing examples are performed outdoors, at Midgley and at Heptonstall, both in West Yorkshire. With some variations, the plays involve a fight between a hero-knight, often St George, and a challenger, usually 'Bold Slasher', who is revived by 'the Doctor' after being slain. A second fight then takes place, and this time Bold Slasher does not survive, and a variety of characters – the Doctor, of course, and a fool or 'Old Tosspot', along with numerous others, including some kind of devil – come in and out of the action to extend the simple plot line until an end is finally reached, the concluding song is sung, and a collection is taken. Although these plays are scripted and in verse, there is much leeway for comic ad-libbing and contemporary references, such as the use of mobile phones or even toy pistols.

Over the years, considerable effort has been made to find origin dates for pace-egging and other mumming plays. A widely quoted strand of research in the twentieth century sought to root them deep in the pre-Christian past, as survivors of pagan rituals. Yet although pace-egging clearly draws on older mumming and miracle-play traditions from the pre-Reformation period, there is no evidence of pace-egging plays before the late eighteenth century. Moreover, the idea that mumming plays are direct descendants of pagan beliefs and fertility rites has been shown to have no basis. Yet the desire to find ancient origins for our folk culture is curiously persistent, and raises some interesting questions. Would the surviving pace-egging plays somehow be more valuable or 'valid' if it could be proved that they contained pre-Christian rituals? And if so, why?

As it is, many of our customs (or at least the written records of them) only date back to the nineteenth century, but that doesn't make them – or our desire to keep them alive – any less worthwhile. Indeed, it's the way in which they are refreshed and updated each year that gives them their vitality. Somehow, traditional 'folk' plays, such as pace-egging, have developed a successful formula that allows endless reinvention to match the mood of the times. And if in the slapstick antics of St George, Bold Slasher and Old Tosspot we imagine a comforting continuity with our ancestors, we are also gathering each year to remake the tradition anew for our contemporary community.

REBECCA WARREN

Chulkhurst Dole

Biddenden, Kent

EASTER MONDAY

It's Easter Monday, and a small group of people are standing in the garden of a white weatherboarded house in the village of Biddenden in Kent. At 10 o'clock precisely, one member of the group detaches from the others and offers a brief welcome. The rest then file up to an open window, through which a previously hidden hand passes out brown paper bags containing a loaf of bread, some cheese, butter, tea and a bottle of mineral water. As people leave with their bags, others arrive to take their turn, but there are rarely more than ten or twelve figures quietly waiting and chatting under the trees. Everyone here knows each other and there are no casual spectators, because there is nothing showy about this tradition – no costumes, no music, no mumming plays, no colourful parades. The sharing of the Chulkhurst Dole is low-key and local, and sensitive to the feelings of those who take part.

Annual doles, or gifts, of food or money have an ancient history, stretching far back to, and beyond, the Middle Ages, when providing charity for others was considered a religious duty, especially at death. Even today, many such small local funds continue to benefit the poor, often unobtrusively and without fuss. In that sense, the Chulkhurst Dole is not unusual; it too originated in a legacy that produced an income in perpetuity, from which help could be given to the needy of the village. Yet the narrative which surrounds this dole is far from typical and has been the subject of considerable investigation, invention and contention.

In outline, the story goes like this: around the year 1100, twin girls – Eliza and Mary Chulkhurst – were born in Biddenden. The babies were joined at the head and hip and yet, almost miraculously, they survived to adulthood. When they died, at the age of thirty-four, they left some land to provide beer, bread and cheese for the poor of the village – gifts that continued to be given out annually thereafter.

Sadly, there is much that is questionable about this story, in particular the very early date for the start of such a legacy; in 1100, most people did not have formal surnames and written records of such gifts were not made, let alone kept. Indeed, almost everything about the legend has subsequently been questioned, dismissed or modified, including the facts that there are no known examples of twins joined in two places who survived, and the first mention of the conjoined nature of the sisters does not occur until the seventeenth century, when it is mentioned briefly in a legal case. Moreover, in the later eighteenth century, the respected historian of Kent, Edward Hasted, argued that the sisters' surname was Preston; the surname Chulkhurst was not attributed to them until the nineteenth century.

Nevertheless, among all the claims and confusion, some verifiable facts remain. The dole was indeed funded from the income of a gift of twenty acres of land lying close to the parish church in Biddenden, known then and now as the Bread and Cheese Lands. Moreover, records show that the distribution of food and drink to the poor at Easter was certainly happening by the early seventeenth century. In the later eighteenth century another part of the tradition emerged: the 'Biddenden Maids' biscuits. Inedibly hard and unsweetened, the biscuits were shaped to represent the two women standing side by side. They were handed out with the rest of the dole which, at that point, was three loaves of bread, a pound and a half of cheese and a quantity of beer. Not surprisingly, when free beer was involved, the distribution of the dole was frequently accompanied by disorder and drunkenness, which led to its transfer away from the church and into the nearby workhouse. Even this failed to stop the revelry, however, which only ceased in the later nineteenth century, when beer was finally omitted altogether from the dole. In 1907, the Bread and Cheese Lands were sold off for housing – resulting, rather predictably, in roads on the new development being named Chulkhurst, Cheeselands and Maids Close. The sale realised a substantial sum that continues not only to fund the Easter dole today but also to provide some financial help for parishioners known to be in need at Christmas.

The village sign in the centre of Biddenden proudly features Eliza and Mary in long blue dresses, their shoulders and hips touching, their faces staring down at the passing traffic. It doesn't matter whether the legend behind them is accurate or fanciful, nor that it has changed over the years, nor indeed that the famous biscuits are produced now as mementoes rather than as edible treats. Somehow, all the layers of fact and fiction have only helped to secure the tradition in the life of the community. And there is something deeply satisfying in a local custom that just gets on with itself, not as a performance that attracts tourists, but as an act of genuine charity towards those who are struggling with income, disability or age.

REBECCA WARREN

Hare Pie Scramble and Bottle Kicking

Hallaton, Leicestershire

EASTER MONDAY

If I tell you there's a game where the only rules are 'No murder, no gouging, no riding on horseback with the bottle', what comes to mind? Perhaps you're imagining a violent free-for-all where only a few cuts and bruises would be considered a good outcome? Throw in thousands of participants, a few spiky hedges, dank ditches and muddy streams, and you've accurately conjured the Hallaton bottle-kicking event.

This chaotic game is the culmination of an annual Easter Monday tradition in the Leicestershire village of Hallaton. The day starts with the Hare Pie Scramble. Thousands of people – many of them returning home from living elsewhere specially for the event – congregate to see a pipe and drum band and children's parade. After a church service, a huge pillow-sized hare pie (made from onions, hare, carrots, celery, garlic, cloves, beef stock, red wine, port, herbs and potatoes, and topped with a golden crust bearing the shapes of two jumping hares) is carried through the streets. The pie is blessed and shared out, and the remains are put in a sack and then thrown into the crowd – hence, the 'scramble'.

So far, so eccentric. But this is where things turn wild. Villagers from Hallaton and nearby Medbourne then converge for the bottle-kicking event. The aim of this game is to get the 'bottles' (small barrels dressed in stripes of ribbon and full of beer) across your home stream. The winners are the side that gets two out of the three bottles over their boundary. Sounds easy enough – but not when you factor in a scrum of 500–1000 people competing for the bottle, and pushing, tackling, elbowing and throwing each other across fields and through hedgerows for three to five hours.

As is often the case with these customs, the exact origins are cloudy. The bottle-kicking element is claimed to be the precursor to the modern game of rugby, and is thought to have begun in 1835 when some Medbourne boys joined the Hare Pie Scramble and stole food and drink. Supposedly a chase ensued, and it has been re-enacted ever since. Although the game is mostly good-natured, the rivalry runs deep and has been known to turn violent – one account describes a man punching an opponent in the face before the game had even started, and a recent photograph shows a young woman wielding an umbrella as a runner tries to get past. This description from the *New York Times* in 1978 highlights an unforeseen peril: 'A pair of trousers was passed out of the scrum. Some minutes later, a young man clad only in underwear was passed back in similar fashion. Presumably there was a reunion.'

The Hare Pie Scramble dates back much further – possibly a thousand years, though records only go back to 1797. The legend is that a gentlewoman on Hare Pie Hill was being chased by a bull when a hare appeared and distracted the animal. The woman was so grateful that she donated the land to the village on the condition that the rector provided two hare pies, twenty-four penny loaves and ale to the villagers every year. Turning your rescuer into a pie seems a strange way to show gratitude, but there we are. It is also possible that this springtime custom developed from the pre-Christian early-medieval practice of worshipping Eostre, a goddess who took the form of a hare.

While locating its exact origin may be impossible, this is undoubtedly one of the oldest ongoing British customs, and it is an important event in the local calendar. During the Second World War, the women of the village took over the event, baking a pie from turnips, barley and food scraps, determined to keep the tradition going. A word to the wise, though: if you go to watch, make sure your trousers are firmly secured, and perhaps arm yourself with an umbrella.

LULAH ELLENDER

Marsden Cuckoo Festival

Marsden, West Yorkshire

LAST WEEKEND IN APRIL

Sumer is icumen in,
Lhude sing cuccu,
Groweth sed, and boweth med,
And springeth the wode nu,
Sing cuccu!

The cuckoo is a deceptive creature. Grey-winged, with a barred front that looks like the ripples of wind on water, it closely resembles the sparrowhawk, to the point that early natural historians such as Pliny were fooled into classifying it in the same family. The cuckoo's mastery of disguise is, in fact, clever mimicry: putting on the appearance of a predator means that smaller birds scatter in panic on its approach. This then gives the cuckoo the opportunity to play its most famous trick: swooping into the nests of other species while they are absent, and laying its own eggs in the clutch. The shells are extremely variable in colour and pattern, because the cuckoos deliberately match them to the eggs of their hosts, an impressive feat of biological forgery. Not only are the surrogate parents then burdened with the considerable demands of feeding and raising the oversized chicks, but the young cuckoos will deal summarily with the genuine offspring, forcing them out of the nest before they can defend themselves.

The mercurial, elusive quality of the cuckoo, the difficulty of pinning it down, seeps into its association with another notoriously changeable entity: the British seasons. One of the earliest songs in English, 'Summer is icumen in', is about the cuckoo's call, and there is still no birdsong more intimately associated with the coming of spring than this fluting two-note melody, which can carry for hundreds of metres on a still day. Cuckoos are migrants, making their long journey to the British Isles from central and southeastern Africa, Sri Lanka and Southeast Asia to arrive from late April onwards. *The Times* used to ask readers to write in on hearing the first cuckoo of spring; nowadays, the movements of a small number of celebrity cuckoos are tracked by the British Trust for Ornithology using satellite tags, with an avid audience following their progress on an online map. For centuries, then, the coming of this bird has been a welcome signal that winter is finally over. Some places still have a tradition of listening out for them on certain days: in many places, 28 April is the lucky time, but in the Colne Valley of West Yorkshire, cuckoos are supposed to call for the first time on 24 April, at the Marsden Cattle Fair.

Local legend says that long ago, the villagers of Marsden decided that if they could only capture the cuckoo, it would be spring for ever. Leaf fall comes early in this part of the Pennines, and ice holds water in its clawed grip late into the spring. So little wonder that people here would want to pin down this seasonal sentinel, suspending time and keeping future frosts at bay. The cuckoo's presence meant a time of plenty, of dappled sunlight, of fresh green and frothy white flowers, of mating, and of ease.

So legend has it that Marsden's residents built a structure to trap the bird, adding layer upon layer of rough sandstone until they had constructed a tower. And as they did so, the cuckoo sat inside, calling, beguiled by the echo that leapt back from the steep-sided stone hills. But just as the villagers were laying the final course of stone, the cuckoo suddenly took fright and flew out of the tower, spreading its wings to the sky. The prison stood empty. Time kept moving. And winter came once more, as usual.

Stories of capturing the cuckoo are also found in other parts of Britain. Along the southern Chilterns, there are a number of ancient earthworks with spinneys of trees above them, which used to be explained locally as the results of similar attempts to capture these birds. Somerset folk used to be ridiculed as 'Cuckoo-penners' by their Wiltshire neighbours, and there are also Cornish stories from Towednack near St Ives about caging these birds. But perhaps the most famous comes from the village of Gotham in

Nottinghamshire, which was proverbial for the stupidity of its residents. As a 1630 chapbook recounts:

> On a time the men of Gottam would have pinned in the Cuckoo, whereby shee should sing all the yeere, and in the midst of the town they made a hedge round in compasse, and they had got a Cuckoo, and had put her into it, and said, Sing here all the yeere, and thou shalt lacke neither meat nor drinke. The Cuckoo as soone as she perceived her selfe incompassed within the hedge, flew away. A vengeance on her said they, We made not our hedge high enough.

Other legends, however, tell a rather more flattering story, presenting this apparent idiocy as a clever ruse. Hearing that King John was going to visit their village and fearing the expense of a royal visit, the inhabitants turned him away, making the monarch extremely angry. As he approached in high dudgeon to punish them, the villagers decided to feign insanity. They pretended to be trying to drown an eel in water, threw cheeses down a hill, and played at hedging a cuckoo in so it could not depart. The King's servants were so put off by this display that they decided not to enter the village. One of the pubs in Gotham is still called the Cuckoo Bush Inn, in celebration of this feigned madness. Subsequently, in the United States, the name 'Gotham' became a byword for a kind of crazed ingenuity. Washington Irving called New York 'Gotham' in the early nineteenth century, and the moniker was subsequently adopted by comic book writer Bill Finger to name a fictitious New York–like city in his *Batman* series.

*

Marsden today is a tiny village, home to just over 3,500 people, yet it has an active calendar of events, thanks in part to the local charity The Cuckoo's Nest, which generously funds a number of neighbourhood organisations. The entire village seems to get involved in the Cuckoo Fair, which is full of local colour and costumes, yet also contemporary in its feel. There's clog and Morris dancing, but also belly-dancing, and alongside the traditional folk and brass band music, there's infectious Brazilian-style street percussion. A plastic duck race raises money for local causes, with the yellow bobbing birds carefully fished out of the river at the end of the course. There are organised cuckoo walks for those who want to hear the birds, and a town trail for visitors of a more urban persuasion. But the highlight of the day is definitely the procession: attendees are treated to a sight of magnificent puppets, including a gigantic articulated flying cuckoo, which flaps proudly over a banner displaying the festival's strapline: 'It were nobbut one course too low', in reference to the tower that wasn't quite high enough to pen in the bird.

This custom now has additional resonance, because cuckoos are increasingly endangered. Across continental Europe, their numbers have dropped by a quarter, but in the UK they have fallen by three-quarters. One of the main reasons so many of us can no longer rely on hearing their cry as the starting gun of spring is because the seasonal clocks of the world are changing. Climate change is shifting the timings of summer and winter across the globe, meaning that, with spring starting sooner, cuckoos now face a choice: cut short the time to gain valuable calories before migration and embark on a risky earlier journey north, or arrive too late, when their host birds have already finished breeding. With the cuckoo's future so uncertain, there has never been a more important time for festivals like Marsden's. They remind us of the joy in natural rhythms – and of our responsibility to fix their contemporary disorder.

KIERA CHAPMAN

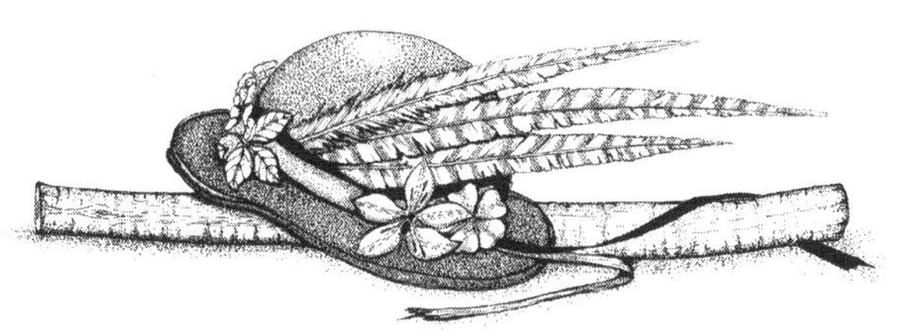

Adderbury Morris Men Day of Dance

Adderbury, Oxfordshire

LAST WEEKEND IN APRIL

At first glance, Adderbury's Day of Dance might look like a mass teenage booze-up, but there is much more to it than that. Held at the end of April every year since 1975, the festival is organised by the Adderbury Morris Men, who spend the whole day dancing in every part of the village.

This Morris side is deeply rooted in the village – to be a member you have to be male, and you have to have been born there (or in a neighbouring parish). It was set up by resident Bryan Sheppard during the 1970s folk revival that was influenced by local folk-rock band Fairport Convention, whose jangly guitars brought traditional music to a wider audience. There had been sides in the village as far back as the 1800s, but the dancing died out when all but one of the Morris men were killed in the First World War. For the lone survivor, dancing didn't seem important any more. Six decades later, however, a group of villagers under Sheppard's direction decided to revive the side. They rehearsed for a whole year, drawing on the detailed records of villager Janet Blunt, who wrote descriptions of all the dances she had seen. Blunt was a folklorist and music collector in the early twentieth century, and through her work the Morris men revived nineteen dances specific to Adderbury, telling stories of war, love, work and ale. By 1975 they were ready to go public.

Now, the Day of Dance is a regular fixture in the village year. The Morris men wear top hats with flowers, white 'kits', bells sewn onto leather pads around their shins, and 'baldrics' (ribbons worn across the chest), and in their hands they hold large handkerchiefs, or willow sticks (depending on the dance). One man in fancy dress (Darth Vader once made a memorable appearance, with a light sabre in place of a stick) dances as the Fool, carrying a pig's bladder on a stick, connecting the audience to the dance in the way a jester would engage an audience. The dancers are accompanied by a fiddle, tabor and melodeon. People line the main village street to watch them perform, with a steady flow of alcohol, a hog roast and a burger stall providing sustenance throughout the day. Drunken teenagers look on with scepticism but also with curiosity.

It is easy to ridicule Morris dancing, but there is a skill, complexity and underlying meaning that makes it one of our most fascinating folk art forms. It is also one of the most mysterious, with little documented history other than the collections of Janet Blunt and Cecil Sharp, who created archives of regional dances and folk music. We can trace it back to the Tudor court, but its origins beyond that are hard to pin down. The earliest English mentions of Morris dancing spell it variously as 'morisk', 'morys' and 'morisse'

– all close to the Spanish *morisca* and French *morisque*, meaning 'Moorish dance'. This could possibly indicate that it may have developed from Berber or North African customs, and then moved across Europe as courtly entertainment. Filmmaker, actor, playwright and Adderbury native Tim Plester describes it as 'a mongrel dance for a mongrel nation', capturing the diversity and complexity inherent in the tradition.

The different elements of the dance may reveal clues as to the custom's roots. Most controversially, Morris sides often wore blackface, perhaps denoting the dance's cultural heritage, but possibly also to disguise themselves when begging or dancing for money. Most modern Morris dancers have replaced this with abstract paint patterns to avoid the offensive racial connotations. Their hankies are thought to represent blossoms or seeds and hopes of a good crop, and we see similarities with Middle Eastern scarf dances. They could also simply be used to emphasise the dancers' hand movements and add a percussive 'snap' to the dance. Their sticks are made from hazel, willow or ash and possibly symbolise weapons or tools, reflecting similar combat-based dances, such as the Basque *makil dantzak* ('stick dance'), which also features white kits and bells. Their purpose could also be to hit the ground and wake up the earth for the growing season, but they could equally be there simply because they make a good noise. Some believe the bells worn around the shins are a way to ward off evil spirits.

The Adderbury Morris Men, with their bells, sticks and hankies, are part of the Cotswold style of dancing. This usually consists of six or eight dancers per set, accompanied by a melodeon or fiddle, and involves dancing unique, highly choreographed dances in a 6/8 or 4/4 step. They perform a mix of jigs, and stick and clapping dances, using their bodies as instruments (as we see in many West African dances). A second style, Border Morris (hailing from the Welsh–English border) is less stylised and more energetic and boisterous. These dances feature loud percussive footwork, 'tatter coats' in place of white kits, and painted faces.

Different again is the Northwest Morris tradition, which developed alongside clog dancing, with similar footwork and heavy shoes. Sides using this style, such as Sussex's all-female Knots of May, have up to twelve dancers, who wear garlands and carry shorter sticks, performing precise processional dances designed to move along the streets. Molly dancing, which is discussed in the 'Whittlesea Straw Bear' entry, and sword dancing are closely related folk dances, but not strictly Morris. Regional variations reflect the different terrain, labour and seasonal festivities of each area.

Superficially, Morris dancing could seem quintessentially nostalgic, but it has constantly evolved and is now enjoying something of a renaissance. In 2024, for the first time ever, the national Morris Ring had a female squire – a maths teacher named Emma Melville – and 50.6 per cent of the UK's 13,000 dancers are now women. Sides are embracing different aesthetics, like the Wolf's Head and Vixen Gothic Border Morris side from Rochester in Kent, who perform around London (including in graveyards), while campaigning sides like Murky Water Morris are using dance and performance as a means of protest.

Groups like Boss Morris are bringing folk dance to entirely new audiences. This young, all-female 'prog Morris' group of artists based in Stroud, Gloucestershire uses traditional dances alongside modern music, performing at festivals, in squash courts, and even at the Brit Awards. Their creativity and joyfulness are infectious – they whoop and yelp as they dance, and their costumes and face paint are full of colour, patterns and pagan motifs. Sometimes they are joined by life-size dancing creatures – an owl, a bull, a goat – adding to their folkloric allure. They are reimagining folk dance, with an inclusive, climate-aware lens and community-driven events. They believe that 'folk is not a museum piece. It is breath, beat, and belonging. It is a shared ritual across time, a collective memory danced into the earth. And now, more than ever, folk must speak to the challenges of our time – ecological crisis, social fragmentation, and the need for community renewal.'

A custom that can embrace such a spectrum of practices, from the Adderbury Morris Men to rock-star dancers, has a hope not just of surviving, but of thriving.

LULAH ELLENDER

Boaldyn and Crosh Cuirn

Isle of Man

30 APRIL

You may be familiar with Beltane, the Anglicised name for the Gaelic festival that marks the start of spring. In the Isle of Man, it is known as Boaldyn, and it takes place on or around 1 May. The root of the word Boaldyn or Beltane may be pre-Celtic, meaning 'bright light', so it is no surprise that fire is a common feature of many of the customs that take place at this time. Yet fire festivals do not have to be large, communal affairs. On the Isle of Man some landowners still practise a small, local custom of Burning the Buitch on the night before May Day, lighting a small bonfire, often of gorse, to frighten off any bad spirits from the surrounding land.

In the past, Boaldyn was believed to be a moment of particularly frenetic activity among the island's spirits or 'little people', known as *mooinjer veggey* in Manx. Placating these difficult little characters has long been a feature of Manx folklore, and it reappears in a slightly different form in a second small custom, known as the Crosh Cuirn, that is still practised by some around their homes. This also takes place just before May Day, and is a uniquely Manx tradition. A small wooden cross is made by sliding one small twig of rowan – or 'cuirn' – through a slit made in the centre of another. The centre of the cross is then bound around with gathered strands of sheep's wool. Metal cannot be used in making the cross, because of its negative resonances with the nails of the crucifixion of Christ, and the wool must have been cast off by the sheep, rather than deliberately cut. The cross is then hung on the door of the house to ward off evil spirits or witches from the property.

Rowan, of course, is a tree that has deep and time-honoured associations with magic and folklore, and it has long been considered a guardian against witchcraft. In the past, in many parts of Britain, its protective powers led people to plant it near the doors of houses. Not surprisingly, it also gave rise to the belief that cutting down a rowan tree would bring bad luck, an idea that also applied to another bearer of red berries, the holly. It is possible that the red colour of the fruit of both trees was adopted by the Christian Church as symbolic of Christ's blood and therefore of possessing a sacred quality; but the likelihood is that the apotropaic beliefs surrounding both rowan and holly trees are more ancient still.

Whatever the origins, it seems that the mystical associations attached to the rowan live on. Sometimes the longevity of customs depends on the ease with which they can be carried out. Burning the Buitch and the making of a Crosh Cuirn are small and simple acts, requiring only what can be gathered easily from the land, and perhaps this is why they have remained woven into the calendar of some people's lives. Well, that, and a preference for staying on the safe side of the *mooinjer veggey* – just in case.

REBECCA WARREN

MAY

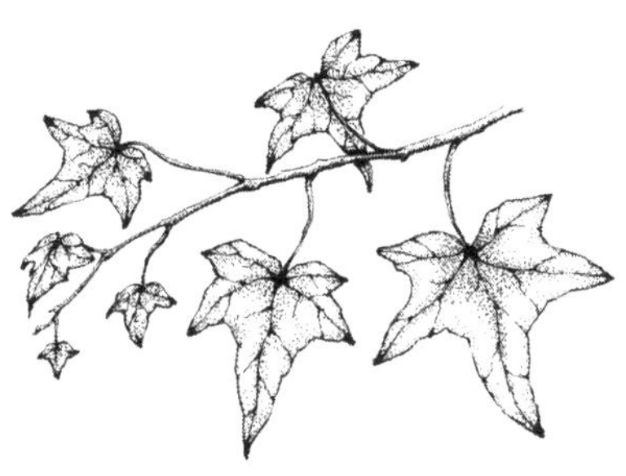

Jack in the Green

Hastings, East Sussex

1 MAY

Bouncing off the walls of the narrow streets, waves of deep, rhythmic drumming fill the air. The blood quickens, feet tap, hips swing and sway . . . the old town in Hastings is awash with people, whooping and cheering, laughing and chatting. And at the centre of the crowds, a huge cone of greenery comes whirling and ducking out of the Fishermen's Museum and into the street, cascading ribbons and leaves, and topped with a yellow and white flower-covered crown. Jack in the Green has been released! And around him, dipping and diving, roaring and leering, circles a posse of men, their bodies covered in leaves, their skin painted a rich green, and their heads garlanded with ivy. These wild men are the Bogies, and they will stay with Jack as he makes his way past the black-timbered fishermen's huts on the seafront, up the old medieval streets and out on to the grassy clifftop overlooking the English Channel. Today is May

Day, and Jack is born and will die on this day – welcoming in the summer and bringing together a community.

The Jack in the Green festival has a forty-year history in Hastings, and over this time it has grown into a four-day extravaganza of celebrations. The culmination of the festivities is a long parade that features all the expected May Day figures, including chimney sweeps, milkmaids and a huge gathering of Morris dancers. Between them move a series of towering model figures: scowling 'Black Sal' and other giants sway above the crowds, a wicker man gazes down with alarming poppy-flower eyes, and grotesque ravens' heads walk behind leering rams' skulls to terrify small children. A wolf strolls past playing a guitar, followed by a gaggle of human toadstools and a mobility scooter moonlighting as a tree. But dominating over all of this are the green-clad wild men and women dancing in and out of the onlookers, clothed in ribbons and cloth-cut leaves, wreathed with flowers and garlanded with foliage. These costumes are labours of time and love.

There is no doubting that Hastings, with its strong alternative culture, has taken the celebration of Jack in the Green on May Day to its heart. Every generation is here, the white-haired as eagerly painted in green as the very young and every age in between. Many of the green-stained women wear flowers and corsets; among the men, there are many beards. This is no dignified procession, no 'them and us'; green face paint, garlands and masks have leaked out into the crowds, so that it is hard to tell who is in the parade and who is not. When asked what is being celebrated, a woman smiles and looks around: 'We're welcoming in the summer and releasing . . .' She laughs and gestures into the sky, '. . . well, whatever.'

Reaching at last the open grass at the top of West Hill, Jack and his followers mount a temporary stage on which the denouement of the procession will be enacted. Accompanied by darkly throbbing drums and surrounded by the white-shirted, red-ribboned Mad Jack's Morris troupe, here, against the magnificent backdrop of the English Channel, Jack in the Green is ritually 'slain'. As he lies helpless and prone on the stage, his green leaves are stripped from him and tossed into the crowd, who catch them eagerly, as a token of good luck for the coming year.

May Day is an ancient focus of seasonal celebration, and many other towns and cities have similar festivities, featuring their own Jacks, their own sweeps, and all the associated music, dancing and drinking that go with such events. Something clearly speaks to us still of the need to mark this moment in the year – the arrival of spring and its heralding of summer. After the long days of winter, the Jack in the Green May Day celebrations allow us to relax, to throw off the shackles of normality and release – well, whatever!

REBECCA WARREN

Bolster Day

St Agnes, Cornwall

EARLY MAY

Many of us have grown up with images of terrifying giants in pantomimes or fairy tales 'fe, fi, fo, fumming' and grinding bones to make their bread. These oversized symbols of chaos and power are represented in a wide range of cultures around the world, and the stories associated with them are often rooted in landscapes that mirror their forcefulness, such as Brittany's *Gargantua* tale and the Basque country's *Jentilak* legend. Cornwall, with its dramatic tors, craggy cliffs and jagged coastline is prime giant country.

This storied, weathered land, with its Celtic connections and isolated geography, is home to tales of giants like Gogmagog, Trecobben, Giant Cormoran and Giant Bolster. It is Bolster's story we are exploring today – a tale with echoes of the Green Man figures of other folk tales, the myths of John Barleycorn, and Norse and Irish legends of blood and land.

We will begin as all good stories do, by anchoring ourselves in a vaguely distant past. .So, once upon a time, a cruel, tyrannical giant named Bolster, who forced his wife to carry boulders all day, fell in love with a beautiful young maiden called Agnes. Fed up with his malevolence, the village mayor and a knight called Sir Constantine tried to kill him, but they were defeated. The villagers were desperate. Quick-witted Agnes tricked the giant, telling him that if he gave her proof of his love, she would love him back. She told him to fill a hole in the cliff with his blood, and he duly sliced open a vein, letting the blood seep into the hole. But Agnes knew something Bolster didn't: the hole opened up into the sea and could never be filled. Bolster slowly bled to death on the cliff, his blood staining the rocks.

The story is retold every year at the Bolster Festival, held over the early May bank holiday weekend in the village of St Agnes in Cornwall. On the Saturday a lantern-lit procession snakes from the village up the 192-metre-high Bronze Age barrow known as St Agnes Beacon for an evening of music, barbeques and a bonfire in which children fire small clay houses they have made. The next day a troupe of characters from the story make their way between the village pubs before processing to the cliffs around Chapel Porth cove. A line of drummers dressed in red and black assembles to summon the giant. It is a light-hearted pageant using people and puppets to recount the standoff between Agnes and Bolster, with long strips of red cloth representing the giant's blood rolling down the hill. This image of blood marking the landscape echoes pan-European fertility myths in which the land is nurtured by sacrificial blood.

What makes this story interesting is the agency of a young woman who takes on the hero's role. Some see Agnes as representing the Cornish people triumphing over the oppression of outside forces, claiming her as the spirit of independence and resistance. Despite the ancient roots of the myth, the custom itself is a fairly recent practice that only dates back to the 1980s. It wears this modernity proudly, not succumbing to faux-medieval pageantry, but instead embracing its status as part of a broader Cornish cultural revival. It is also a grassroots event, organised by volunteers and focusing on creativity and community rather than commercialisation.

Time is a constant presence in this event thanks to the percussive drumbeats that accompany the pageant. Drums summon Bolster and give him a breath and a pulse. They frame key elements in the story and unite the procession, giving everyone a beat to march to. This unifying and synchronising effect is an ancient part of human ritual, used across cultures to create a kind of sonic architecture that connects bodies, communities and myths.

The earliest drums were found in China and date back 7000 years, though it is thought that people could have made percussive sounds even earlier by stamping on holes in the ground that were covered with wood or animal skins. Drums appear in Egyptian murals from the Middle Kingdom, and they play a crucial role in indigenous cultures around the world. Canadian First Nations don't consider them objects; instead, they believe drums are sacred entities, the heartbeat of Mother Earth that connects them to their ancestors. The Sámi people of Lapland and northern Scandinavia see drums as reindeer or boats that transport the spirits, while Siberian Chukchi and Evenk communities feed, thank and rest their drums. Amazonian peoples link drums to forest spirits; Australian Aboriginal groups use clapsticks to connect song, land and Dreaming stories; and Burkina Faso's Dagara believe the drum is a speaking spirit.

We feel drums in our body, and they can generate feelings of safety and life (a reminder, perhaps of the steady beat of our mother's heart from the womb), as well as arousing our more violent, warlike tendencies. Like many shamanic traditions, old European drum patterns may also mirror natural biological rhythms to create 'entrainment' – the synchronising of body and brainwaves that sends us into an altered state. Much like staring into the flickering flames of a fire, absorbing a drumbeat is as elemental and ancient as the Cornish cliffs.

LULAH ELLENDER

The Clootie Well of Inverness

Munlochy, Scotland

MAY DAY
AND ALL YEAR

One person's time-honoured ritual can be another person's nuisance, and so it is with the Clootie Well at Munlochy, on the Black Isle near Inverness. The well itself, dedicated to St Curidan (also known as St Boniface), has an ancient lineage associated with healing, but if you didn't know better, the approach through the surrounding woodland might suggest that you have stumbled across a fly-tipping site. Every tree and bush is festooned with swags of faded fabric, dripping mournfully in the damp air alongside decomposing scarves and grubby socks. Here and there a decaying doll or bedraggled teddy bear, tied on to a low-hanging branch, stares sightlessly at the ground, legs dangling, head lolling. If part of your healing ritual is to commune, unmediated by modernity, with the beauty of the natural world, this may not be the place to come. And yet, where some people see the jumble surrounding the Clootie Well as an eyesore, symbolising our spoliation of the natural environment, others see it as a vibrant illustration of an ancient therapeutic tradition still flourishing in the modern world.

Whichever side you take, this custom shows no sign of dying out. And despite the slightly chaotic appearance of the well, it enjoys all the usual trappings of a carefully managed tourist attraction: there is a well-signed car park, a well-maintained access path, a friendly information board, and a notice requesting that synthetic fabrics should not be left in the trees. One might wonder whether these attempts to 'manage' the site threaten its intrinsic spirituality. But perhaps they offer welcome guidance for those who come in search of comfort and reassurance.

Either way, the well at Munlochy is widely believed to have curative qualities, and the tradition goes something like this: you bring to the well an item of clothing – a 'clootie' – that relates to a sick person, and you tie it on to a branch as near to the water as possible. And there it is left to decay. Some people say the clootie must also be wiped over the ill person before dipping it in the water and leaving it to rot. Others assert that the clootie must be soaked in the water before wiping it over the ill person, and still others say it is sufficient just to bring a clootie that represents the ailment to dip in the well before leaving it nearby. Whichever method you favour, everyone agrees that as the clootie rots away, the sickness will vanish too.

From the number of scarves and socks draped in the undergrowth, it might appear that most supplicants have sore throats or bunions – but closer inspection reveals other items too. Fading shirts clasp their empty sleeves passionately around tree trunks, boots and trainers swing on fraying laces next to shapeless bath towels and soggy ties, and a smattering of knickers, bras and underpants dangle demurely between tattered flags, flannels and dish-cloths. All body parts, it would seem, are represented here, damply decomposing in the forest air.

The Clootie Well at Munlochy attracts visitors from across the world, and, indeed, the tradition of healing wells, pilgrimages and the leaving of offerings that relate to bodily ailments is both ancient and cross-cultural. At first glance, there is something unsettling about the fact that people are investing their hopes for health and comfort in a place where so many tokens of illness and suffering are dangling in the undergrowth, stained with bird droppings and mould. It is hardly a sight to cheer the hearts of the sick and anxious, and you'd have to be very brave – or very desperate – to drink the well water, as some versions of the tradition recommend. But maybe the grim surroundings of the well are entirely appropriate. Illness and pain are not beautiful and tidy, but ragged and challenging and often unpleasant to observe. Our desire to sanitise sickness is a luxury our ancestors did not have and, perhaps, would not have understood. After all, for those who visit the well in genuine distress, what matters is hope. So perhaps the experience of seeing the hundreds of garments that others have left speaks of hope shared, and of belonging to a community of those who also want to believe.

There is also a lighter side to the Clootie Well tradition, of course. The best time to visit is said to be around May Day or, for the neo-pagans, Beltane. And from the number of football-related clooties left to rot, and the scatter of coins dropped in the stone cistern that catches the well water, it must be assumed that many visitors are less interested in healing than in garnering good fortune for their favoured team or cause. It seems that here the line between a healing well and a wishing well is hazy at best – but then, who can say what might work?

One thing that isn't working, however, is the plea for visitors to leave only natural materials that will rot away. Hand-scrawled notes tied among the rotting garments reveal a desire to heal the damage caused by our pollution and destruction of the natural world. It is a bitter irony that many of the offerings at the well are made of synthetic fibres, which will not rot for decades or, in some cases, centuries.

Recently, the charged feelings around the tatty appearance of the Munlochy well found dramatic expression, when all the clooties were removed overnight. Clearly someone could bear the mess no longer, and the resulting publicity highlighted the divided nature of our approach to such places and customs, where one person's healing well can be another person's eyesore. And maybe that's OK? Many of our folk customs seek to shake up the everyday, to subvert the acceptable – so, in this way, the Clootie Well at Munlochy is continuing a fine tradition – both comforting us and disturbing us at the same time.

REBECCA WARREN

Tissington Well Dressing

Tissington, Derbyshire

ASCENSION DAY
(FORTY DAYS AFTER EASTER)

In the warmth of late May, a smooth sheet of spring water slides unobtrusively out of a shallow circular pool below a garden wall, into a small stone basin, in which a scatter of votive coins glitter and shine. Brimming over the lip of the basin, the water trickles on down a cobble-lined channel to join a narrow stream that hugs the road on its way past the village church. Back at the pool, a crowd of onlookers has gathered to hear members of the local clergy, eye-catching in their white cassocks, recite psalms and lead hymns in a Christian blessing of the waters. And above the spring itself, where the water drops into the pool, stands a large board, decorated with colourful scenes, biblical sayings and worthy phrases – for the village of Tissington, in the heart of the Peak District, has 'dressed' its wells and, for a brief few days, it has become a place of both secular and religious pilgrimage.

Water is a feature of this village, oozing out of the underlying limestone in a series of springs before feeding into the Bradbourne Brook and eventually joining the river Dove. Generations of Tissington's residents have benefited from this underground water supply, protected from the threat of drought and disease by the upwelling of safe, clean water from the rocks below. How long the village has been decorating and celebrating its wells, however, is unclear. Antiquarians in the nineteenth century pushed the origin of well dressing, rather romantically, back to the Roman period, arguing that it emerged from the ancient festival of Fontinalia, celebrating Fons, the god of wells and springs. Others claimed it had roots in the pre-Christian worship of 'Celtic' water deities. More plausibly, it has been suggested that Tissington's well dressing began as a Christian thanksgiving ceremony for the pure water that had enabled the villagers to survive the Black Death in 1348. Of course, we now know that this plague was spread by lice and fleas or infected breath rather than by unclean water, but perhaps Tissington's clean water saved its inhabitants from the water-borne diseases that occurred elsewhere as a result of rotting, plague-ridden bodies? An alternative thanksgiving origin dates from 1615, when the village springs continued to run despite a widespread drought. Whatever its beginnings, the custom itself is an old one, although the use of decorated boards does not appear in the records until the nineteenth century, when they are noted as an addition to the use of floral garlands.

*

Tissington is not alone in dressing its wells; the geology of the Peak District gives rise to many springs, and other villages in Derbyshire and beyond have similar water-related customs. At Tissington, the wells are dressed on Ascension Day, the fortieth day of Easter, but elsewhere community well-dressings take place throughout the summer. Whenever it happens, the popularity and longevity of the practice of well dressing is impressive, and perhaps in part this is a result of the team effort required to build the decorated boards: large oak frames are soaked for several days before being covered in a layer of clay. The designs are pressed into the clay with small brown alder cones or even coffee beans, before the rest of the colours are filled in using only natural items, such as petals, leaves and stones. The process takes several days and relies upon cooperation and experience. Community enterprises on the scale of those involved in well dressing clearly help to cement social relationships and enhance a sense of belonging.

Yet perhaps there is something deeper at play here, too. The sight of water welling up out of the ground still has us enthralled; it is a strong will that can resist throwing a coin into a pool while muttering a wish. Whether it is a garden pond, a waterfall or a riverbank, water draws us towards it. It is a focal point, a gathering place, an 'other world' reflecting reality back at us, changed but the same. It is not hard to understand why older traditions saw pools as portals to the underworld. Water, as they say, is the fountain of life, so perhaps the celebration of springs, however small and tamed they may be, speaks to something primitive in us all.

REBECCA WARREN

Levellers Day

Burford, Oxfordshire

17 MAY

There aren't many towns as relentlessly pretty as Burford, sitting on the edge of the Cotswolds in West Oxfordshire. The golden sandstone of the buildings that line its prosperous high street imparts a cosy and timeless serenity to the place. There is a palpable feeling of affluence here: antique shops jostle for space with clothing boutiques, art galleries and upmarket pubs. At the foot of the hill, discreetly tucked out of sight, a crowded coach park betrays the extent of the tourism that bolsters the town's income, for this is a place which unashamedly services those with wealth and leisure. All of this imparts a delicious irony to the annual celebration of Levellers Day in mid-May, when Burford's pact with Mammon is briefly challenged by a parade of resolute but cheerful figures waving banners in support of socialism, communism and workers' rights. The contrast between the event and its location feels incongruous – and poignant.

Levellers Day commemorates the execution of three soldiers in Burford churchyard during the mid-seventeenth century, and it has taken place annually since its inception in 1975. The custom harks back to the 1640s, when the Civil Wars were raging between King Charles I and his parliament. The social upheaval that accompanied the fighting triggered an explosion in radical political and religious ideas, which found particularly fertile ground within the rank and file of the army. By 1647, many ordinary soldiers had come to believe that hazarding their lives for Parliament entitled them to greater political power and more religious freedom. As parliamentary leaders struggled to reach a settlement with the now-imprisoned king, some of those who called for profound political and religious change coalesced into a faction known as the Levellers, who published their demands for reform in a manifesto called *An Agreement of the People*.

The *Agreement* demanded the vote for most men over the age of twenty-one, as well as annual parliamentary elections, legal reforms, fairer taxation and the abolition of military conscription. Not surprisingly, it was opposed by both parliamentary and army grandees, who feared a breakdown in political control and a collapse of the wider social order. Arguments over the *Agreement* continued until January 1649, when Charles I was finally executed. In the chaotic aftermath of the regicide, however, the Levellers and their manifesto were sidelined by Parliament. The result was that simmering resentment in the ranks turned into outright rebellion. Finally, in early May, three months after Charles's execution, several hundred soldiers quartered in Banbury set out to rendezvous with other troops in Salisbury. Fearful that this would lead to a general mutiny, the army commanders, Sir Thomas Fairfax and Oliver Cromwell, intercepted the soldiers at Burford, imprisoning some of them in the parish church. On 17 May, three of the ringleaders, Private John Church, Cornet James Thompson and Corporal Perkins, were led into the churchyard and executed. The rest of the men were pardoned and returned to their regiments.

History, they say, is written by the victors, and after the restoration of the monarchy in 1660, the events that accompanied the radicalism of the Levellers' movement were conveniently forgotten. For the next three centuries they remained a minor footnote to the idea of the 'natural progression' of capitalism, remembered only at moments of social upheaval, such as the Chartist riots of the mid-nineteenth century. In 1975, however, the Oxford branch of the Workers' Educational Association chose to redress the disappearance of the Levellers from public consciousness, holding a commemoration service in Burford churchyard and affixing a memorial plaque naming the executed soldiers. The success of the event generated such enthusiasm that Levellers Day has been celebrated there every year since.

Despite the seriousness of its theme, Levellers Day is a cheerful occasion. The march down the high street is a colourful, if noisy, parade. People in jeans waving large decorated banners mix with others in seventeenth-century costumes. Some years there are Morris dancers, and often a local choir, the Sea Green Singers, performs freedom- and green-themed anthems throughout the day. The atmosphere is good-natured, but there is a slight frisson of defiance among many of those who attend, for no one can be unaware of the painful irony of proclaiming socialist ideals in the moneyed setting of Burford. A few desultory policemen chat to onlookers who perhaps wonder what these law enforcers are doing there, for it would be hard to find a less threatening political march. Indeed, Levellers Day is as far from a violent expression of outrage and rebellion as it is possible to be, and yet the brightly coloured banners reveal that this is a gathering of people supporting some of the most fundamental issues of how we treat – and mistreat – each other as human beings. The trade unions are well represented, as are local branches of the Labour Party, local peace groups, Amnesty International and CND. The red flags of Communism flutter alongside those of the Woodcraft Folk, and the Green Party's presence is evident from the many green banners fluttering on poles.

One might say, in fact, that green is the unofficial colour of the event, for the original Levellers wore twigs of rosemary in their hats and green ribbons to identify themselves. There is a sweet irony in this: in Shakespeare's *Hamlet*, rosemary was hauntingly given by Ophelia to her brother Laertes 'for remembrance; pray, love, remember . . .', and Levellers Day is, at its heart, about exactly that: prayer, love and remembrance for the executed soldiers and their idealism. More overtly, each year's event has its own theme – defending democracy and the right to protest; resisting poverty and oppression; learning lessons from history; seeking justice – around which talks and debates led by high-profile campaigners and politicians are given.

Levellers Day is the epitome of a custom that reflects contemporary events. Its emergence in Britain in 1975 surely reflected the numerous crises of the year before, when the country entered an economic recession, the miners' strike resulted in the 'three-day week' to save energy, the IRA undertook an extensive bombing campaign in England, and inflation soared to 17 per cent. More recently, the day's focus has been on such issues as the crackdown on the right to protest peacefully, lack of action on climate breakdown, the impact of 'fake news', and the experience of obscene wealth alongside abject poverty within modern Britain. In the seventeenth century, the Levellers were rebelling against political impotence and inequality; it seems that in the twenty-first century there is much, still, in our society that they would recognise and decry.

REBECCA WARREN

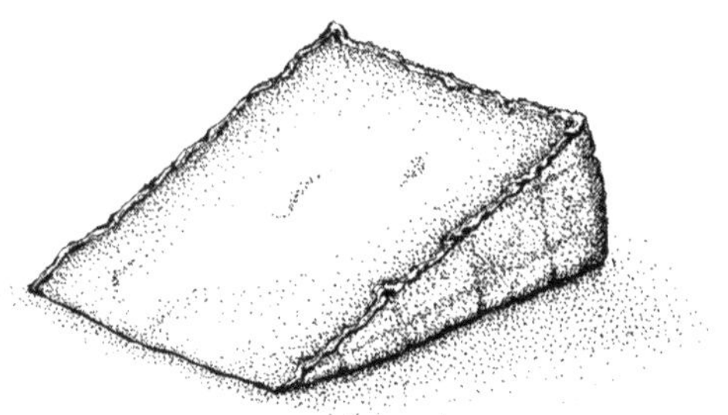

Cheese Rolling

Brockworth, Gloucestershire

LATE MAY BANK HOLIDAY

Let's begin with some numbers:

- 8 pounds – the weight of the Double Gloucester cheese rolled down a hill
- 1:2 – the hill's gradient
- 54 metres – the hill's drop in elevation
- 90 metres – the distance the cheese travels
- 75 miles per hour – the speed the cheese could reach
- 7 – the number of races where people chase the cheese down the hill
- 25 – the maximum number of people in each race
- 1 second – the length of the cheese's head start
- 8–12 – the number of cheeses made specially for this event
- 5 – the number of double-crewed ambulances in attendance in 2025

Now for the action. On the last bank holiday Monday in May, a crowd of spectators gathers around the edges of Cooper's Hill, a steep grassy slope just outside the village of Brockworth in Gloucestershire. Competitors jostle in a line at the top, looking over the precipice as they await the signal. At the bottom, volunteers stand by with first-aid kits and blankets to shield the injured from the hundreds of onlookers. In a field beyond, an air ambulance helicopter crouches in readiness. The Master of Ceremonies cries, 'Are you ready for the cheese?' and the crowd chants in response, 'Cheese! Cheese! Cheese!' The cheese is let loose, closely followed by the competitors.

The aim is to chase the cheese and get to the bottom of the hill first. The race is a furious jumble of flying limbs, bouncing bodies and muddied faces as the competitors run, roll, hurl, fly and tumble down the hill. Broken bones are common, and bruises are inevitable. The winner is presented with the cheese, which they hold aloft to great cheers, doubtless feeling not just a huge adrenaline rush but a wash of relief, too, for making it down in one piece.

There are several men's and women's downhill races over the course of the day; children's and occasional uphill races are sometimes held separately. Locals train for weeks beforehand and have the advantage of knowing the hill's tuffets and holes, while eager tourists take their chances with fate. A twenty-three-times winner says the best tactic is to try to stay on your feet, but there are a variety of other – possibly unintended – techniques for getting down the hill, ranging from professional-looking army rolls to haphazard ragdoll tumbles. In 2025, a twenty-two-year-old man dressed as a wizard took such a spectacular somersault that he was knocked unconscious for three hours (luckily, with no long-term injuries) – and became an internet sensation as a result. The first written record of the event dates to 1826 (some claim it dates back much further, to pre-Roman times, but evidence for that is scant), and in all these years there have been no deaths. For public safety and insurance reasons, the event was declared unsafe in 2010 and has continued in an unofficial capacity since, classed as an 'extreme sport'.

Winners often choose to donate their prize cheese to charities, and some become local heroes. The ashes of one previous winner, Steve Brain, are scattered on the hill. The event is a source of pride (and welcome income) for the community – not just in the bravery of the participants, but also in the cheese itself. For the last twenty years the Double Gloucester cheeses used in the races have been handmade on nearby Smart's Farm. This type of cheese is made from milk from the rare Old Gloucester breed of cattle, which nearly became extinct in the 1950s after years of rationing had crippled dairy businesses. The breed was revived in the 1970s by farmer Charles Martell. Not only is Double Gloucester produced locally, its semi-hard texture (the result of a long ageing process) makes it a sturdy choice for this demanding custom. Schoolchildren help prepare the cheeses for the event, wrapping them in cardboard and paper, and then finishing them with a red and a blue ribbon.

The role of cheese in human culture runs deep. While this Gloucestershire event is one of its more eccentric manifestations, evidence of dairy processing dates back to around 3800 bc. While we now have over 750 varieties in Britain alone, early cheeses would have been soft and curdy, with firmer kinds developed by monks across Europe in the Middle Ages. Traditional Double Gloucester production is part of the Great Cheese Renaissance of recent years, whereby dairy producers have rejected large-scale slab manufacture in favour of skilled artisan cheese-making.

Cheese also features in transhumance festivals such as Austria's *Almabtrieb* and Switzerland's *Alpabzug* (Descent of the Cows); and across Italy on Easter Monday, towns and villages hold *Ruzzola del Formaggio* competitions, where men roll large pecorino cheeses to see who can get theirs the furthest, launching them with strings like liberated yoyos. While these festivals celebrate cheese with ritual and pageantry, Gloucestershire's Cheese Rolling embraces chaos and competition.

There is something about the combination of cheese made from local cows' milk and the vertiginous landscape of Gloucestershire's wolds that makes the Cheese Rolling so unique. Formed in the Jurassic era, these limestone hills and valleys have inspired writers from J. R. R Tolkien to J. K Rowling, but they were perhaps most famously brought to life by local author Laurie Lee. His descriptions of Gloucestershire village life, often written with a heavy dollop of nostalgia, put this quiet area on the cultural map. While he later acknowledged that life wasn't 'all rising fields of poppies and blue skies' and talked about the grinding poverty and lashing rain, his work conveys a deep and often sentimental love for the landscape's 'long shadows in tufts and hollows'. There is an enchantment and harshness about this rippling countryside that makes it the perfect setting for the chaos of the Cheese Rolling.

The real winner of the event? The cheese. It has survived near extinction and has become a global symbol of courage and derring-do – and it always gets to the bottom of the hill first.

LULAH ELLENDER

Hunting of the Earl of Rone

Combe Martin, Devon

LATE MAY BANK HOLIDAY

Authenticity is a tricky concept. One meaning of the word associates it with continuity: something is said to be authentic if it can be traced directly back to an origin in a distant past, on which a faithful tradition is built. Another definition, however, associates authenticity with a break from history, when energy is applied to achieve a change towards something that is more genuine than what came before, which is now pictured as stultifying and old-fashioned. As literary critic Lionel Trilling has noted, the second usage draws on the word's linguistic roots in the ancient Greek term *authentēs*, which means an originator, someone who acts under their own authority – though it also has a darker side, denoting someone who commits a killing. *Authentēs*, according to Trilling, means 'not only a master and a doer, but also a perpetrator, a murderer'.

Arguments about whether authenticity lies in the persistence of the past or in a rift with it permeate the study of folklore, too. Some scholars distinguish between 'folklore' and 'folklorism'. In their view, folklore is something that emanates organically from the life of a locally settled community, preserved for a length of time in more or less unchanging form. Folklorism, on the other hand, refers to a custom that has been adapted or altered in some way. Sometimes the latter word has a neutral meaning, but it can also be used more pejoratively, to signal a 'fakelore' that is judged to be kitschy, fallen or inauthentic in some way.

One event that raises questions about authenticity, as well as exemplifying the utterly bonkers nature of some British customs, is the Hunting of the Earl of Rone. Held at Combe Martin, a village on the north coast of Devon, on the spring Bank Holiday, this four-day festival offers a smorgasbord of British folkloric elements. The Friday, Saturday and Sunday of the holiday see processions through the streets, but the climax of the weekend comes on Monday. It is then that the Earl of Rone himself makes an appearance, wearing a black, white and red mask over a hessian costume stuffed with straw padding. Around his neck is a string of twelve huge sea biscuits: dense dried crackers made to store on long voyages. In the early evening, at around 6 p.m., the earl creeps into the local woods to hide in the undergrowth. A group of people dressed as redcoat grenadiers then march down from the village to the sound of military drums and assiduously hunt for him. On the discovery of his whereabouts, there is a mock fight, but the outcome is always the same: the earl is captured and a volley of shots is fired to signal the moment, while the crowd boos the prisoner and cheers the soldiers.

The earl is then made to sit backwards on a donkey, which also wears a necklace of sea biscuits, along with garlands of flowers. One year, this element of the procession had to be abandoned because the donkey refused to move, transfixed by a nearby female in heat, and the earl had to walk around on foot instead. But normally, donkey, earl and grenadiers march back into the village to the accompaniment of a folk band. Eventually, their ranks are swollen into a procession, which follows a set route around the village.

At certain points the grenadiers force the earl to dismount, and then fire their muskets at him. They are delighted when he falls, but there are terrible laments from two other characters – the Hobby-horse and the Fool. Fortunately for the earl, the Hobby-horse, a stalwart of mumming plays, has miraculous healing powers and can leap in and revive the dead, allowing the procession to continue to its next stop, where the whole scene is repeated. The masked fool, meanwhile, solicits financial contributions from the audience, sprinkling them with dirty water from a broom if they refuse. The Hobby-horse also carries inducements towards generosity: it brandishes a pair of jaws, called a 'mapper', that can snap at any delinquents who don't pay up. The donations used to be spent at local hostelries, and the generosity of the village was such that the custom was banned in 1837 for causing 'rough horse-play and drinking habits'. Local stories tell of an intoxicated member of the party falling down some steps at Lynton Cottage and breaking his neck – and even today, the procession falls silent as it passes this location.

Finally, actors, musicians and spectators wend their way to the beach, where everyone forms a large circle, inside which the Fool, the Hobby-horse and the attendants dance. The earl himself is finally 'shot' and then flung into the sea and ceremonially 'drowned', scapegoat-style, in the breaking waves.

What are the origins of this strange custom? One theory is that its central character is based on the Irish aristocrat Hugh O'Neill, the Earl of Tyrone, a rebel against the English who fled Ireland in 1607. Yet there is no record of the historical earl ever going anywhere near Combe Martin – according to the official histories, he fled to Spain. There were Irish miners in the village, however, who may well have sympathised with O'Neill's views, so the name may have something to do with their legacy. Other writers think the ceremony is older, reflecting medieval May Day festivities, or even pre-Christian Green Man customs.

The current incarnation is relatively recent, having been revived in 1978 after a gap of 140 years. In the decades since, the event has shifted and evolved, making it an interesting example of the ways in which customs get adapted, bit by bit, to fit the world around them. For instance, the person who plays the earl has to be a minor (so as not to overburden the donkey), and changes to child safeguarding now mean that they have to be accompanied by two adults while hiding in the woods. However, this adult supervision first happened for very different reasons: one year, a group of enterprising children stole a march on the grenadiers and found the earl themselves, upsetting the whole celebration. Similarly, chaos created by young boys riding in and out of the procession on their bikes was avoided by adding a rope to the front of the procession, carried between a number of women and decorated with ribbons and flowers. A pretty garland in the shape of a flower-bedecked pole was also incorporated, integrating what was formerly a separate May Day tradition into the weekend. This, too, has a pragmatic use: there are now so many participants that a visual signal – hoisting the pole – is needed between the front and rear of the cavalcade to ensure that everyone stops simultaneously at the right places.

A new group of characters has also emerged: the Horse Maidens ensure that the Hobby-horse, who wears a gigantic rigid hessian-covered circle around its neck, does not collide with the growing crowds of spectators. The horse maidens each wear a corsage of lily-of-the-valley flowers after one of the organisers spontaneously brought a bunch from their garden one year. Other sartorial elements have also shifted: in the 1970s most women wore an approximation of a nineteenth-century costume, with shawls over long dresses, or a blouse combined with a long skirt, but today many wear contemporary floral dresses. Early in the revival, instructions to wear a mob cap provoked a revolt among the younger generation of participants, with some choosing to go bare-headed rather than don the unflattering hat. When one woman placed a garland of flowers in her hair, however, it caught on with other participants, and a new tradition was born. Cross-dressing also became part of the new custom when some of the grenadiers decided to start exchanging clothes with women in the procession halfway through the event. Finally, 'the Death Run', a madcap rush by the Hobby-horse and the Fool down a steep local street, has now been outlawed. Rumour has it that it was a victim of health-and-safety concerns.

For Tom Brown, a folklorist who vividly documented these changes in a series of often amusing accounts, these shifts in the custom are evidence of it moving from folklore in the nineteenth century to folklorism in the 1970s revival, and then back again to folklore as repetition bedded in the new version. But this raises more questions than it answers. When the custom was revived in the 1970s, was that first event somehow less authentic simply because so much time had passed since its last performance in 1837? Is authenticity just about constant repetition, so something becomes progressively more authentic, in linear fashion, every time it recurs? And if so, how do we define that magical point when folklorism becomes folklore once again? How many repetitions does it take? And do we start counting afresh when new elements are added?

As Trilling reminds us, the word 'authenticity' can connote both tradition and its violent rupture. And if there is a form of killing involved in the constant pragmatic reinvention of folklore, then perhaps there's no more appropriate custom to illustrate this than the Earl of Rone. It is, at root, all about symbolic murder.

KIERA CHAPMAN

JUNE

Appleby Horse Fair

Appleby-in-Westmorland, Cumbria

EARLY JUNE

Appleby Horse Fair might be the most stigmatised custom in this book, for the simple reason that there is an enduring prejudice against those who wander. The Gypsies and Travellers who gather annually in the town of Appleby-in-Westmorland, Cumbria, for this horse fair have long been a target for legalised abuse. When Romani people first began to arrive in Britain in numbers in the early sixteenth century, their itinerancy, their poverty, their association with fortune telling, and their refusal to bow their knee to the dictates of waged work all exacerbated existing alarm around 'vagrants'. In 1530, Henry VIII tried to banish them from the kingdom as a threat to moral order. Further laws to control their presence followed, in

1554 and 1562, which made Gypsies vulnerable not just to deportation, but even potentially to execution. These pieces of legislation were known as the 'Egyptians Acts': the word 'Gypsy' derives from 'Egyptian' and refers to a mistaken belief that Romani people came from northern Africa. Modern genetic evidence instead suggests that they originated from northern India.

The Egyptians Acts were not repealed until 1783, but the intervening period saw a shift in the perception of Gypsies. By the Romantic era (about 1770–1830), they were seen as an evocative presence in the landscape, with works by writers like Byron, Wordsworth and Clare featuring them as exoticised 'others'. Sometimes they were portrayed as a relic of a pre-modern and irrational past, ill-adapted to the new industrial and urban world. But they could also be represented as the source of an alternative and mysterious culture that was closer to nature, community and virtue than mainstream society. Whatever view they took, writers on both sides of this debate now agreed on one thing: Gypsies were a part of the British landscape. They belonged.

In the nineteenth century, particularly after the potato famine, another group with a similarly nomadic lifestyle arrived from Ireland. Irish Travellers are ethnically distinct from Gypsies, and have a separate culture. One striking element of this is a secret language, or 'cryptolect', called Shelta (also known as 'the Cant' and 'de Gammon'). Shelta words are often formed from Irish or English ones by transposing letters, adding sounds to the start or end of words, or substituting consonants. It's as if the roving lifestyle of the group found expression in a language that also refuses to stand still. Shelta has a clear purpose: it helps members of a persecuted community to identify one another and converse without interference from outsiders, known as 'Buffers'. Consequently, those who speak it are often reticent about sharing its meanings with those outside the community, making this a difficult language to study.

As the nineteenth century wore on, however, perceptions of both groups of nomads shifted once again. Despite nostalgic depictions of Gypsy life in work by prominent writers like George Borrow, the growth of nationalism and biological racism led to a hostile argument that Gypsies and Travellers were a 'lesser race' who existed at a more primitive stage of history than dominant white Europeans. What had seemed to many Romantics to be a charmingly nostalgic lifestyle from the past began once more to be depicted as a threat to mainstream society. The ultimate consequences of this belief were unimaginably tragic: as many as 500,000 Gypsies were murdered in the Nazi Holocaust in the name of racial purification.

While Gypsies and Travellers today are ostensibly protected from discrimination, they often face hidden forms of prejudice as the targets of a racism that is all too often normalised as acceptable. A 2018 report found that 44 per cent of British people were prepared to express negative attitudes towards Gypsies and Travellers, compared with 22 per cent who aired discriminatory views against Muslims. While racism is generally condemned in our society, not all of its forms are treated equally.

Responses to Appleby Horse Fair are often clouded with similar prejudice, and many people may therefore be coming to this custom through a haze of negative media coverage.

Newspaper reports frequently highlight anti-social behaviour, disruption, criminality, noise and mess: in 2024, the *Daily Mail* sent a reporter to the town, publishing their report under the headline 'Appleby Ground Zero: Fighting in the street, urine through letter boxes and locals terrified into silence'.

Despite such inflammatory coverage, the fair is a well-established event on the cultural calendar (it has greater antiquity than some of the other customs in this book) and continues to be enjoyed by thousands. It began as a drover gathering to sell livestock in the late eighteenth century, but by the turn of the twentieth century, it had become a major public event, and today attracts between 30,000 and 50,000 visitors and 10,000 Gypsies and Travellers. Some of the latter arrive in traditional hand-painted vardos, or wagons, others in more modern and roomy caravans. And there are horses *everywhere* – in particular, the distinctive cobs and vanners, with their feathered ankles, powerful necks and waterfall manes.

Appleby Horse Fair has its own geography, and its organisation is carefully coordinated between the town council and the 'Shera Rom', or head of the Gypsies, who acts as a spokesperson. Together, they arrange the considerable infrastructure that a custom of this scale requires: toilets, rubbish collection, water, and grazing for the animals. The main area for accommodation is at Fair Hill, though other, private fields are rented out nearby by local farmers. Market Field is the centre for catering and stalls, while horse trading takes place at a nearby crossroads called Salt Tip Corner and along Long Marton Road. The latter is known in the community as 'Flashing Lane' or simply 'The Flash', and it is here that you can witness spectacular horsemanship, since the long, straight, narrow lane makes it possible to get up a heart-thudding, breakneck gallop. Horses are taken down to the banks of the river Eden, known as 'the Sands', for washing, which is said to bring both the animal and its rider good luck. Navigating these waters on horseback is a feat: the river runs deep and cold, with a strong current.

The fair acts as a powerful affirmation of Gypsy and Traveller identity, and it is especially important for teenagers, given that children from these communities often experience bullying at school. Social media has created new opportunities to push back against some of the stereotyping they face, and there are now influencers who use video platforms such as TikTok and YouTube to promote a more contemporary image. Many are articulate young women with large followings, who describe their lifestyle to a fascinated audience, including behind-the-scenes tours of their caravans, and extensive content about the clothing, hair and makeup they choose for Appleby. Dressing up to the nines is part of the fun, and the image of femininity that they present is a long way from the romanticised image of flowing skirts, fringed shawls and shining gold headpieces. Yet this contemporary representation does not always work in their favour, being interpreted in some quarters as a sign of inauthenticity. Those being criticised cannot win, caught between accusations of backwardness and charges of being fake.

But it's not just cultural forms of discrimination that are a problem: legislation that singles out Gypsies and Travellers continues to be enacted. In 2022, the government passed the Police, Crime, Sentencing and Courts Act, which restricts the right to hold peaceful political protests, and also redefines the legal definition of 'trespass' in ways that impact the travelling communities. People who stay on land without permission, living in or with a vehicle, and who cause, or are deemed likely to cause, significant damage, disruption or distress, are now, according to this Act, committing not a civil offence, but a criminal one – punishable by a £2500 fine, prison time or seizure of property by the police.

At first sight, it might sound reasonable to evict someone from an unauthorised campsite where they are staying without leave. But bear in mind that travelling to Appleby with a horse entails a very different rhythm from travelling by car or train, since journeys must be broken into small and manageable stages. Local councils have a duty to provide designated places for Gypsies and Travellers to stop, but many are failing to support the community in this way, meaning that legitimate sites are simply not available. Meanwhile, toleration of traditional stopping places has eroded, with landowners increasingly challenging their use in this way. The 2022 Act has effectively criminalised the traditional Gypsy and Traveller way of life, and the cumulative effect is that many families are now left with no option other than to camp in unlicensed places.

This is just the latest in a centuries-old attempt to force these two communities to stay still, including late-twentieth-century efforts to rehouse them in bricks-and-mortar homes, 'sedentarising' them in the name of assimilation into mainstream society. The onslaught has taken its toll: many of those still on the road are now semi-nomadic, journeying only for holidays, special events like weddings, and, of course, Appleby Horse Fair.

But why do we as a society have such a problem with mobility when it is a traditional way of life? Its millennial equivalent, van living, is seen more positively as the assertion of a freedom to travel, as is the leisure pursuit of caravanning. The answer is complicated, but the perceived economic subversiveness of refusing both waged work and the debt associated with property ownership may be part of the answer. Another possibility is that we have too restrictive an idea of folk culture, seeing it only as something that emanates organically from a community, a 'natural' result of long-term rootedness in a particular location, rather than as something that can be nomadic and roaming. But if we adjust our lens to include cultures that are all about movement, then we might just see that Appleby Horse Fair is not just another fair or festival like the others in this book. Instead, it's a unique event that reflects the history, resilience and identity of two remarkable groups – and provides an important space for exchange and sociability between them.

KIERA CHAPMAN

Knollys Rose Ceremony

All Hallows-by-the-Tower and Mansion House, London

EARLY JUNE

Here's a cautionary little tale that goes back to 1381. In that year, Lady Constance Knollys, living just around the corner from the Tower of London, found herself with a knotty problem. Just to the north of her rather smart house on Seething Lane was a corn market, and all too often, wheat for the market was threshed on the land opposite her house, filling the air – and her home – with chaff and dust. Lady Constance, who had a practical turn of mind, eventually solved her problem by buying the offending piece of land and building another house upon it, with a dear little garden for good measure. However, her difficulties did not stop there: the threshing may have ceased, but the street between her two houses was still dirty and muddy in winter, dusty and foul in summer; worse still, it was frequented by common people and animals at all times of the year. What to do?

Her husband Robert was no use; having recently helped King Richard II to put down the Peasants' Revolt, he had immediately hot-footed it back to France to continue fighting in the Hundred Years' War. So once again, Lady Constance took matters into her own hands; this time she built a footbridge right over Seething Lane, so that she could access her new property without befouling herself in the muck and mayhem of the street below. Problem solved, she must have thought.

But no! The city council, which, even in the fourteenth century, was rather keen on planning control, took umbrage at her actions, which it claimed had been carried out without its permission. And perhaps Lady Constance trembled at the thought of punishment – her feelings at this point in the proceedings were not, alas, recorded – but she need not have feared. In the end, the council rolled over and granted her and Robert a retrospective licence to build their footbridge – or, as they termed it, their 'Haut-pas' – at a 'height of 14 feet extending from the house of the said Robert and Constance his wife on the west side thereof to another house to them belonging on the east side thereof'. Perhaps Robert's fearsome reputation as a commander of English forces in France had some bearing with them, or his popularity with King Richard may have swayed their decision. Or perhaps they agreed with Constance that Seething Lane was just too unpleasant for a well-bred lady to cross – who knows? All they asked for their generous concession was that, in return, she and

Robert should give a red rose to the 'Chamberlain of the Guild Hall' [today the Lord Mayor] every year on 24 June, the feast day of St John the Baptist.

That, at least, is the story that has come down to us over the centuries. Not surprisingly, there is no longer an 'haut-pas' over Seething Lane, but, strangely enough, there is still a garden on the east side. This cannot be the direct descendant of Lady Constance's garden, however, since it is on the site of what was once the Navy Office, famously the place where the seventeenth-century diarist Samuel Pepys worked. And, of course, neither Lady Constance nor Sir Robert – nor, indeed, Sam Pepys – would recognise Seething Lane today, since what wasn't damaged by the Great Fire of London, whose greedy flames licked up as far as the houses along its western side, was mostly destroyed in the Blitz of the Second World War. Yet somehow, even though the buildings are long gone, the custom has survived, having been revived in 1924 after a gap of 250 years.

Nowadays, the garden in Seething Lane near the site of the Knollys' former property belongs to the City's Company of Watermen and Lightermen of the River Thames. And every year, in early June, members of the Company, the Knollys family and other dignitaries gather at All Hallows-by-the-Tower Church, just to the south, before walking in procession to the garden, where a single red rose is picked. Placed carefully on a blue cushion, it is then carried in procession to the Mansion House, where it is formally handed to the Lord Mayor as rent for the non-existent footbridge.

That's not quite the end of the story, however. In 1514, another Sir Robert Knollys, a distant descendant of Sir Robert and Lady Constance, was gifted Greys Court in

Oxfordshire by King Henry VIII, in return for an annual red rose. This floral remittance passed down to his son Sir Francis, who also paid a rose to Queen Elizabeth I in turn for the manor. Somehow and somewhere in the retelling, however, the gift and recipient appear to have become confused, so that now the rose is believed to have been paid *by* the Crown *to* the Knollys family, and the phrase 'a Knollys rose' has become a synonym for a royal grant or pension. It seems curious that by chance two separate members of the Knollys family were charged a rent of a red rose by the Crown, so perhaps Henry VIII asked for the red rose by way of an allusion to the Knollys family's existing form of rent for the property in Seething Lane?

And yet, the payment of a rose as rent was, and still is, not unique. In 1436, William Clopton, Lord of Toppesfield Manor in the Suffolk town of Hadleigh, granted land there for a guildhall and market, initially in return for an annual rent of one mark, later converted to a single red rose. Today, a ceremony still takes place in the parish church of the neighbouring village of Long Melford, where William's tomb lies; at this ceremony, a single red rose is 'paid' by the mayor of Hadleigh to a representative of Long Melford Parish Council, standing in for the absent Clopton family, who now live abroad, and the rose is placed on the tomb. Other examples of such floral token rents also exist, so it turns out that the payment of the Knollys red rose is not a one-off example of British whimsy, but part of a once-standard payment method similar to the better-known 'peppercorn rent'. No doubt there are many people today who would be more than happy to pay their landlords in flowers or spice, rather than hard-earned cash.

REBECCA WARREN

The Common Riding

Selkirk, Scotland

MID-JUNE

Early on a Friday morning in mid-June, the streets of Selkirk in the Scottish borders are ringing with the sound of horses' hooves. It's only 7 a.m., but already it's been a busy day: Selkirk Flute Band was up and piping at 4 a.m., and at 5.30 a.m. a wreath was laid at the war memorial. By 6 a.m., the centre of the town was filled with people on foot and on horseback and, at the beat of a drum, the town provost handed over the Selkirk standard – a heavy blue and white flag on a long pole – to a young man from the town, chosen to carry the standard for the year. The provost ended his speech with the familiar send-off: 'Safe oot and safe in!'

Now, at 7 a.m., a second drum beat sounds out across the town and the cavalcade is off, a long line of horses clattering across the tarmac, followed on foot by what must be the majority of the town's residents. Heading down the hill, the cavalcade splashes through the Ettrick Water, which once provided power for the local tweed mills, before heading up into the hills to follow the boundary of a vast swathe of common land still belonging to Selkirk. Pausing at three stone cairns – the Three Brethren – high up on the moors, the standard bearer drapes the flag briefly across one of them, before turning for the long ride home. As he does so, a long line of horses can be seen below, still making their way up to this spectacular viewpoint.

By mid-morning, the road into Selkirk from the river is thickly lined with people, waiting for the sound of horses' hooves rattling on the tarmac, as they thunder back up the hill into the marketplace. Once they are there, the second part of the tradition requires the standard bearer and several others to climb up on to a stage, where they 'cast the colours', swinging their flags in a carefully choreographed display to the sound of time-honoured songs, concluding with the slow lament, 'Flowers o' the Forest'. By lunchtime, the casting is over, the standard has been handed back to the provost 'unsullied and untarnished', and the ceremony is complete.

For Selkirk, the Common Riding and Casting of the Colours customs have a deep emotional resonance, defining the community's history. In 1113, King David I gave a large area of land to the town, which was extended further over the following centuries. The extent and value of the donated land meant that its borders had to be continuously defended from raiders and encroaching neighbours, and this is now re-enacted ceremonially every year by the riding of the boundaries. To this ancient tradition was later added the Casting of the Colours, which commemorates the return to Selkirk of a single soldier from the nearby Battle of Flodden in 1513; the rest had been killed fighting under the Scottish king James IV against the armies of Henry VIII.

Today, the Selkirk Common Riding attracts hundreds of participants, and it is one of many similar events held across the Scottish borders. Some of these Ridings, such as those of Hawick and Langholm, also have their origins in the distant past, while others, including those of Jedburgh, Melrose and Kelso, are more recent. In essence, however, the tradition of 'Ridings' – either of common lands, or, as at Berwick-upon-Tweed, of the extent of the town's ancient jurisdiction – emerged from the lawlessness for which the borders were known. For much of their history, after all, Scotland and England had been separate nations and uneasy neighbours, and the border country between them had been too vast and too unpopulated for either side to control effectively. In the resulting power vacuum, dominant local clans held sway over as much land as they were able to defend, carrying out brutal and damaging raids into each other's estates.

Today the landscape on both sides of the borders is still littered with once-fortified stone 'pele towers', built in the Middle Ages to defend their occupants against these violent incursions. Indeed, the rugged landscape to the west along the estuary of the river Esk, up into Eskdale and Liddesdale, was considered so unmanageable by sixteenth-century Scottish and English monarchs that in 1551 they jointly washed their hands of any responsibility for the area. Declaring the inhabitants to be outlaws, they announced that 'all Englishmen and Scottishmen . . . are and shall be free to rob, burn, spoil, slay, murder and destroy all and every such persons, their bodies, buildings, goods and cattle as do remain or shall inhabit upon any part of the said Debatable Land without any redress to be made for the same'. Just a year later, however, a formal border between England and Scotland dividing up these 'Debatable Lands' was finally agreed, and a measure of control was slowly exerted over the warring families. Nevertheless, this violent history gave rise to intense loyalties among the inhabitants of the border region, reinforcing bonds of security, kinship and common purpose.

The Common Ridings now attract riders from far afield as well as large crowds of onlookers, but at their heart they are still local expressions of community and of independence. More recently, the dubious heritage of raiding or reiving – the stealing of beasts and land – that originally led to the need for town Ridings, has emerged as a cause for celebration. What was once a violent tradition of theft is now a source of pride, commemorated with a popular annual festival at Hawick – although the orderly programme of lectures, re-enactments and concerts seems a very long way indeed from the cattle-rustling, murder and pillage upon which the festival is based.

REBECCA WARREN

Solstice at Stonehenge

Salisbury Plain, Wiltshire

21 JUNE

Some years ago I tried to become a magician. I had lessons with an old professional magician, read books on sleight of hand and misdirection, practised on friends, performed at talent-show parties. But even though I learnt some impressive tricks, discovering the prosaic mechanics behind the 'magic' killed the mystery for me. Once you know how something is done it loses its appeal. Which is why I am glad we don't know everything about Stonehenge on the Wiltshire plains. For centuries we've been obsessed with establishing who made this incredible monument and what it was for. Yet the mystery remains.

From the writings of Geoffrey of Monmouth through to studies by mid-twentieth-century researchers, we have been given many conflicting explanations as to what Stonehenge was, and how it was made. In his book *How to Build Stonehenge*, the archaeologist Mike Pitts puts forward a compelling case for focusing on the *how* of Stonehenge instead of the *why*. He asks us to celebrate the magnificent endeavour of building it, to wallow in the extraordinariness of the achievement, rather than picking apart the latest theories.

So, in brief, what *do* we know about Stonehenge? The story begins around five thousand years ago with an earthwork enclosure and a ring of fifty-six chalk pits, possibly once holding upright bluestones (distinctive spotted dolerites) from the Preseli Hills in Wales. Most archaeologists believe the stones were hauled on sledges and floated on rafts, though various legends attribute their arrival to the Arthurian wizard Merlin or the power of song. The sarsen stones that form the larger uprights and lintels were added centuries later and were sourced more locally from Wiltshire and Dorset. Though shorter distances were involved, their immense size – some weighing over twenty-five tonnes – makes the feat of their transport and positioning no less astonishing.

While the summer solstice draws the biggest crowds to Stonehenge today, archaeological finds suggest it was a site of winter feasting. Pig bones recovered from nearby Durrington Walls show the animals were slaughtered at around nine months old, pointing to midwinter gatherings. Stonehenge was also a major burial ground, with over fifty cremation burials discovered, making it one of the largest such cemeteries in Neolithic Britain. The site speaks as much of darkness and death as it does of light and renewal.

One of the most pervasive beliefs about Stonehenge is that it was built by the Druids. But the stone circle predates Iron Age Druids by over two thousand years. The

Druidic association arose in the seventeenth and eighteenth centuries and was a reasonable guess at the time, given how little is still known about pre-Roman British history. The site's striking alignment with the midsummer sunrise and midwinter sunset, along with its perfect and complex geometry, led to theories that it was an early computer. Associations with the Druids also gave rise to suggestions that it was a temple for human sacrifice and cannibalism, though Pitts argues that these reflect colonial encounters with other cultures more than any form of historical evidence.

There is confusion, also, around exactly who the Druids were. Modern-day Druids who gather at Stonehenge are part of a contemporary spiritual movement rooted loosely in the beliefs of Iron Age Celtic Druids, who probably served as religious leaders, teachers, judges and advisors, and who were said to train for up to twenty years. They may have practised animism, honoured natural spaces and observed seasonal rites. Historical records are limited, but the idea of Druidism was revived in the eighteenth century and again in the twentieth, possibly in response to disillusionment with institutional religion. Today's Druids are diverse, but they share a reverence for nature and for the turning points of the year. They are one of three types of Druids, distinct both from the Welsh bardic cultural tradition and from fraternal societies like the Ancient Order of Druids, of which Winston Churchill was once a member, and which were rooted in skilled workers' mutual societies.

Despite being a relatively recent fixture at Stonehenge, the contemporary summer solstice ceremony is famous around the world. Every year on 21 June, huge crowds descend on Stonehenge, bringing traffic on the nearby

A303 to a halt and transforming the hushed monument into a chaotic festival site. People from all walks of life come to watch the sun rise over the majestic stones, some clapping and cheering as it emerges from the shadow of the huge Heel Stone (a fifteen-foot block of stone just outside the entrance to the circle), while others dance and drum in celebration.

For the Druids, the solstice ceremony begins with a midnight vigil before they process, dressed in white robes and headdresses and carrying banners, to a barrow near the stones. They link hands, chant an invocation and walk back to the stones. Just before dawn, they divide into four groups and stand at four points around the stone circle, facing the rising sun. The Chief Druid, carrying a shepherd's crook dressed with oak leaves, collects the sacred elements (bread, salt, a silver cup, incense, a rose) and says a prayer to the rising sun. The Druids place oak branches on a fire, sprinkle blessed water and hold prayers for peace. They hold another service at midday, in which a sword that was previously placed in a crack in one of the stones is withdrawn (a nod, perhaps, to the legendary King Arthur pulling the great sword Excalibur out of a stone). Today, the Druids give offerings and meditate, gathering energy and strength from the sun.

I spoke to ex-Chief Druid Philip Carr-Gomm, on what felt like rather an anachronistic Zoom call. He explained to me that the ceremony is constantly evolving, with different Druids bringing their own unique creative expressions to it. When he came into the role, he brought an interest in Jungian ideas, incorporating myth and the power of story. Creativity is central to the solstice celebration, which Carr-Gomm points out is not confined to Stonehenge (in fact, he says that Stonehenge is too crowded and unpleasant now, and he prefers to mark the solstice at Avebury stone circle or Glastonbury Tor). For him, whether it involves people on stilts in illuminated costumes or a silent disco, the form of the ceremony is not important. It is about marking the eight points of the year, in community.

However Stonehenge got here and whatever feasts and customs it has witnessed, its hold over our imaginations is enduring. As the crowds gather sleepily at dawn, surrounding the enormous stones, holding each other, taking photos, or dancing quietly to the beat of a drum, it is hard not to be moved by the sight of the sun slowly climbing into view. It is a collective moment of hope, wonder, relief and gratitude.

LULAH ELLENDER

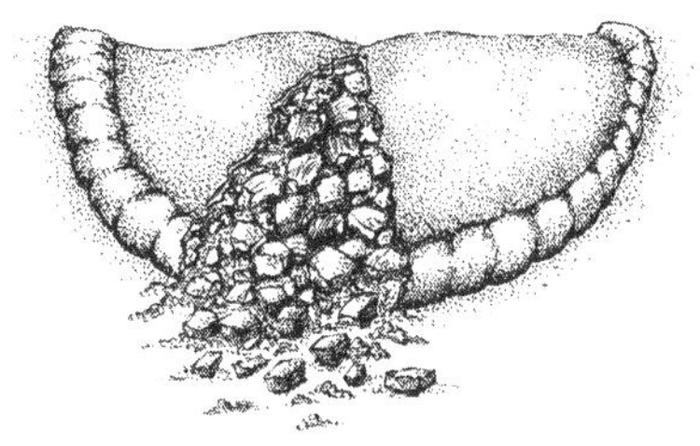

Midsummer Eve Bonfires

Redruth, Cornwall

23 JUNE

On Carn Brea, a chilly hilltop above the town of Redruth in Cornwall, a modest gathering of mainly elderly people is standing loosely around an equally modest bonfire of sticks, old paper and dried furze. A temporary flagpole has been stuck into the ground between some nearby exposed boulders, and Saint Piran's Flag, the Standard of Cornwall – a bold white cross on a black background – is flapping in the evening breeze. Not far away, a few cars are parked on the turf. There's a slight air of self-consciousness among the group members, as if they are a little embarrassed to be there. But slowly, a few more people arrive until, eventually, someone steps forward and introduces the event: its history is recounted, thanks are politely given to those who have helped to set it up, and a short Cornish translation of all of this is read out rather awkwardly.

Eventually the bonfire is lit by the mayor or mayoress, and an appointed 'Lady of the Flowers' throws a bunch of flowers on to the flames – an easy-enough duty if the bonfire is built on the ground, but a Herculean task requiring numerous retries if the fire is burning three metres up on the beacon. However, it's all very decorous – polite applause accompanies the speeches, and in some years a length of binder twine keeps people from standing too near the flames; it's hardly the Bacchanalian festival that might be expected from a midsummer party with a bonfire on a hilltop. But as the fire takes hold, someone brings out an accordion and people join in with a halting rendition of the Cornish 'anthem', 'The Song of the Western Men'. Like most singing at communal events, the voices rise and fall alarmingly, as no one can remember all the words, but determination overcomes uncertainty and everyone joins in with the rousing line, 'Here's twenty thousand Cornish men will know the reason why!'

As the evening light fades and the fire casts its warmth out into the darkness, more people arrive, the average age drops significantly and the awkwardness dissipates. Now, the laughter is warm and heartfelt, someone has provided pasties, and beer is circulating, as well as mugs of tea and coffee. The intentional 'Cornishness' of the celebration has given way to a relaxed community gathering.

Midsummer bonfires are not restricted to the south-west of England – indeed, many European countries also have similar traditions – but after centuries of celebrating the summer solstice with fire and music on 23 June, St John's Eve, most of these bonfire gatherings in Britain died out in the nineteenth century. By the 1920s, however, the loss of local traditions and language in Cornwall was causing alarm. The response was the establishment of several 'Old Cornwall Societies', some of which resuscitated the midsummer bonfires, using them as a vehicle to reinvigorate a sense of Cornish identity and knowledge of its language. Today the tradition is alive and well across the county, each celebration unique to its area but all of them broadly similar in the essentials: fire, flowers, warmth and celebration – and, of course, an impressive smattering of Cornish words too!

REBECCA WARREN

Bawming the Thorn

Appleton Thorn, Cheshire

THIRD SATURDAY IN JUNE

Hawthorn is so readily associated with the spring that its blossom is called May. Traditionally, on 1 May, people would decorate the outside of their houses with armfuls of its flowering branches, though it was considered extremely bad luck to bring them indoors. This is perhaps because the sweet-smelling blooms contain a chemical called trimethylamine, which is also present in rotting flesh after death. Those who lived through the plague, like the philosopher Francis Bacon, complained that hawthorn smelt of the pestilence.

Alongside these folk customs, however, some hawthorns have a strong Christian resonance – perhaps most famously the Glastonbury Thorn in Somerset. It is a variety known as *Crataegus monogyna 'Biflora'*, and it flowers not once, but twice a year – in May and again around the winter solstice in December. There are several of these trees in and around Glastonbury, and since the seventeenth century, a winter-flowering sprig of the specimen in St John's churchyard is ceremonially cut and then sent to Buckingham Palace for the royal Christmas table each year. Such was the connection between the Glastonbury Thorn and the royals that during the Civil War in the mid-seventeenth century a Puritan demonstrated his anti-monarchical fervour by chopping one of the trees down.

The twice-flowering thorn is also a potent religious symbol for the resurrected Christ. Many of Glastonbury's legends make this connection via Joseph of Arimathea, one of Jesus's followers, who took down his body from the cross, bound it in linen with spices and ointments, and conveyed it to a nearby cave. But how did a Middle Eastern saint come to be linked to a British shrub? The answer may lie in the power of religious storytelling to produce its own scrubby thicket of symbolism. In the thirteenth century, enterprising Glastonbury monks sought to increase the prestige of their abbey by inventing a series of associations with various disciples. William of Malmesbury argued that Philip the Apostle had come to spread the Gospel in Britain, and when his manuscript was copied in 1247, a marginal note was added, imaginatively suggesting that Joseph of Arimathea had also travelled to these shores. This idea, in turn, grew into a wider mythology centred on a visit to Britain by Jesus himself. In William Blake's 1804 poem 'Jerusalem', the opening question, 'And did those feet in ancient time / Walk upon England's mountains green?' refers to the young Christ, who is said to have accompanied Joseph on his travels to Britain.

A cult of pilgrimage around Joseph subsequently developed in the Glastonbury area, weaving together Christian and Arthurian mythology by figuring the saint as a keeper of the Holy Grail. The first mention of the hawthorn in connection with these tales lies in the *Lyfe of Joseph of Armathia* published in 1520 by Richard Pynson. Here, the winter-flowering tree is just one of many miracles that Glastonbury has to offer:

Thre hawthornes also that groweth in werall
Do burge and bere grene leaues at Christmas
As fresshe as other in May whan þe nightyngale
Wrestes out her notes musycall as pure as glas
Of all wodes and forestes she is þe chefe chauntres
In wynter to synge yf it were her nature
In werall she myght haue a playne place
On those hawthornes to shewe her notes clere.

Later sources had Joseph arriving in Glastonbury with the Holy Grail and clambering up a steep local hill. At the top, he declared, 'We are weary all,' giving the place the name it still carries today: Wearyall Hill. Thrusting his staff into the ground, Joseph went to sleep, only to wake the next morning to find that it had magically metamorphosed into the sacred hawthorn tree.

The village of Appleton Thorn is nearly 200 miles north of Glastonbury, in Cheshire. It, too, has a legendary hawthorn tree, which is reputed to be the offspring of the Glastonbury Thorn. Legend has it that it was carried to the village in the twelfth century by Adam de Dutton, a knight of the Crusades and local grandee. Its carefully pruned descendent today sits at the heart of the village, behind a low protective railing. Also behind bars are the inmates of HM Thorn Cross Prison, located just a few metres up the road. Like the thorn, however, the restraint they endure is light: this open prison allows prisoners to help out with a colourful local ceremony called 'bawming the thorn'.

The custom of bawming (which means 'adorning' or 'decorating') dates back at least as far as the early nineteenth century, but fell into abeyance in the 1930s. It was revived in 1971 by the headmaster of the local primary school. During the ceremony, local children dressed in red and white process towards the tree, which has been decked with ribbons in advance. A child dressed as Adam de Dutton in full crusader attire ceremonially 'plants' the tree, declaring: 'I, Adam de Dutton, raise this thorn, on this morn, in Appleton Thorn.' The children then dance around it, singing a special bawming song composed by Rowland Egerton-Warburton in the mid-nineteenth century. Confusingly, the lyrics refer to May Day, to midsummer, and to a July date for the festivities. The old date for the celebration was actually St Peter's Day, 29 June, but like many modern variants of these customs, the bawming ceremony has been moved to the weekend for convenience and now happens on the third Saturday in June. Stalls, brass band music, Morris dancing, and even a Spitfire fly-past ensure that the event is well attended, raising funds for local projects.

Perhaps something older than any of this still inhabits these ceremonies to honour the tree, however. After all, in pagan lore, hawthorn is considered sacred to the fae, or fairy folk, and harming it carries severe penalties. In 1999, construction of a new Irish bypass had to be rerouted to avoid displeasing the 'little people', as it would have destroyed an old *Crataegus* that was said to be the meeting point where Munster and Connaught fairies would do battle. The story is often repeated by way of ridiculing 'credulous' Irish folk, but there is, in fact, great contemporary wisdom in the environmental care that it teaches. Hawthorn has exceptional value in terms of biodiversity, providing leaves for butterflies and moths, nectar and pollen for insects, haws for birds and mammals, and scrubby shelter for a host of creatures. In our current nature crisis, the custom of bawming the thorn offers an opportunity to celebrate hawthorn – and to connect to the webs of life on which we all depend.

KIERA CHAPMAN

Blessing of the Fisheries

Folkestone, Kent

LAST SUNDAY IN JUNE

The rain had set in earlier that afternoon as the wind picked up. Now, at 9 p.m. on 8 October 1904, Folkestone's fishermen still haven't returned. Their families have assembled at the harbour, anxiously staring into the darkness, hoping for a sight of the fleet. The roiling sea, whipped up by a hurricane, looks ominous, and the gale has been raging all evening. Wives hold tight to their children. Suddenly they see lights, surging up on huge waves before tumbling into the black. It is 9.45 p.m. when the first boat makes it back to the harbour. The families count the returning boats – one is missing, and there are still three offshore. Two red flares blaze near the rocky Copt Point. The onlookers know there are crews out there fighting for their lives, and they can only watch and pray.

The lifeboat crew try to launch, but the force of the waves is too strong and the vessel is turned broadside, battered by the sea and unable to move. A group of men and women stand on the pier tugging the lifeboat with ropes, trying to get it seaborne, and eventually they manage to push it the right way round with a long pole. It heads off towards the fishing boats, and disappears.

That night three boats were lost and three men drowned. Some of the lifeboat men pitched into the sea but managed to clamber back into the boat. The survivors and their families were lucky, but they knew that every time the fishing boats went to sea, their luck could run out. Globally, there are around 100,000 fishing-related deaths every year – the majority in smaller fleets with unsafe boats.

For communities like Folkestone's that have been so dependent on a dangerous and unpredictable livelihood, protection rituals have long been a way to retain hope and recognise the shared endeavour. In Folkestone, the Blessing of the Fisheries serves a dual purpose – praying for the safety of 'all who go down to the sea in ships', and for a good catch for the year ahead. Held on the last Sunday in June, this custom begins with a bagpipe-led procession of the clergy from St Peter's Church down to the Stade (part of the harbour). The short sermon is followed by a hymn, and a bishop (usually the Bishop of Richborough) gives a blessing, shaking incense and holy water into the waves, offering thanks for the sea and its bounty and praying for the protection of the fisheries. It is a celebratory affair, with onlookers watching with interest, as well as pipers and a brass band. In the past, all the fishing boats would have been decorated and the houses covered with bunting; today, it is a more low-key event with a strong Christian emphasis.

Although the first written record dates only to 1883, this is a much older tradition, and an interesting example of the Christianisation of a pagan ritual. In ancient cosmologies, the sea was regarded as a sentient force or as the home of the gods, and travelling on it without permission or an offering was seen as inviting danger. Some traditions involved lighting fires to ward off evil spirits or making an offering of food, while others centred around water-purification rituals. Although Christianity put an end to many of these practices, some elements remain – like the use of holy water in the Blessing of the Fisheries.

Although we are an island nation, the closest many of us get to a prayer for the safety of those at sea may be listening from our beds to the much-loved nightly *Shipping Forecast* on BBC Radio 4, an incantation of names and weather patterns. It is a poetic, hypnotic aural map of far-off places that punctuates the liminal space between Britain and her neighbours. In recent years, the sea has become politically charged, whether it's as a result of sewage releases, pro-Brexit campaigns that promised a return of control of the waters surrounding the country, or the heated debate over migrant crossings in the Channel. Coastal areas are poorer and have worse health outcomes than inland regions, with many dependent on the seasonal tourism that has replaced fishing as a source of income.

Fishing communities often have long histories of displacement and migration, from people escaping the Highland Clearances of the 1750s–1860s, to those forced to leave their homes in the Western Isles of Scotland when the kelp and herring trade collapsed, to Grimsby's mass unemployment after the Cod Wars and the EU Common Fisheries Policy destroyed the town's livelihood. The sea is a provider of essential resources, a place to play, a contested space, a tourist attraction, a dumping ground, a deadly danger, a border, a depleted ecosystem. The Blessing of the Fisheries is a reminder of its power and of the vulnerability of those who live by it.

LULAH ELLENDER

JULY

Holsworthy Pretty Maid

Holsworthy, Devon

EARLY JULY

Early in July, the town of Holsworthy in Devon holds its annual St Peter's Fair. The celebrations are kicked off by a church service, followed immediately by the announcement of the name of the coming year's 'Pretty Maid'. The young woman chosen must be able to demonstrate an active contribution to church and community, and she will have to take part in various civic engagements during the coming year. In return, she receives a financial award of several hundred pounds. Depending on how you feel about beauty contests, the Pretty Maid ceremony appears to be either a charming custom that benefits a young woman who has shown herself to be participating in local life, or an embarrassing hangover from less enlightened times. Of course, rewarding women for being attractive has a very long history, one strand of which remains the crowning of a 'carnival queen' at fairs across the country, and on the face of it, the choosing of the Pretty Maid at Holsworthy seems to be in the same tradition. Yet a closer look at this particular custom reveals a rather different backstory.

Unlike many of our traditions, the Pretty Maid custom has a precise date of origin. In 1841 a local clergyman called Thomas Meyrick wrote his will, in which he left £1000 in annuities from which to fund an annual gift of £3 10s to the 'young single woman resident in [Holsworthy] being under thirty years of age and generally esteemed by the young as the most deserving and the most handsome and most noted for her quietness and attendance at church'.

He added that a smaller sum was also to be given to a 'spinster not under sixty years of age and noted for the like virtues and not receiving parochial relief'. These were not, however, his only charitable bequests. With no direct dependants of his own, and after leaving only modest sums to his brother, sisters and nieces, he went on to bequeath over eight thousand pounds to charities that helped the poor and furthered Christian worship, including the Society for Promoting Christian Knowledge, the Incorporated Church Building Society, and the Society for the Encouragement of Faithful Female Servants.

Notwithstanding the notorious difficulties of comparing prices in the past with those of today, Meyrick's bequests, if handed out now, would equate roughly to a staggering half a million pounds at least. Moreover, his gift-giving was clearly guided by deeply held principles of promoting Christian morality and supporting the deserving poor, for which he drew heavily on the teachings of the Bible. Preceding each bequest, he provided the Gospel entry that guided his decision. For example:

> *St Matt[hew], chapter 6, verse 20: Lay up for yourselves treasures in heaven; ch. 25, v. 36: I was in prison and ye came to me*: In like manner . . . I give £1000 . . . to the Society for the Discharge of Small Debts, [until] imprisonment for debt shall be happily abolished.

His concern for those in poverty continued with a further bequest of £1000 to the Society for Bettering the Condition and Increasing the Comforts of the Poor, which was to pay the rent of 'seven or more country labourers' for whom the local vicar could confirm their 'sobriety, quietness, and industry and attendance at church', in one-off sums of up to five pounds.

Finally, there was a third strand to Meyrick's generosity. As a member of the ancient and wealthy Meyrick family of Bodorgan on Anglesey, he clearly felt a deep affinity with Wales, because he left significant sums specifically to Welsh causes, including the Welsh Charity School in London, and female servants in Wales who had a proven record of good church attendance.

Meyrick was hardly the only Victorian gentleman to leave money for charity, but his will is unusual in also explaining that through his bequests he wished to encourage 'rulers to see and know that subjects are better directed and fed by harmless amusement and by judicious reward than by the fear of punishment'. What prompted this very specific explanation? Was there some particular injustice or institution to which he was referring?

The last decade of Meyrick's life was one of great social upheaval. As the Industrial Revolution brought huge wealth to some through the labours of the many, there was increasing unrest among the working classes at their poor conditions and lack of political representation. In 1830, the desperation felt by agricultural workers suffering poverty and unemployment led to widespread rioting, for which the punishments included hanging and transportation. Despite the increasing political unrest, however, the 1832 Reform Act refused to extend the vote to those who were not property owners, and two years later the Poor Law Amendment Act refused financial support to any who would not enter the dreaded workhouse. The same year, six agricultural workers from Tolpuddle in Dorset were transported to Australia for forming an early trade union and refusing to work unless they received a minimum wage. By 1838, the increasing calls for political representation and social reform had been published as a People's Charter, sparking a major demonstration in South Wales, which ended in several deaths, and in transportation for its leaders. In the same year, the author Charles Dickens published his novel *Oliver Twist*, exposing the harrowing conditions of the urban poor to the wealthier middle classes.

Even in the depths of Devon, it would have been hard for an educated clergyman like Meyrick to be unaware of the acute social deprivation and political unrest sweeping the country. It seems likely, therefore, that his will was shaped by concerns about the government's brutal responses to the disorder and rioting that resulted from the miserable conditions of the poor. Perhaps it was this which led him to articulate his hope of influencing the country's rulers to treat their subjects well rather than inflicting punishment upon them.

*

It may seem that we have wandered rather far from the Pretty Maid award at the fair in Holsworthy, but here's the thing: in the light of Meyrick's other bequests, it turns out that what, at first glance, might seem to be a custom with a rather old-fashioned and uncomfortable focus on female beauty is something rather different. This is not to deny that he thought 'attractiveness' was an acceptable part of the requirements of both the 'young single woman' and, indeed, the 'spinster not under sixty years of age' who were to receive his charity; but read alongside the other stipulations that they should be the 'most deserving' and 'most noted for [their] quietness and attendance at church', the emphasis on their appearance is much reduced. Seen against the rest of his bequests, it is quite clear that the Pretty Maid bequest was part of a very substantial provision of genuine help for a wide range of impoverished people, from servants to children, from agricultural labourers to debtors. And yet somehow, in the years following his death, it is the single clause 'most handsome', now translated as 'pretty', that has come to dominate the custom's public face. Perhaps, if we are uncomfortable with the beauty-contest aspect of this tradition, we should ask why it has been allowed to continue unmodified? Rather than raise our eyebrows at Meyrick, maybe it is ourselves whom we should question first?

REBECCA WARREN

Swan Upping

River Thames, Berkshire

JULY

In 1592, a court made a judgment that still underpins modern statutes relating to wildlife and property claims. The Case of Swans was brought by Queen Elizabeth I, who claimed two men had taken 400 unmarked swans that, by law, belonged to the Crown. The court found in her favour, ruling that all unmarked swans on open waters were by default her property, and establishing the foundational principle of qualified property. This means property rights are not absolute, but are conditional or limited based on use, legal status or context. The case affirmed a broader common law principle: ownership of wild animals could be claimed by taking, taming or reclaiming them.

Rather like cattle branding, people purchased official

'marks' to show who owned them. Each mark was unique to the owner, registered with the Crown, and etched on to the birds' beaks. Between 1450 and 1600 there were around 630 marks, and from 1482, swan marks were restricted to landowners or those of recognised wealth and status – a rule that effectively excluded the lower classes.

These lines and geometric shapes ensured that the wealthy could keep track of their mute swans, and special 'Swanmoots' were set up to decide legal cases of contested ownership. Ordinary people were forbidden from handling, owning, eating or engaging with swans. They could simply watch from the shore as these floating symbols of grace, elegance, nobility – and property – swam past. Punishments for killing or stealing swans were severe, ranging from a year's imprisonment to deportation and even death. In this way, swans gained an equivalence with other wild animals like deer, rabbits and game, which could not just be caught or taken by anyone.

The monarch's connection to swans goes back even further, to at least the twelfth century. In medieval times, swans were a culinary delicacy and status symbol. There are records of Henry II ordering forty swans for a Christmas feast in 1247, and in 1295 the formal position of Swanmaster (later known as Keeper of the Swans) was created – joining other delightfully specific-sounding ceremonial offices, like Piper to the Sovereign and Yeoman of the Glass Pantry. The job of overseeing the swans was split into two roles in 1993: Warden of the Swans and Marker of the Swans. One of the key duties is Swan Upping, an event that takes place every year on the river Thames, starting in Sunbury on the Monday of the first week in July, and ending downriver in Abingdon on the Friday.

This ancient custom involves wooden boats, or 'skiffs', representing the Crown and two livery guilds, the Worshipful Company of Vintners and the Worshipful Company of Dyers. The boats fly crested banners and flags bearing the different insignia, and the men wear red, white or blue, depending on their guild. There are two oarsmen and a leader in each boat, sporting white swan feathers and embroidered badges. The flotilla sets sail, looking for cygnets. When they find a mother swan and her young, they shout, 'All up!' and circle their boats around the birds, lifting them carefully on to the shore. Here, the cygnets are weighed and checked, before being ringed to indicate ownership: a Vintners' or Dyers' ring to match the mark on the mother's leg, or a Crown ring if the mother is unmarked. It is dangerous work – the swans' wings are so powerful they can be heard flapping up to half a mile away, and their feet can cause nasty scratches.

So, why do it? The practice used to be about asserting ownership, but now it serves a more ecological purpose. Swans are vulnerable to getting tangled in fishing lines and swallowing poisonous lead weights. Despite the 1987 ban on these weights, they still cause six per cent of swan deaths. Before the ban it was estimated that around 4000 swans died every year from lead poisoning. Swan Upping provides a way to monitor the health of the recovering swan population – a little like a census if you also got a quick health check at the same time.

The tradition features in a painting by Cookham-based artist Stanley Spencer, who witnessed the event in his home village. In 'Swan Upping at Cookham' (1915–19), he portrays less of the pageantry of the custom, instead creating a sense of the physicality of lifting the birds out of the water and inspecting the boats. He began the painting before going off to fight in the First World War and finished it after his return. The later sections are darker, perhaps reflecting the shift in his perspective after the horrors of the conflict. Perhaps there was some comfort for him in this annual custom; or perhaps by then it seemed impossibly archaic and irrelevant.

While today Swan Upping is doubtless concerned with conservation and care, its roots are more troubling. This assertion of ownership over the natural world reflects a long tradition of extending property rights into the realm of living creatures. Swan Upping, in this light, can be seen to celebrate a narrow version of guardianship framed as possession. While its role in conservation is real, the ritual sits uneasily beside contemporary efforts to recognise rivers and their ecosystems as entities with rights of their own. It could be that the Thames comes to have more rights than the birds who make it their home.

LULAH ELLENDER

Honiton Hot Pennies

Honiton, Devon

TUESDAY AFTER 19 JULY

Marking the start of the Honiton Fair, the Hot Pennies custom takes place on the first Tuesday after 19 July. At midday, the Honiton town crier, dressed in gold-trimmed black, with a waterfall of white lace at his throat, walks down the high street ringing his bell and calling out, 'Oyez, oyez, oyez!' Immediately, the crowds around him shout back his words, 'Oyez, oyez, oyez!' He continues, 'The glove is up!' and the crowd sings back, 'The glove is up!' and the pattern continues for the rest of his announcement: 'The fair is begun!' . . . 'No man shall be arrested . . .' 'Until the glove is taken down!' . . . 'God save the King!' The glove in question is mounted on top of a tall pole, which is itself covered in tightly packed flowers and is carried by the crier down the street.

In the past, the raising of the glove indicated, as the crier proclaims, that those who attended the fair need not fear arrest. This leniency is widely explained as having been a means of encouraging attendance, especially among those who lived outside the town. But, thought about more carefully, this doesn't feel quite right. After all, it's hardly likely that the town would welcome a free-for-all of violence, theft and debauchery during the fair, no matter how many people such a temporary amnesty attracted. An older, now rarely remembered, explanation was that the lifting of the fear of arrest applied only to debtors. This sounds more likely, and it would certainly have allowed more people to attend the fair, but it begs the question of how many debtors there were in the hinterland of Honiton. One other explanation might be hazarded: that the raised glove once indicated a period when the town's normal restrictions on trading within its boundaries would be lifted, allowing other sellers to operate for the duration of the market. Honiton Fair seems to have been held since 1221, and a royal charter for the holding of a market in the town was granted in 1257. Markets were the lifeblood of medieval towns, but there were tight restrictions on who could or could not take part, and those who were allowed to trade paid a range of tolls and taxes for the privilege. Moreover, anyone who attempted to buy up goods as they entered a market, in order to resell them at a higher price at the same market, would face a heavy fine, or even find themselves in jail. So perhaps an alternative explanation might be that the raising of the glove at Honiton Fair originally communicated a brief lifting of trading restrictions.

Whatever the original significance of the raised glove, there's plenty of laughter and excitement in Honiton High Street today as the crier makes his announcements. But it is when he walks back to the middle of the town that the real fun begins. From the upper windows of the pubs along the road, hands appear, showering pennies down on to the waiting crowds below. Of course, children are the best at gathering up the scattered coins, ducking easily and deftly between the adults, their quick fingers scooping up the treasure. Some have come with buckets or containers, hoping to catch the pennies before they hit the ground, but this attempt to cheat the system is largely unsuccessful, as most of the coins still end up on the tarmac.

Notoriously, in the past, the pennies were heated up before being thrown down to the crowds, making their collection a more painful process, but today they are simply warmed. The standard explanation for this odd aspect of the custom is that watching the poor burn their fingers as they scrabbled for the money was an amusement for those handing it out. Well, perhaps. But equally it might have been a way of slowing down the rate at which any one person could collect the coins, enabling more people to share the pennies. Who knows? At Honiton, as with so many of our traditions, the logic and nuances behind the custom may have been altered or lost over the years of its existence, yet the high street is filled today with happy shrieks, squeals and giggles from children clutching pennies, a fitting start to the town's summer fair.

REBECCA WARREN

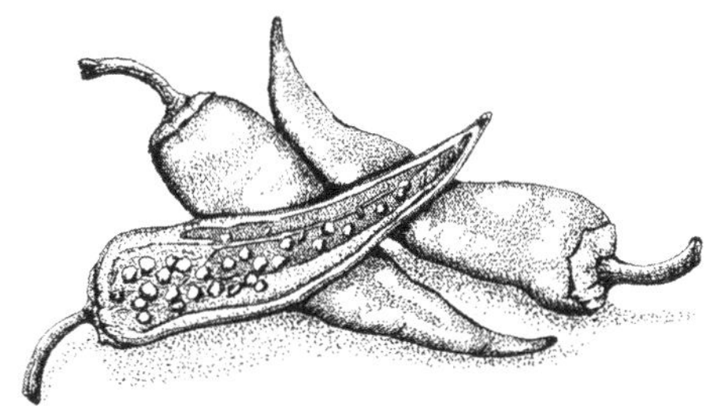

Bradford Mela

Bradford, West Yorkshire

MID-JULY

On 14 January 1989, the northern English city of Bradford found itself at the forefront of an international media storm. A group of 1000 Muslims had gathered to protest the recent publication of Salman Rushdie's novel *The Satanic Verses*, and in the course of the event, as the video cameras of eager journalists whirred, one group set the book on fire. The images were seized upon by the global media: behind the literal flames, argued commentators, lay a fiery ideological conflict between conservative, intolerant, 'fundamentalist' Muslims and the intellectual and liberal democratic values of modern Europe. These representations were only reinforced a month later when the Iranian revolutionary leader Ayatollah Khomeini introduced a global *fatwa* calling for Rushdie's murder. The fact that those torching the novel did not represent the entire British Muslim community was lost in the noisy rhetoric as

Islam came to be seen as a locus of cultural confrontation in Britain. And Bradford was now its epicentre.

Yet just a few months later, Bradford hosted a festival that centred on a very different image of the Muslim community: the Mela. The word is Sanskrit in origin, and simply means a meeting or gathering. The custom has its roots in religious festivals traditionally held across the Indian subcontinent. Some melas are specific to a particular faith, celebrating Eid al-Fitr or Holi, but others are secular, aiming to create a sense of shared identity across different communities and faiths, bringing Hindus, Sikhs and Muslims together in a celebration of music, dance and food. The 1989 event was the second time that a mela had been held in Bradford, and it took place in Lister Park.

Today, melas happen right across Britain. Many of the festivals are funded through a combination of local government grants, arts funding and commercial sponsorship. Music and performance are a central focus, with a strong emphasis on homegrown talent, and diverse programming that includes both traditional and modern forms of music and dance. You might see tabla folk drumming, in which musicians play two different-sized drums with intense rhythmic precision, followed by bhangra rap, which fuses traditional Punjabi music with hip-hop. You might witness the elegant storytelling of Kathak dancing before enjoying the latest in Bollywood moves. Performers are often exuberant, dramatic and very engaged with the audience: this performance style is sometimes called 'tamasha', after a flamboyant type of folk theatre from Maharashtra, India.

Curating a festival that is premised on the idea of multiculturalism is, however, a tricky and politically sensitive task. Mela organisers have to strike a careful balance between programming for older and younger tastes; in 2010, young people at the Bradford Mela showed their displeasure with a somewhat old-fashioned lineup by protesting loudly, waving Pakistani flags and blowing strident plastic horns. But critics have also raised questions about the cultural breadth of the acts that are on offer, asking whether they overrepresent some communities and neglect others (or, indeed, whether they simply reflect the preferences of white arts organisers). Finally, concerns about policing and fears that certain performers could invite the 'wrong crowd' (meaning young, male and Pakistani) sometimes influence the choice of lineup. At its base, the debate about programming is as much philosophical as it is practical: it asks what concepts like 'inclusion' and 'diversity' really mean, and what image of 'the community' the mela organisers seek to convey.

Perhaps the greatest threat to melas, however, is the post-2010 environment of austerity, which has brought swingeing cuts to local government and arts funding. As early as 2010, the Bradford event was shrinking in size, and in recent years it has ceased to prioritise music and performance, instead focusing on food. However, at the time of writing, sizeable festivals continue in the urban settings of Camden in London, Birmingham, Belfast, Middlesbrough, Leicester, Newcastle, Cardiff and Glasgow, while the celebration in Southampton is currently expanding from a one-day to a two-day event. The largest festival at present is the Boishakhi Mela in Tower Hamlets, London. Held in May, it has marked the Bengali New Year since 1997, and now hosts some 80,000 visitors.

Whatever their multicultural politics might be, melas exist because migrant movement across borders quite literally brings new rhythms to contemporary British life. These festivals not only celebrate and consolidate a sense of local community, they offer opportunities to showcase the varied musical and poetic traditions that make up our multicultural society.

KIERA CHAPMAN

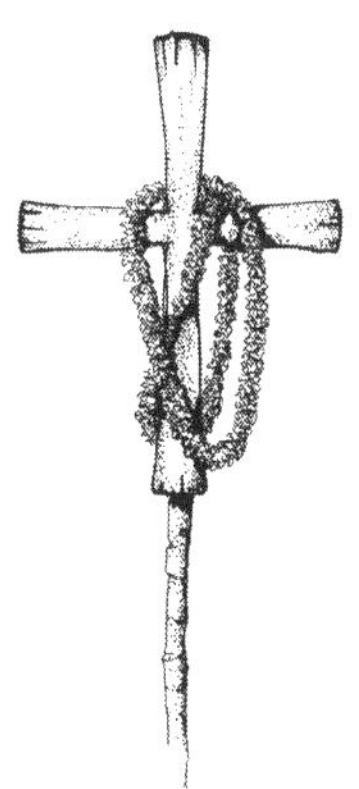

Tamil Pilgrimage to Walsingham

Walsingham, Norfolk

MAY–AUGUST

What does it mean to go on pilgrimage in modern Britain? One conventional view is that this ritual represents a reconnection with the medieval past, stretching back to a time before the sixteenth-century Reformation replaced Catholicism with Protestantism as the state religion. This was an era when salvation could be earned by visiting churches richly decorated with statues, gold and gems, where the cool air smelled of heady incense, where priests chanted Latin masses in kaleidoscopic, soft stained-glass light, and where saints might shed a miraculous tear for your sins as a sign of your redemption. The religious world was filled with purchasable indulgences, and ordinary people might travel to shrines and other places of religious visitation where the dividing line between the human and divine worlds became wafer-thin, bringing the believer closer to God.

The conventional narrative says that this connection was broken in the Reformation, when Protestantism ushered in a more direct, less mediated relationship with God. This meant that religious experience no longer required travel: Christ could now be encountered by sitting at home and reading the Bible in English. But this is a simplification of a more complicated history. Although some of the more zealous Protestant reformers did campaign against pilgrimage, the tradition of journeying for religious inspiration did not suddenly die when Henry VIII's iconoclasts came crashing through the monasteries in the 1530s. It dwindled, certainly, but many people continued to travel, and the sense of sanctity that surrounded particular places in the landscape still held meaning. Later, in the nineteenth and twentieth centuries, pilgrimage underwent something of a rebirth, as large numbers of people used new transport networks to revitalise the practice of visiting the old sites. Many of these religious sites experienced a rapid growth in visitor numbers – including Walsingham in Norfolk, which had been an epicentre for religious travel in the Middle Ages.

In 1061, just a few years before the Norman Conquest, the Virgin Mary appeared three times in the dreams of Richeldis, a wealthy widow of Walsingham. The holy mother transported Richeldis to Nazareth, showed her the house in which the immaculate conception had happened, and instructed her to build a copy on her large Norfolk estate.

But where on the estate should Richeldis locate her reconstruction? Fortunately, divine guidance was forthcoming: a night of silvery dew miraculously left two patches of ground inexplicably dry, enabling her to narrow down her choices. She picked one, and set carpenters to work on the wooden frame of the building. But the geometry of construction kept going wrong: wood refused to meet wood, joints inexplicably sprang apart, and neither measure nor mark would put things right and true. Richeldis stayed up all night, praying for guidance from the Virgin, and while she kept her vigil, a company of angels quietly built the house – on a different site two hundred yards away. Clearly, this heavenly host was not in the slightest bit interested in architectural fidelity, because the building that resulted was nothing like real Palestinian buildings. Instead, it was an Anglo-Saxon house, roughly twenty-four by thirteen feet in size, built from wood, wattle and daub rather than limestone, and with a pitched roof rather than a flat one.

At least, that's the story of Walsingham according to the later-medieval poet Richard Pynson, who wrote a ballad in the latter part of the fifteenth century recounting its foundation as a place of pilgrimage. However, some historians – those terrible sticklers for facts! – argue that his dates are wrong, and that Walsingham's shrine was probably built nearly a century later than he suggested, sometime between 1130 and 1153, which is roughly when the nearby priory was founded.

This was also the time when pilgrimage was starting to become a major religious pursuit. Walsingham quickly became one of the most visited shrines in the Catholic world, a site so important that it attracted visitors not only from across Britain, but from overseas too, with boats landing at Kings Lynn and other locations along the Norfolk coast to avoid travelling through the lawless Fens of East Anglia. During the fourteenth and fifteenth centuries, the practice of going on a religious journey became so popular that there were fears that people were just doing it to have fun, shirk work and neglect their family responsibilities. Consequently, the devout were soon required to get permission from their bishop before departing. In the allegorical poem *Piers Plowman* written in the late fourteenth century, William Langland disapprovingly records people dressed as hermits with a train of women in tow, who are supposedly on a Walsingham pilgrimage, but who are clearly enjoying a jaunt. Those who made it to their destination, in whatever spirit, purchased badges showing that they had worshipped there, the equivalent of today's Instagram selfie (though modern visitors can also still purchase a brooch showing a scene of the Annunciation).

The Walsingham shrine was destroyed by Henry VIII during the Reformation in 1538, and thereafter pilgrimage visits decreased. But, like many of the other customs in this book, the ritual of visiting the shrine has enjoyed a modern revival. Walsingham's Anglo-Catholic priest Father Hope Patten rebuilt Richeldis's Holy House in 1931, with the architecture replicating a fourteenth-century Italian shrine at Loreto, which was itself supposed to be the actual Holy House that had been miraculously transported from Nazareth to Italy. The new Holy House immediately proved popular, and in 1938 a more elaborate shrine church was subsequently constructed to accommodate an increasing stream of Protestant pilgrims.

People can visit Walsingham at any time, but there is a

special day for Protestants, the National Pilgrimage, which takes place annually on the Whit Monday bank holiday. However, this ritual is controversial: for decades, a small group of Protestants calling themselves 'Walsingham Witness' have gathered to protest the mixture of Anglican and Catholic theology on offer in this custom, travelling from as far afield as Northern Ireland to make their disapproval known. They stand at the village pump and object loudly to the procession as it carries a statue of the Virgin Mary, brandishing banners proclaiming a hard-line theological stance: masses are a 'blasphemous fable', and 'idolatry' is to be deplored. As the procession nears the group, the Anglo-Catholic priests in their richly coloured fabrics and lace contrast strikingly with the ordinary, modern clothes of the evangelicals, the Latin singing of the first group competing with street preachers decrying the evils of worshipping intercessory saints and declaiming the need to accept that salvation is by faith alone. Watching the confrontation from the sidelines, it feels like the Reformation is not so much a centuries' old historical event but a fervent debate that is still unfolding. Ironically, the protesters are effectively enacting a kind of paradoxical 'anti-pilgrimage', travelling to Walsingham to object to the folly of placing one's faith in religious journeys to sacred shrines. Two competing ideas about the religiosity of place, as well as two different theologies, stare each other down in this confrontation.

Among the modern pilgrims to Walsingham are Indian Tamils, who visit in such numbers that two separate dates in the calendar are devoted to them, one in May, the other in July. This is because a small but significant proportion of the population of India's southernmost state, Tamil Nadu, and of the neighbouring country of Sri Lanka, are Catholic. Their presence is a result of European colonialism in the region: in 1505, the Portuguese arrived in Ceylon (modern-day Sri Lanka), and by 1522, they had established a permanent presence along the eastern coast of India, designed to forge and defend commercial links, particularly around the lucrative spice trade. In the mid-seventeenth century, they were displaced by the Dutch East India company, which was in turn gradually forced out by the British in the late eighteenth and early nineteenth century. The brutality of colonial rule under all three powers should not be underestimated: indentured slavery on plantations was common. There was strong resistance to all of these European groups from local populations, running simultaneously alongside waves of violence between local kingdoms, making this a turbulent period of history for this part of India.

In this context, Christianity became a cultural weapon, a way of consolidating European power by converting local rulers and their subjects. Missionaries were consequently an important presence in the region, and the religion they propagated laid heavy emphasis on the Virgin Mary. She was a sympathetic figure because devotion to female deities was already common in the Hinduism of the Tamil region: there is a rich vein of South Indian religion that believes that the original creator was female, and that she gave birth as a virgin to the major male gods Brahma, Shiva and Vishnu. Simultaneously, a folk faith in the area worshipped more menacing female deities of blood and power, such as Mariyamman, the village goddess of smallpox, who had to be appeased to protect the community from disease.

There was therefore a degree of familiarity among the local population about the idea of a powerful female divinity whose independence and fertility were bound up in her virginity, and whose vocation was caring for the sick.

Parallels were furthered by the early missionaries, particularly the seventeenth-century Jesuits, who encouraged an approach that accommodated the new Catholicism to these older, more established Hindu beliefs, rather than trying to assimilate the population into a separate Catholic belief system. A set of Indian customs around the Virgin quickly developed: the Tuticorin festival began in Thoothukudi, Tamil Nadu, in 1720, with the community building a magnificent cart to pull a statue of the Virgin through the streets.

So the Tamils come to Walsingham because the European powers, including the British, came to Tamil Nadu. The three visits paid by this community to the shrine each year continue a 'twinning' of places and cultures that are geographically distant, yet culturally long interwoven. As a result, pilgrimage at Walsingham today invests this remarkable local place with a shared and global history.

KIERA CHAPMAN

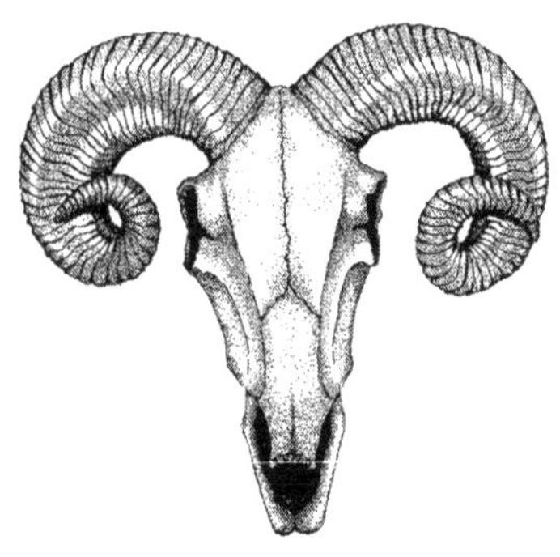

Ebernoe Horn Fair

Ebernoe, West Sussex

25 JULY

Anyone for cricket? If so, the tiny village of Ebernoe in West Sussex might be the place for you – as long as you don't mind avoiding the occasional car tootling along the lane that crosses the outfield of the pitch. But the hazard of traffic is not the only unusual feature of Ebernoe's cricketing tradition. On St James' Day, 25 July, the annual village fair takes place, at which a 'fair day' cricket match is the main event. Nothing unusual there, you might think, until you discover that the cricketer who scores the most runs is awarded a pair of sheep's horns. What's more, during the day, two sheep will be roasted and then carried ceremonially across the pitch. One will be given to the cricketers at lunchtime, while the other is shared out between the players and spectators at the end of the day.

The Horn Fair, along with its peculiar sporting trophy, is widely believed to have its roots in the distant past, but the first definitive evidence of the tradition is not until 1864, when there is a record of the fair's 'revival'. Since then, although paused during the two world wars and the recent COVID-19 pandemic, it has been robustly maintained, and continues to be a popular annual event. The horns used in the ritual today, however, are no longer those belonging to the freshly roasted carcasses; those have been replaced by a permanently mounted sheep's skull, topped with fine curled horns, which is reused every year. The change is said to have come about some years ago, after a dog ran off with the roasted sheep's skull before the horns could be awarded to the winning batsman, although one wonders whether modern health-and-safety concerns may in fact have played a part.

The only other known horn fair used to be held at Charlton in southeast London, between Greenwich and Woolwich, from at least the seventeenth century until its abolition in 1872. This was a very different kind of event, with a well-documented history. The fair took place at Cuckold's Point on the south bank of the river Thames, and was widely known for its debauchery: the wearing of cuckolds' horns by some of those attending was recognised as a blatant advertisement of the 'availability' of women there. In 1675, the author of a scurrilous book, *Mercurius verax*, mockingly noted that Charlton Horn Fair offered 'Stallions of all Sorts, Coachmen, and Gentlemen-Ushers for great Ladies; Monkeys and Island-Curs for private Uses, Licences for Poligamy; Cures for crack'd maiden-heads . . .'

Two hundred years later, however, the social climate was changing and the more priggish Victorians succeeded in closing down what had become known as the Charlton Pleasure Fair. In 1869, the *Morning Post* reported that the 'midnight masquerading and other absurd customs [were] at last likely to be discontinued', although it took another three years for the government to abolish the fair altogether.

Ebernoe Horn Fair has no known links to the Charlton Fair except, tenuously, in the 'Horn Fair' song that has been sung at Ebernoe since the 1950s. This is clearly a distant cousin of the bawdier songs that were widely associated with Charlton, its theme being the attempted seduction of an innocent young woman, who protests to her assailant in suitably euphemistic terms:

If you would see Horn Fair you must walk on your way,
I will not let you ride on my grey mare today,
You'd rumple all my muslin and uncurl my hair,
And leave me all distrest to be seen at Horn Fair."

'O fairest of damsels, how can you say No?
With you I do intend to Horn Fair for to go,
We'll join the best of company when we do get there,
With horns on their heads, boys, the finest at the Fair.

They are the finest horns you did ever behold,
They are the finest horns and are gilded with gold.'

Although the song only became a formal part of Ebernoe Fair after the Second World War, it was apparently known locally well before that. So are we seeing here an echo of a salacious reputation once possessed by this local Sussex fair? Or did the existence of another fair of the same name lead to the adoption of one of its associated ballads, in a desire to claim more ancient roots and greater authenticity? As is so often the case, it is difficult to distinguish hard fact from idealised fiction, but no one seems to mind, and each 25 July, Ebernoe happily continues to reward its most successful cricketer with a pair of mounted sheep's horns.

REBECCA WARREN

AUGUST

Llansteffan Mock Mayor

Llansteffan, Carmarthenshire

2 AUGUST

Think of recent political satire and you might picture *Spitting Image*'s terrifying Maggie Thatcher puppet, or the hard-hitting cartoons of *Punch*, or perhaps the lampooning of modern leaders in *Private Eye*. The British have a long history of parodying public figures, as seen in the work of writers such as Geoffrey Chaucer, Jonathan Swift and William Hogarth. Parody is also fundamental to the ongoing custom of electing 'mock mayors'.

The Welsh village of Llansteffan upholds this tradition in its village hall every August. Some believe the custom goes back to the thirteenth century, but the first record of this popular event occurs in a description of the mock mayor's procession in William Waters's 1881 *History of Llanstephan*.

Today, the candidates for the mock mayoral election canvass for votes before the big day, campaigning for implausible things like hiring mermaids in the bay to attract bachelors to the village, building a 'Stink Tank' for the village's dogs, or gold-plating all the cockles. As well as making exaggerated promises, they often take on an invented persona, bringing their own individual creativity to the event. After a light-hearted campaign, the election result is announced in the rowdy village hall, with the five candidates waiting on stage to hear which one of them has succeeded. The winner dons a red robe, a heavy gold chain and a large red bicorne hat that they can personalise with their own embellishments. They then process through the village in an open-top car (previously a horse and cart) in celebration. It is all very good-natured and tongue-in-cheek, but it is part of the lineage of Welsh satire that brought us Dic Siôn Dafydd, poet John Jones's imaginary eponymous literary character from the early nineteenth century who rejects his Welsh heritage in a bid to make it in England, as well as the protest songs popularised by singer-songwriter Dafydd Iwan (who was also leader of the Welsh Nationalist Party, Plaid Cymru, from 2003 to 2010). Iwan's nationalism was rooted in the controversial forced flooding of Capel Celyn by Liverpool Corporation, when the Welsh-speaking village was deliberately submerged to create a reservoir. He saw the destruction of the last community where only Welsh was spoken as a symbol of Welsh decline, and wrote several political songs in the 1960s that followed the bardic tradition of being the spokesperson for local people. His most famous song, 'Carlo', satirises Prince

Charles's investiture as the Prince of Wales in 1969, lambasting his privileged life playing polo and attempting to learn Welsh.

Llansteffan's election of a mock mayor continues this tradition of carnivalesque rebellion, as candidates lampoon the incompetence, self-importance and buffoonery of political and civic leaders. For those with little power, this is a moment when the tables are turned on those who have too much.

LULAH ELLENDER

Bonsall Hen Races

Bonsall, Derbyshire

FIRST SATURDAY IN AUGUST

'How do chickens wake up on time?' yells the compere. 'Alaaaaaaarm clucks!' Everyone in the crowd grins and groans, except for the competitors, who are hovering nervously at the yellow-sprayed start line, clutching bemused-looking chickens. This is the world hen racing competition, an annual egg-stravaganza that happens in early August at the Barley Mow pub in Bonsall, Derbyshire. The latest iteration of this race dates from 1991, but there are records of hen racing as a sport going back to the mid-nineteenth century, and perhaps beyond.

The 'race track' is a narrow thirty-foot area of the car park that has been fenced off with crowd barriers and the type of orange plastic safety netting that acts more as a warning than a barrier on building sites. The spectators are packed in on both sides, and most have been drinking for a while, with local yolk-els teasing visitors from further afield. Quite a few are balancing a pint in one hand, with a bag of hen treats, from mealworms to corn, in the other.

If you haven't got your own hen, you might be able to rent one from a local outfit called Henterprise. And the puns don't stop there. Some of the chickens have monikers with comedic pop-culture references (previous years' contenders include Cluck Norris and Cindy Clawford), while others bear names that are definitely not vegetarian (Drumstick, Colonel Sanders).

It's a sport with rules, too: any 'fowl play', such as chicken-on-chicken fighting, is met with an immediate yellow card. Repeat offenders face disqualification. It's not clear whether the same rules apply to human altercations, though there are definitely some chicken hats on display that deserve a red card in the fashion 'hensemble' stakes.

And they're off! 'Egg-cellent start!' announces the compere. 'Im-peck-able timing!' The chickens immediately move off in all directions, attracted by everything but the finish line. Their human counterparts shake favoured snacks to entice them onwards, but are mostly ignored. The fastest recorded winning time for the race is three seconds, but the athletes this year look like they will be a long way off that pace. You might even call them 'hendurance' runners. One of them is going round in circles, and another is more interested in an insect it has found in the dirt. The moment any of them put on speed, the crowd starts to cheer enthusiastically. Despite this fuss, the competitors remain quite literally unflappable.

After a few of these heats, featuring some fifty birds, there are quarter- and semi-finals, and then it's the big deciding race . . . The starting gun fires, and the finalists amble forward at a distinctly leisurely pace. A black bird with a mop of head feathers bolts for the line, but two feet from it, comes to a bemused halt. A cockerel called Peckish strides out in stately fashion, but then hesitates, looking haughtily side to side as if acknowledging his admiring public, before becoming distracted by the gravel underfoot. Eventually he resumes his forward movement, pacing delicately across the finish line to an immense roar from the crowd. The prize for being fastest in the pecking order is distinctly 'poultry' however: a trophy and a bag of grain await the winner. All in all, the Bonsall hen races are a delightful celebration of the contagious absurdity and eccentricity – or should that be eggcentricity? – of British humour.

KIERA CHAPMAN

The Burry Man

South Queensferry, Lothian

SECOND FRIDAY IN AUGUST

It's just before nine on a quiet, still morning. Down an alleyway beside the Staghead Hotel in South Queensferry, the hulking cantilevers of the Forth Bridge brace against the softest of grey skies. The industrial solidity of these orange girders makes itself felt throughout the town, anchoring even the places where the bridge is not visible. A webbed geometry of modernity, this engineering feat pulls the world into its stark, sharp-angled, shadowless way of seeing.

Suddenly, the morning calm is shattered by the ringing of an old-fashioned handbell. A few seconds later, a figure lumbers out of the hotel. The confidence of the modern world suddenly collides with something anachronistic, bringing factual certainties to a shrieking halt on their well-oiled tracks. A small crowd cheers. Passersby stop to gaze. Dogs bark. Small children stare, frozen with surprise, then turn quickly to the adults around them for reassurance. One toddler bursts into tears.

The first thing you see is the odd outline, a stylised cartoon of a human figure swaying unsteadily from side to side. The proportions are wrong, the limbs too stocky. The arms are held rigidly out at shoulder height, each grasping a staff that has impossibly burst into flower. Over the whole body, including where the face should be, the skin has been replaced by hundreds of hooked seeds. Like green barnacles, they have mossed over the entire form, eradicating all evidence of individual human identity. The mouth is closed by rows of hooks. On top of the eyeless head perches an absurdly comic hat of flowers and fruit.

Two men flank the figure, each grasping one of the two staffs that he holds. At first they seem to be restraining him from committing acts of terrible violence. A few moments later, it becomes clear that they are needed to guide his sightless, wordless path over the hard stone cobbles, and on through the town.

This figure is the Burry Man. He does not speak. He tells no one why he is there, or what has brought about this strange vegetal metamorphosis. Any answer he could give seems to matter very little to the group of volunteers who assemble at this pub to create him every year. The wearer of the costume, who needs to be strong, is sewn into a fabric suit consisting of a balaclava, a T-shirt and under-trousers. Some 11,000 seedheads of greater and lesser burdock are then attached to this base layer, from preassembled sheets that are picked up and patted on to the costume. The Burry Man will walk seven full miles in this heavy, hot outfit, a procession that can take as long as ten hours. Fortunately, local residents are on hand to help, dishing out regular sips of fortifying whisky at houses and pubs. Since his spiked hands cannot easily raise a glass, they feed this to him, with gentle kindness, through a straw.

The Burry Man's taciturnity hasn't stopped people from speculating about him. Some say that this event commemorates Queen Margaret's visit to the town in the eleventh century. A pious ruler, she established the more spiritual forerunner of today's calculative bridge: the ferry across the Firth of Forth for pilgrims wishing to get to the religious centre of St Andrews. Others argue that the custom is a cleansing ritual and the Burry Man is a scapegoat, gathering all the town's bad luck from its evil corners and carrying it beyond the boundaries. Learned people say that his presence relates to other old customs in nearby places, where people used a costume made of burdock seeds to raise the herring in a bad fishing year. The Burry Man listens to the theories but keeps his silence. You cannot even tell whether he is smiling or frowning at all this hypothesising.

Every year, though, this embodied presence enacts a kind of magic. As the procession moves from the older parts of town to newer, carefully planned modern streets, people still gather with their friends, colleagues and neighbours to participate in something old, something unexpected, something that breaks with the routine, the prosaic and the everyday. Nor does the uncertainty about the meaning of this ritual stop members of the audience from gathering a sticky burr from the Burry Man's costume as he passes and taking it home, for good luck.

KIERA CHAPMAN

Boys' Ploughing Match

St Margaret's Hope, South Ronaldsay, Orkney

MID-AUGUST

Surprisingly few British customs focus specifically on children, but in the middle of August on the Orkney Islands, an annual event takes place where young people take centre stage. The village of St Margaret's Hope sits at the head of a small bay on the north coast of South Ronaldsay, overlooking the natural harbour of Scapa Flow. Dotted across the landscape around these waters are numerous concrete structures left over from Orkney's time as a major naval base in both world wars, while the huge oil terminal on the island of Flotta, just west of South Ronaldsay, demonstrates the continuing industrial role of the area. Yet the custom at St Margaret's Hope relates neither to the navy nor to the oil industry, but instead to the islands' agricultural history.

Dating back at least to the nineteenth century, the South Ronaldsay Boys' Ploughing Match is now the only remaining example of an annual contest that used to be found right across Orkney. The challenge is to plough a 'flat', which is a square of sandy beach measuring four feet by four feet, keeping the furrows as straight and evenly spaced as possible. Originally the boys used little ploughs with wooden handles and ploughshares carved from cow horns or even hooves. In 1920, however, the first miniature metal plough was made, and today all the boys use similar versions of these simple hand ploughs, roughly three feet long, some of them wooden, but most made of metal. Many of these are family heirlooms, used by generations of boys before them.

Ploughing furrows across flat, damp sand may sound easy; in fact, it's anything but. Although the soft and even consistency of the sand makes it easier to turn over than soil, it also shows every slight wobble or hint of unsteadiness. At the start and end of each furrow, the merest tremble or hesitation by the ploughboy leaves a telltale mark on the otherwise perfect surface of the sand, and each flaw will count against the final score. Intense concentration – not always the strongest suit of small boys – is required to complete the task within the allotted time.

Only boys may participate in the contest, but these days there is also a competition which is open to, and enjoyed by, the girls: before the ploughing match begins, a parade of 'horses' is held and judged. These are not real horses, however, but children dressed in beautiful and complex 'horse harness' costumes made of black fabric and trimmed with red, white and gold. Although the details are a matter for personal invention, certain components resembling genuine horse harnesses are expected to feature, including the heavy collar, some form of bridle with blinkers, and various straps and buckles. Around their ankles, many of the children wear ornate straps with thick white fringes in imitation of the long hair around the hooves of the heavy horses that were once the mainstay of Orkney's agriculture. From a distance, paradoxically, they resemble the costumes worn by the rather more urban Cockney Pearly Kings and Queens, whose annual parade in September is discussed below in its own entry.

If you are familiar with Orkney, its annual celebration of local ploughing skills will come as no surprise, for, unlike the wild and craggy Hebrides on the west coast of Scotland, most of the Orkney Islands are softly rolling, and large swathes of their fertile soils are intensively farmed. Only Hoy, in the south-west of the archipelago, reveals the dramatic volcanic origins which formed its towering sea cliffs and central uplands. Elsewhere, even the central areas of hilly moorland on both Mainland and Rousay are gently rounded, their rocky heights smoothed off by glacial activity in the last ice age.

In fact, the landscape of Orkney is remarkably benign, its open farmland interlaced with watery expanses of inland lochans and coastal bays. People have been living here since the Stone Age, but the farming of Orkney began about six thousand years ago, when small Neolithic communities emerged, cultivating oats, barley and even wheat, and raising cattle, pigs, goats and sheep. It is to them that we owe the rich legacy of dramatic megaliths, evocative turf-covered tombs and ancient stone buildings that still punctuate the undulating landscape. Over the centuries that followed, different peoples arrived and were assimilated, including the Picts and the Norse Vikings, followed by an increasing Scottish influence. In the sixteenth and seventeenth centuries, however, the 'Little Ice Age' affected Orkney, as it did the rest of Britain, bringing in colder temperatures. Coupled with the gradual exhaustion of the overworked soil, this resulted in a decline in agricultural output, and famine became an ever-present possibility. Eventually the climate warmed again and new ideas on agricultural improvement penetrated the region: the old 'runrig' system of communal farming was abandoned in favour of the piecemeal enclosure of farmland, and more recently, many of these initial small fields were then enlarged. Even so, despite the cultural and climatic changes of the past millennia, the agriculture of the islands remains a patchwork of intensive stock raising and arable production, alongside areas of unimproved, species-rich grassland. And the plough, albeit now towed by large, gleaming tractors, is still essential to the local economy. It is a tribute to their ancestors' manual skills and to the horses upon which they depended that young and old still gather each year on the sands at St Margaret's Hope, overlooking the calm waters of Scapa Flow, to celebrate the passing on of these skills that are so essential to the future of the islands.

REBECCA WARREN

Ras Beca

Preseli Hills, Pembrokeshire

MID-AUGUST

In the middle of August, the slopes of the Mynydd Preseli (Preseli Mountains) come alive with panting, sweating fell runners, whose exertions over the tough terrain are rewarded with panoramic views out over the Irish Channel or down across the stunning Welsh countryside. The scale of these magnificent hills, smoothed over by glaciers in the last ice age but still rising to impressive heights, dwarfs the tiny figures, who quickly disappear against a vast backdrop of rock-strewn slopes. The course is waymarked periodically, but the exact route is not delineated, so runners must make their own decisions about how and where to cross the boggy, tussocky ground. This is no parkrun.

After a long and punishing climb up towards the summits and an equally punishing descent back down, the front runner is draped in an item of women's clothing and, while still running, handed a toy axe. At the finishing line, they bring the axe down with whatever energy they have left to symbolically chop up the gate and claim their victory. 'Rebecca's Daughters' have struck again!

Ras Beca – Rebecca's Race – has been run every year for nearly half a century. It takes its unusual name from a famous period of social unrest that took place in the nineteenth century in the Preseli area – the Rebecca Riots. Before the arrival of the railways in the 1850s, this part of south-west Wales was one of the poorest and most remote parts of Britain, and the only feasible means of transport for people or goods was by roads, which were notoriously slow and sometimes virtually impassable. By the late eighteenth century, serious attempts had been made to improve travelling conditions by building 'turnpiked' roads, which provided superior surfacing and maintenance, enabling faster and more reliable passage. The turnpikes were funded, however, by private turnpike trusts, which recouped their capital expenditure through the imposition of a toll on road users. Those who could not – or would not – pay were not allowed to continue along the road. Not surprisingly, turnpikes were usually constructed over the existing highways between major settlements, which meant that people with livestock or other goods to sell suddenly found themselves having to pay several tolls just to reach their usual markets. And Pembrokeshire in particular found itself subject to a plethora of small turnpike trusts, which increased the number of gates through which road-users had to pass as they crossed from one trust's jurisdiction into that of another.

The financial burden of these tolls on already-impoverished communities was substantial, and bitterly resented, but the final straw was that by the 1830s an

Englishman called Thomas Bullin had leased the running of many of the north Pembrokeshire turnpikes from the local trust. Bullin already managed a portfolio of toll gates, stretching from the east of England across into west Wales, and the imposition of these hated tolls by a 'foreigner' roused particular fury among Welsh farmers. In the spring of 1839 matters came to head with the erection of a new tollgate at Efailwen, on the road between Narberth and Cardigan. Late in the evening on 13 May, a large crowd of armed men, blowing horns and bugles, crashing drums and firing shots, hacked the Efailwen toll gate into pieces and then demolished the adjacent tollkeeper's cottage. The terrified inhabitants reported that the gang was led by a man on a big white horse. He was dressed in a white dress and bonnet, and sported a wig of gold ringlets, which framed his blackened face. After destroying the house and gate, the gang retreated without causing further harm.

The Efailwen toll gate itself was quickly rebuilt, but within days it had been demolished again by the same men. This time, the guards who had been employed to protect the re-erected gate – fruitlessly, as it turned out – heard the gang calling the ringlet-wearing leader 'Rebecca' and referring to themselves as her 'daughters' – *Merched Beca*. After these violent episodes, nothing further happened until 1842, when, out of the blue, the toll gates at St Clears were demolished, again by Rebecca and her daughters. Thereafter, the destruction spread rapidly. Throughout 1843, numerous toll gates were destroyed across south-west Wales, only to be re-erected by the trusts and then demolished again by Rebecca and her daughters a few weeks later. In fact, the turnpike trusts were fighting a losing battle; in the mid-nineteenth century there was no means of instant communication to call for help, no proper police force, and absolutely no local sympathy for their plight. And as the attacks escalated in frequency, so too did the number of participants and the range of their targets. In late June 1843, several thousand armed and angry men and women descended on the county town of Carmarthen, where they not only destroyed the toll gates but also gutted the hated workhouse. The rioters were only overcome when soldiers of the 4th Light Dragoons finally appeared and dispersed them, arresting several of the ringleaders.

Despite this setback, the 'Rebeccaites', as they had become known, did not give up. Only days after the riot in Carmarthen, the gates at St Clears were demolished yet again, the well-armed, black-faced assailants dressed almost universally in white dresses and bent on destruction and revenge. Many more attacks followed across Pembrokeshire, including the demolition of the numerous gates around Cardigan, twenty-five miles north-west of Carmarthen, and of those around Fishguard, forty miles to the west. As shown by the destruction of the Carmarthen workhouse, the retribution perpetrated by Rebecca and her daughters was sometimes extended to other injustices too, usually those involving the exploitation of the very poor.

Despite the efforts of local constables and drafted-in soldiers, the toll-gate riots continued until 1844. The mystery of Rebecca's real identity, and the damage, danger and occasional death that accompanied her activities, produced, almost overnight, a frisson of horrified but romantic fascination with the movement and its leader. Her exploits were reported in newspapers across Britain, in tones of both moral outrage and sneaking admiration, perhaps because the vandalism was often accompanied by a strong sense of theatre and even comedy. *Merched Beca* usually announced their arrival at a target with a carnival of music, whooping and drumming, while one night, they arrived with a coach and horses at the house of a man who had made his servant-girl pregnant. Rebecca herself got out of the coach dressed in a ballgown and handed over the resulting baby to the horrified man, warning him that if he did not look after the child properly over the coming years, she would take her revenge.

But most of the hundreds of attacks carried out by *Merched Beca* were upon the punitive toll gates. Today, this might seem like an overreaction to a relatively minor nuisance, but the impact of these tolls on the poor could be severe. The journalist Thomas Foster, sent by *The Times* in June 1843 to investigate the riots, confirmed that the gates were so numerous in Pembrokeshire that he personally had counted eleven of them along a stretch of road just nineteen miles long. Foster added that the replacement of 'parish relief' for the poor by the brutal new workhouse regime had stoked further resentment, especially in a period of economic recession. Other factors also underlay the unrest: thanks to Thomas Bullin and his like, the toll gates were widely seen as an English imposition, as was the hated legal requirement that everyone must pay tithes to support their parish church, even though most Welsh people attended Nonconformist chapels. And all this was set against the backdrop of the national movement against poverty and disenfranchisement known as Chartism, that was sweeping the country. This potent mix of poverty, fear and resentment undoubtedly accounted for the widespread local support for the campaigns carried out by Rebecca and her daughters.

And the real Rebecca? Several men were identified as this charismatic leader but, of course, she was not a single person throughout the years of her activity. After the first wave of attacks, she became a persona taken on by a number of different men, and groups of her 'daughters' sprang up spontaneously where grievances were deemed to need redress. And she almost certainly took her name not from some local figure, as some sources say, but from the biblical verse in Genesis, so familiar to the chapel-going poor: 'And they blessed Rebekah, and said unto her, Thou art our sister; be thou the mother of thousands of millions, and let thy seed possess the gates of those which hate them.' It was an exhortation that men and women in Pembrokeshire took literally.

On the whole, the punishments inflicted on most of her 'daughters' who were caught were remarkably lenient, reflecting perhaps a recognition that the aim of Rebecca and her daughters was common justice, not personal gain. Indeed, the movement, although short-lived, did have some lasting success. The turnpike legislation was quickly reshaped to reduce its harsh excesses, and slowly the 1834 Poor Law was reformed.

But what of the link between Rebecca and her daughters and the stalwart runners of *Ras Beca*? The connection may at first seem purely geographical, but there are deeper resonances. Fell running developed as a sport in the 1950s, harking back perhaps to earlier village sporting competitions, such as the still-played Haxey Hood game of Lincolnshire described in the 'January' section. The first fell races were generally run by working men and boys at local fairs and markets. As fell running began to be regularised by the athletics world, however, it attracted an 'educated elite' who had trained in cross-country racing and steeple-chasing at public schools. The resulting tension between the two groups clouded the early days of the sport, only dissipating slowly, as running became more popular in the later twentieth century. Class tension no longer explicitly exists in fell running, of course, but the *Ras Beca* is still very much a local race, whose participants are exercising not just their hearts and lungs, but also their right of access to the wilder parts of their local countryside. *Merched Beca*, too, were working men, exercising what they perceived as their right of access to their country. The battle between private ownership and public access is still being fought to this day, and in the destruction of the toll gates, which restricted this right of access and charged people for what had previously been free passage along the highway, perhaps we are seeing a progenitor of contemporary conflicts over free public access to the countryside and the right to roam.

REBECCA WARREN

Notting Hill Carnival

Notting Hill, London

AUGUST BANK HOLIDAY

It is 1948. You are a passenger on HMT *Empire Windrush*, travelling away from everything you know. Away from Trinidad, where strong sunshine throws stark shadows, where colour takes on an additional vibrancy, where the streets are filled with bustling people, piles of goods, and ice barrows filled with tempting bottles of bright syrup. Your life there, however, was not without its stresses and strains – so you have decided to make your destiny elsewhere, in the metropole. Britain needs a workforce after the war, and you have read pamphlets circulated by the government begging you to start a new life in London. You are about to answer their plea.

After thirty days on board ship, finally you dock at Tilbury, Essex. You put on your Sunday-best clothes and smartest shoes, ready to step off the ship and into a new life. The arrival is anticlimactic, though. The dockyard is a brutal piece of anonymous-looking infrastructure. There is no welcoming urban skyline whispering untold possibilities, no Statue of Liberty to reassure you that your soaring dreams are a real possibility. Just mist and marsh, an oily smell, and the clanking of chains and the keening of seagulls. First impressions aren't everything, but as you travel into the city, you notice the buildings blackened by smoke and the people hurrying with heads bowed down in their dark suits and hats. Even at midday, the streets look flat and grey.

You need to find a place to live. You find an advert for a room and speak to a friendly-sounding woman over the telephone. As soon as she opens the door, however, her face falls. She shuffles her feet and tells you that the room has already been let. That slight attempt to spare your feelings is more than you get at the next lodging house, where a surly man points to a sign that reads 'No blacks, no Irish, no dogs'. Eventually, you realise that your choices are reduced to a few streets of rickety housing in Notting Hill, where landlords have subdivided the old Victorian blocks into cramped, unsafe tenements, for which they charge an extortionate rent.

After a while, you settle, but it takes far longer to feel at home. As the years go by, Notting Hill's streets change around you. Oswald Mosley's fascist Union Movement gains a stronghold here, and gangs of Teddy Boys begin to mill around the entrance to the tube station. Their hostility is palpable. In 1958, ten years after your arrival, tensions boil over into a searing week of race riots. And even when the violence is brought under control, nocturnal hands scrawl 'Keep Britain White' on the walls you pass every day.

How did this bleak experience of post-war immigration conjure the Notting Hill Carnival, with its fiercely affirmative, creative and joyous spirit? In seeking an explanation, some historians look back to the celebrations that emerged out of the brutally regimented world of the Caribbean plantations, where tropical space was divided into grids, and time into disciplined units of labour. In the eighteenth century, French slaveowners held a Mardi Gras ball just before Lent, in which part of the 'entertainment' consisted of mocking the dress and mannerisms of their African slaves.

However, the enslaved Africans soon began staging their own celebration, with tolerated festivities that mocked their colonial oppressors. On 1 August 1838, to commemorate Emancipation Day, they began to burn sugar canes, reclaiming a harvest festival practice in which the fields were set on fire. This gave the festival its name: burned canes, or *cannes brûlées*, became 'Canboulay'. Drumming, singing, dancing and chanting were central to its celebration, ultimately giving rise to calypso music. In the early 1840s, Canboulay was moved to carnival season, just before Ash Wednesday, where it has remained in the Trinidadian calendar as a celebration of freedom that includes contributions from members of the many nationalities and ethnicities who call the island home. Repeated attempts to suppress the custom only led to subversive creative responses: when the British banned percussion instruments in 1881, the black community answered by creating tuned instruments from bamboo sticks. The gradual addition of improvised metal instruments over time led to the birth of steelpan bands.

The Notting Hill Carnival was born of the same

call-and-response structure that underpins reggae music, with white violence calling forth black creativity. In January 1959, in the wake of the racial violence of 1958, the pioneering left-wing journalist Claudia Jones organised an indoor celebration of black music and dance acts at St Pancras Town Hall, including a steel band run by well-known musician Russ Henderson. Jones used the programme to issue a plea to the black community to make the celebration an annual affair, and the tradition continued until her untimely death in 1964.

Seven years later, in August 1966, community activist Rhaune Laslett decided to start a festival celebrating the multiculturalism of London, and when Russ Henderson's same band began an impromptu march around neighbouring streets, the first outdoor carnival procession was born. The popularity of the event quickly grew, and by 1975, tens of thousands of attendees were dancing to a static sound system that boomed modern reggae, dub and ska alongside calypso.

The Notting Hill Carnival is now the biggest street event in Europe, with as many as three million attendees each year. Costumed masquerade, or 'mas', is its centrepiece. A mas player does not simply wear a costume – they inhabit it from the inside, and interpret the role that it confers for the audience. The cast of possible characters is endless: there are satirical figures, for example, mocking British and American sailors; there are historical personae from around the world; and there are awards recognising special artistry, such as the carnival king and queen. On this day, angels and devils will battle for supremacy on London's streets, to the crowd's delight.

There are also growing numbers of 'pretty mas' participants, whose gorgeous sequins, feathers and bikinis lack any apparent intention to create a narrative or make a social or political comment. Rather than playing a character, they display and dance in a sexy, gyrating style called 'wining'. Some perceive this as a commercialisation of carnival since many of the outfits are made by profit-seeking companies to generic patterns, which they consider to be a betrayal of the custom's roots in political resistance and African forms of performance. Others point out that this critique of 'pretty mas' positions female participation as 'inauthentic' and ignores the fact that many of the leading carnival roles are exclusively male. Bikinis and beads, they retort, offer women an important avenue to participate and express agency.

Mas performance is inherently spatial; it unfolds in dialogue with the streets of Notting Hill. Yet this is an area that has also changed beyond all recognition since the *Empire Windrush* first landed: what were once desperately run-down streets now form one of the most gentrified neighbourhoods of London, and the rise in house prices has displaced many of the post-war settlers to other areas. Recently, too, the carnival has incorporated moments of silence, anger and protest in memory of the seventy-two lives lost at nearby Grenfell Tower in 2017. The inferno that destroyed the building was able to take hold because of incorrectly specified and poorly installed cladding, and the complicity of multiple private companies and public authorities in creating this disaster has become a potent symbol of the wider racism that the black community continues to suffer.

Every year, with wearisome regularity, members of the

British establishment try to associate the Notting Hill Carnival with violence and disorder, arguing that it should be shut down. Financial worries also loom increasingly large, in the shape of budget cuts to local authorities, the police and the arts organisations that support Notting Hill's festivities (see the 'Bradford Mela' entry for more on this). Yet this event represents one of the most significant and valuable pieces of intangible cultural heritage in the British Isles today – a gyrating, unabashedly loud celebration of diversity, inclusion and the enduring strength of migrant communities.

KIERA CHAPMAN

SEPTEMBER

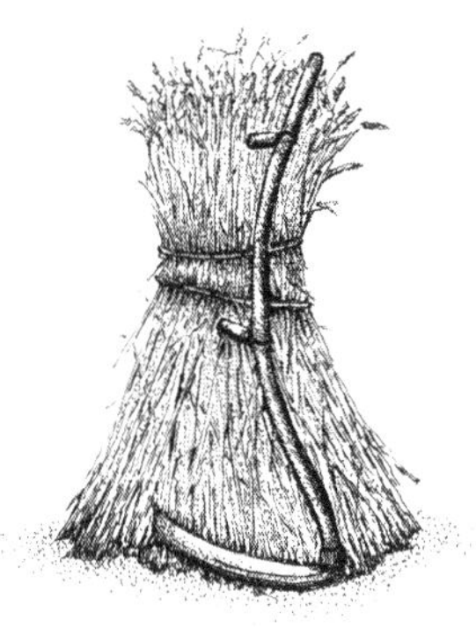

Crying the Neck

Cornwall

AUGUST–SEPTEMBER

The COVID-19 pandemic revealed fundamental weaknesses in the global food-supply chain, particularly in low- and middle-income countries where hunger and malnutrition result from less resilient systems. It has been said (albeit speculatively) that the Caribbean is three weeks away from food collapse and the UK is just nine meals away from anarchy, highlighting the fragility of modern supply chains in extreme scenarios. But for millions of people in Britain, food poverty is already an everyday experience, and for many, the most pressing question they'll ask themselves each morning is, 'Can I afford to eat today?'

This is the situation in a highly developed, industrialised society with global trading networks and imports. For people living in pre-industrial Britain, before intensive farming, things were even worse. Their survival depended largely on the local weather and climate; with limited means of storage and preservation, no back-up imports and subsistence-level production, a poor harvest could result in famine. Generations of growers and farmers looked to the skies, the soil, superstition and animal behaviour to predict the weather. They might use the direction in which smoke drifted, the way their cattle stood, the swarming of bees, and the weather conditions on certain days (as in such rhymes as, 'When April blows its horn, it's good for hay and corn'), as well as rituals to adapt to conditions or ensure a good crop.

One of these harvest customs was revived in Cornwall in 1928 after dying out in the late nineteenth century. 'Crying the Neck' takes place in St Just, Zennor, Madron, Liskeard, St Ervan, St Austell and Mullion, as part of 'Guldize', Cornwall's harvest festival. Unlike many folk customs, there is no fixed date for Crying the Neck – it is traditionally a spontaneous response to local weather conditions and crop readiness – but now it usually takes place around the end of August or the beginning of September.

People gather in windy stubble fields sometimes accompanied by a local band. They say prayers and sing hymns around a patch of barley or wheat that has been left uncut. This is then cut with a scythe and gathered into a 'stook'. The harvester takes a bundle in their hand, touches the ground with it and raises it in the air, crying (in Cornish), '*Yma genef! Yma genef!*' ['I have 'n!' or, 'It is with me!'] three times. The crowd responds with, '*Pandr'us genes?*' ['What have 'ee?' or, 'What is with you?'] three times, and the farmer replies, '*Pen yar!*' ['The neck!'] thrice. The crowd finishes with, '*Houra! Houra! Houra!*' ['Hurrah!

Hurrah! Hurrah!']. At this point, traditionally the man would run to the farmhouse, where he had to dodge a maid holding a bucket of water. If he got past her, he was allowed to kiss her, and if not, he'd get a drenching. The neck was then kept in the farmhouse and fed to the best cow at Christmas. In some places it was twisted or plaited into a harvest token (similar to a corn dolly) and taken to the village church to be placed on the altar. In an early example of trolling, some farmers who had finished harvesting would send their tardier rivals a corn dolly, or leave one in their field, leaving them to deal with the spirit. Today, the neck and accompanying crowd return to the village hall for more hymns and a feast of saffron buns, pasties and tea.

As with many customs, Crying the Neck's beginnings are disputed. One theory was put forward by the Scottish anthropologist and folklorist James George Frazer in his influential 1890 book, *The Golden Bough*. Frazer described how European agrarian societies believed in a regenerative vegetation deity – the Corn Mother – said to be embodied by the last stook of corn. He positioned Crying the Neck as a way of safeguarding the spirit over winter and ensuring a good crop the following year, drawing on descriptions of harvesters in Yorkshire throwing their scythes at the final stook out of fear of reprisal from the corn spirit, or harvesting blindfold to avoid malevolent magic. Similar traditions across Europe do contain superstitious or magical beliefs about a Corn Mother, sometimes represented as a vision, or in the form of a female stranger, and sometimes as a religious icon. We also have records of ancient Egyptian reapers taking part in a similar practice, but instead of celebrating the final stook they lamented the first one. This is thought to have been a way of mourning the death of the corn spirit and praying for its return.

Others argue that Crying the Neck was simply a light-hearted celebration of the end of the toil of harvest. In this explanation it functions as a social mechanism reinforcing collective labour, and a way to mark the transitions between seasons.

The origin of the name 'neck' has been variously claimed to hail from the corn's resemblance to a hen's neck, or to be a hangover from an ancient part of the custom that involved sacrificing a hen. However, in other areas the 'neck' is called a 'tail', and in a similar Dumbartonshire custom it is a 'head', so the name seems more related to the physical form rather than to a specific sacrificial animal. Some villages also introduced a competitive element, with different farms racing each other to finish the harvest first and 'cry the neck' before their rivals. It was seen as bad luck to be the last ones to finish.

The revival of Crying the Neck can be seen as part of a wider Cornish movement for self-determination. After centuries of decline, the Cornish language was given new life in 1904 when Henry Jenner published his *Handbook of the Cornish Language*. In 1924, the formation of the Federation of Old Cornwall Societies in response to the disastrous closing of Cornish tin and copper mines encouraged renewed interest in old customs. Today, Cornish nationalism is on the rise, with 14 per cent of the population in Cornwall identifying as only Cornish, not British, in the 2021 census. In 2017, 51 per cent of schoolchildren in the region self-identified as ethnically Cornish, and the UK government has recently reaffirmed its commitment to recognising Cornwall's national minority status.

With their Cornish chants and focus on local agriculture, these customs reinforce the sense of a separate Celtic cultural and political identity. Where once they might have determined whether a community had enough to eat, now they reflect the strength of Cornish pride and nationalism. In a world grappling with the fragility of food systems, Crying the Neck also reminds us that survival has always been rooted in the land, labour and luck.

LULAH ELLENDER

The Horn Dance

Abbots Bromley, Staffordshire

WAKES MONDAY, EARLY SEPTEMBER

One day, a long, long time ago, someone killed a reindeer. Perhaps it happened on a glittering early autumn day in northern Scandinavia, as the first gentle frost created a delicate fractal geometry among the birch twigs, the low sun striking rainbow sparks from the whitened ground. Perhaps the reindeer and its herd were grazing quietly on the green vegetation, digging down to devour crunchy roots in earth still warm enough for them to move. And perhaps, while they quietly ate, they were being watched, a little way off, by a human who was thinking that the time for the reindeer slaughter had arrived. It has to happen this time of year, before the rut has tainted the taste of the meat, before the year has turned towards the long, dark cold.

Our reindeer inhabited a northern part of the world now known as Fennoscandia, which stretched across the territory now occupied by several modern countries whose boundaries were not yet formed at this early point in history: Sweden, Finland, Norway and the western part of Russia, including the Kola Peninsula. The human hunter could have belonged to one of two peoples: the Sami, a collection of indigenous nomadic groups whose lives revolved around the movements of the deer, or the Norse, the majority of whom had already settled on small farms.

The Sami and Norse cultures mutually influenced each other: in the ninth century, a Norseman called Ohthere visited King Alfred's court, a meeting that the English king recorded in a manuscript that still survives in the British Library. Ohthere told of his wealth, and in particular of his herd of 600 tame reindeer, which he called *hranas*. His account explains that the indigenous Sami paid him tribute in the form of animal skins, whalebone, ropes and feathers, and that the wealthier nomads offered reindeer. In the new Norse way of living, you can perhaps feel the early beginnings of a world that would ultimately come to threaten the fluid spatial and seasonal rhythms of the indigenous Sami. Ohthere describes the roots of an era when property that was formerly owned by everyone came to belong exclusively to one person, whose power over territory would be represented by legal documents and, later, by inviolable lines on maps. A time, also, when deer would become more domesticated, rather than roaming with the changing year. The impacts of these shifts are still felt today. For centuries, the Sami have faced a system of land ownership that fails to recognise their journeying way of life. In 2020, they finally won an important legal battle for recognition of their ancestral right to graze reindeer over a strip of land around an area called Girjas Sameby, in modern Sweden.

We will never know for sure whether it was a Sami who killed the reindeer, or a Norse. But we do know that, after the reindeer's death, its antlers went on an extraordinary journey. Perhaps as part of the international trade network that supplied materials for specialist crafts, such as the making of Viking combs, the horns travelled across the sea, all the way from Fennoscandia to Staffordshire. And when they arrived in this rural corner of the Midlands, they became the centre point of one of England's oldest customs: the Abbots Bromley Horn Dance. This unusual folk ritual takes place on Wakes Monday (more on which in the next entry) in early September, when a Morris troupe wearing the antlers repeats a series of deer-like ritual movements at various locations around the parish, starting at St Nicholas' Church at 8 a.m., and continuing until darkness falls.

The venerable age of the Abbots Bromley antlers was determined with radiocarbon dating. Living things absorb a radioactive form of carbon called carbon-14 during their lifetime on earth. When they die, this process stops and the carbon-14 in their bodies starts to decay, which happens at a uniform rate over time. Calculating the amount left over in an organic object can therefore tell us how old it is. This opens up an intriguing question: if the antlers are a thousand years old, then how long have people been celebrating the Abbots Bromley Horn Dance? The earliest written accounts date from the seventeenth century, but there is often a considerable lag in ritual customs like this being recorded in writing. Many folklorists think that this custom is earlier in origin, with some arguing that it is a truly ancient fertility rite.

Our reindeer's antlers form one of a set of six, all of which were mounted on to painted wooden sculptures of deer heads sometime in the sixteenth century. They are braced crosswise for stability and supported with poles, which is necessary because the largest pair measure over a metre across and weigh over twenty-five pounds (eleven kilos). Each pair is carried by one of six dancers, who are accompanied by a further six mumming figures: a Fool, who strikes at the assembled crowd with an inflated pig's bladder; Maid Marian, often represented by a cross-dressing man who carries a cup and stick to collect donations; a Hobby-horse, who is pursued by a child firing a bow and arrow; a musician who plays the special song for the dance; and a child playing the triangle, which is a later twentieth-century addition to the band.

The dance itself begins with the horn bearers forming two moving circles of three, while the six folk figures move around them in a figure of eight. This then flows into a large clockwise-moving circle, which becomes two parallel inward-facing lines of six. A surprisingly stately pacing now begins, in and out, in and out, with a clashing of horns in the centre (recently replaced by a careful raising of antlers to avoid breaking these precious old bones). The whole thing is graceful, but in an animalistic way: watching it feels very different to the violent energy of the punitive mock stag hunt, or *charivari*, to which it bears a passing resemblance. Nor does it have the swagger of a hunting celebration, which proclaims human mastery over nature. Instead, there are obvious visual similarities between the dance and the fights that take place between stags during the deer rut.

Yet as the same series of movements is repeated over and over at different locations through the village, it feels like something more magical than animal mimicry is happening. The ritual seems to thin the boundaries between the human and non-human worlds. Despite its clearly social function, the antler-wearers, in some strange way, *become* deer. In this stately dance, something crosses over: human-being is concealed and then revealed, and deer-being emerges and retreats. But the transformation is incomplete; it flickers, hovering uncertainly between life-worlds, within the dance. A bridge is crossed, but only to the centre of the arch, with human banter pulling it back if it all becomes too disturbing. Yet as the light falls at the end of the day, and the shadows cast by the horn dance creep longer in the twilight, the reindeer who died a thousand years ago is somehow present once again, its stark antlers defying the darkening sky.

KIERA CHAPMAN

Whitworth Rushcart

Whitworth, Lancashire

WAKES WEEK,
EARLY SEPTEMBER

Modern life, at least in the Global North, is upholstered. We luxuriate on soft sofas, we rest on sprung mattresses and we cocoon ourselves under blankets, with our feet buried in deep carpets. Yet all of this padding is a relatively recent affair; life used to be far less swaddled. Until the eighteenth century saw the adoption of suspended timber floors, most buildings, from homes to churches, had compacted earth underfoot. Tiles, bricks or stone were set straight into the soil, but in the absence of a vapour barrier, the surface often became moist and sweaty. Churches did not have seating in the same way that they do today, and people would likely have stood and knelt through services, with benches around the edge of the church for the elderly and infirm, which gives us the origin of the phrase 'the weakest go to the wall'.

This is where rushes came in. Their grass-like leaves may have been freely strewn or cleverly woven into mats, but either way, they provided a layer of dry vegetation to act as a barrier between the body and the earth in homes and churches. Native species were often used, but in the sixteenth century, sweet flag, *Acorus calamus*, a native of central Asia, was introduced to provide a new material for this purpose, adding a pleasant scent and useful insect-repellent properties. The plant's current distribution in the UK, which tends towards the north-west, may be partly due to deliberate planting for strewing, though it can also propagate by seed, as well as vegetatively, when its roots break off and travel down water courses.

This organic carpet could be easily renewed, though changing it often was seen as an indulgence. When Cardinal Wolsey fell out of favour with Henry VIII in the late 1520s, one of the complaints against the minister was that he imported an extravagant quantity of sweet flag to use at his residences in London. On the other hand, the continental scholar Erasmus, who visited England several times, thought that rushes were not changed nearly often enough in this country: 'The floors too are generally spread with clay and then with rushes from some marsh, which are renewed from time to time but so as to leave a basic layer, sometimes for twenty years,' he complained. Underneath, he explained, festered 'spittle, vomit, dogs' urine and men's too, dregs of beer and cast-off bits of fish, and other unspeakable kinds of filth. As the weather changes, this exhales a sort of miasma which in my opinion is far from conducive to bodily health.'

The renewal of the rushes that strewed the floors of churches was an important date in the ritual year, though different places celebrated it at different times. In St Mary Redcliffe in Bristol, the ceremony happens on Whit Sunday, but in Bishop's Castle in Shropshire, it takes place on or around the summer solstice, and in Barrowden in Rutland, it occurs on or around the eve of St Peter's Day (28 June). Several Cumbrian towns and villages also have rush festivals in late June and July. However, in the Lancashire town of Whitworth, and in the wider north-west of England, where there is a particularly strong tradition of rush renewals, it is celebrated in late August or early September, coinciding with a day of holiday called 'the Wakes'. The name comes from the Old English word *wacu*, which means 'to watch', referring to the vigil kept to honour the feast day of the saint attached to the local church.

By the Industrial Revolution, the Wakes had become a much-valued day off in the northern mill towns. The rhythm of production in the new factories relied on processes that ran from machine to machine, meaning that mill owners relied on most of the workers being present at the same time. Everyone therefore had to take their holiday simultaneously, and it was unpaid, almost strike-like in character: workers would simply refuse to come in. Instead, people across a whole area would scrub and paint their houses and buy new clothes to welcome visiting friends and relatives. Travelling fairs would visit, giving the community something to do, alongside bloodsports like bull-baiting and cockfighting. There was inevitably a lot of heavy drinking, too, with a whole town or village simultaneously *en fête*. In Lancashire, West Yorkshire and parts of Cheshire, older customs like the renewal of rushes in the church were rewoven into this new rhythm of working-class urban life, leading to a hybrid kind of holidaymaking that combined sacred and secular, as well as pre-industrial and industrial, elements.

Communities would gather together to build and decorate 'rushcarts' – two-wheeled wagons that were pulled through the local streets by humans rather than horses, as Morris dancers performed around them. To fund the ritual, donations were solicited from the surrounding community, and particularly from the upper and middle classes. The carts were filled with vegetation, often piled up in a pyramid and partly covered by a sheet, to which shining gold and silver ornaments were added, symbolising the communal wealth of the local area. In the early nineteenth century, when rushcart customs were in their heyday, their decoration was a competitive affair, with villages vying with one another to produce the most splendid vehicle. Sometimes different districts within the same area each produced their own, with chaos and occasional fights ensuing when they came head to head on narrow streets. According to a censorious account of the Saddleworth Wakes from 1858:

> groups of rough, half-drunken, disorderly young men, from what is familiarly called 'the lower end' of Greenfield yoked themselves to 'rushcarts' by long ropes and poles, or 'stangs', by which they drew them through their different districts, and to Uppermill, to the evident delight of themselves – judging from

> their uproarious laughter and merry-andrew capers ... Four carts were thus drawn through Uppermill; and as is usual on such occasions, the parties drawing the different carts came into contact with each other, and fully sustained the true character of their affair by kicking and striking one another.

The practical utility of bearing rushes in rushcarts declined in the later nineteenth century, as churches were restored by the Victorians and seating was added to enable people to sit in relative comfort and give more serious attention to the sermon. Yet the custom lived on as a secular expression of local pride, though its popularity did begin to wane. Attacks from factions within the monied classes who condemned rushcarting as a source of disorder may well have reduced the donations on which its continuance relied. Rushes also became harder to find, as farmland was drained to enclose new land and improve its agricultural productiveness, getting rid of the marshy conditions that these plants enjoy. Incoming town dwellers did not always feel the same attachment to the area and its traditions either, which could have further diluted enthusiasm for participation. Rushcarting also started to require more organisation, making it increasingly expensive; in some places, the response was to replace large, elaborate vehicles with smaller 'grove carts' containing garlands of foliage.

But as the nineteenth century wore on, there were wider changes afoot in the way leisure time was spent. The advent of more secure incomes and improved working conditions and hours allowed people to enjoy their time off. The coming of the railways and the beginning of cheap seaside breaks expanded horizons and meant that people could consider taking a longer holiday and travelling further afield. From the mid-century onwards, new savings clubs, often organised within workplaces, were set up to enable families to pay for these trips. Attitudes among employers shifted, too, with many moving towards sanctioned, though still unpaid, leave. At first, these new periods of holiday remained quite collective, often with whole communities going to the same resort together during what had become 'Wakes week'. By the later twentieth century, however, changes to production methods meant that people could take periods of leave at their individual convenience. And with this shift, Wakes week was reduced to a shadow of its former, collective self, and rushcarting dwindled.

Yet many towns have chosen to keep rush-bearing customs alive, renewing them for an era where the rhythms of labour are changing once again with the advent of internet-enabled homeworking. In Whitworth, the rushcart celebrations have been revived several times between the 1970s and the 2000s, and the festival is now a much-loved part of the local calendar. The rushcart is particularly distinctive, decorated not with rushes but with a huge bishop's mitre full of heather from the nearby moors, some of which is sold as a lucky charm once the procession has ended. The parade through the streets is accompanied by brass and folk bands, a group of women armed with brushes who ceremonially sweep the streets, and colourfully dressed Morris and clog dancers. There's even a unique folk dance for the occasion.

While there are many reasons to be grateful that we no longer have to strew rushes on hard, cold church floors, our modern working lives leave us with fewer opportunities to connect with the social world around us. Perhaps the reason rushcarting customs remain relevant is that they respond to a deeply felt social need for community – even in our swaddled modern world of air travel and holidays to exotic, far-flung destinations.

KIERA CHAPMAN

The Crab Fair

Egremont, Cumbria

MID-SEPTEMBER

One of Britain's oldest fairs, the Egremont Crab Fair, has nothing to do with crustaceans. Instead, it is a celebration of the crab apple harvest.

The crab apple is an ancient species that has been present in Europe for around eleven thousand years, since the end of the last ice age. It supports at least ninety-three insect species and is steeped in mythology, associated with fertility rites and revered in Celtic traditions. It has also influenced the genome of our domestic apples, boosting their cold hardiness and enhancing cross-pollination. It is no surprise then, that its harvest would be an occasion for local celebration. Established by Lord Egremont and dating back to 1267, the Egremont Crab Fair is part of the medieval tradition of fairs that grew into wild and wonderful mêlées of feasts, entertainment, sport and processions.

In addition to a dog show, fell running, equestrian events, ferret shows, fair rides and a concert, apples still feature heavily in the fair, as they are thrown into the crowds that line the streets to see an apple cart parade through the town. But the apple component of the fair is also thought to have given rise to a rather unique custom: since the 1500s, the Egremont Crab Fair has been home to the World Gurning Championships. It is hard to describe gurning if you haven't seen it – imagine folding your face while impersonating a gargoyle. Apparently, having false teeth is a distinct advantage. It is said that these weird facial contortions stem from the grimace that often follows a bite into a sour crab apple. Another theory of gurning's potential origin is that it was a form of entertainment performed in exchange for tobacco at ports; but however it started, it is a serious business here, with some competitors practising for hours a day to soften their facial muscles in the lead-up to the fair.

These facial distortions and exaggerations echo the work of mime artists like Charlie Chaplin and Buster Keaton, and we can even find similarities in Leonardo Da Vinci's drawing, *Grotesque Heads*. As a physical expression of disgust turned into a theatrical performance, gurning is part of a heritage of 'misrule' traditions that temporarily subvert social norms and rules. From questionable freak shows to wacky Snapchat filters, people have long enjoyed exploring ideals of beauty and its opposite, and the Egremont Crab Fair is a whole-hearted celebration of this absurdist form of amusement.

LULAH ELLENDER

Hop Hoodening

Canterbury, Kent

MID-SEPTEMBER

Have you ever been up close and personal with a hop? I mean, really got your fingers and nose into it? A fresh hop flower looks like a soft green pine cone. Pull off some of the sticky green 'petals' and bury your nose in the cone. Suck in the acrid scent: it's an olfactory tour de force, opening up nasal passages you didn't know you had, at once repellent but intriguing. Indeed, everything about the hop is a physical experience: the aroma, yes, but also the stickiness of the flower petals, produced by a waxy oil in the plant tissue called lupulin. Spend any time picking and processing hops and your fingers will carry the scent throughout the day, like a chemical memory. Even the hop's leaves and stems – or bines – will not let you pass them by unnoticed, for they are covered in tiny hooks and hairs that catch at your skin, raising red weals of irritation if you get too close for too long. Pity the hop-pickers of old, who spent hot, weary hours among the hop bines, their arms and faces scratched and raw from close contact with the abrasive, rope-like stalks.

Hops have been grown in Kent for half a millennium. Coming in only slowly from continental Europe, where their role in flavouring and preserving ale had long been recognised, they were generally shunned in Britain until the seventeenth century, when the unique qualities of hopped ale, especially its longer life, were finally recognised. By the later nineteenth century, Kent had over 77,000 acres under hop cultivation, and the hop harvest relied upon such large numbers of people that an annual influx of poor families from London arrived to join the local labour force in the county's hop gardens as a working 'holiday'. During the twentieth century, however, changing tastes in beer, the impact of war, and competition from other hop-producing countries reduced the acreage dramatically. Today, Kent's hop gardens amount to about just 1000 acres, supplying specialist breweries with local varieties and interior decorators with swags of pungent dried foliage. The once-ubiquitous sight of rows of tall poles criss-crossing a field, bleakly bare in winter but swathed with dense foliage in summer, is now all but a memory.

Yet the practice of hop cultivation is still hardwired into Kentish identity, and perhaps this is why in the latter part of the twentieth century two local traditions gradually coalesced to form a cheerful custom that takes place in Canterbury. In the middle of September each year, the precincts of the city's ancient cathedral ring with the sounds of Morris dancers, celebrating the Hop Hoodening ceremony. The event then moves into the cathedral, which is decorated with garlands of hops, where a service takes place, during which one of the local Morris sides dances in front of the high altar. The service is also attended by a girl dressed as the 'Hop Queen', who walks within a portable hop bower, supported by green-clad 'princesses' who offer baskets of hops to be blessed by the officiating clergy. Later, the Hop Queen and her attendants will parade through the streets beyond the cathedral precincts, handing out hops to bystanders.

So much for the hop blessing, drawn from the agricultural history of the area – but what of the Hop Hoodening? This part of the custom draws on the widespread tradition of the hobby-horse. In many parts of the country, a hobby-horse was a key component in Christmas customs that featured some kind of mumming play, and it is related to other similar plays, such as the Cheshire soul-caking custom. Most hobby-horses were constructed with a wooden horse-head, or even a horse's skull, as in the Mari Lwyd custom, described in our December entry, held up by a person swathed in a voluminous cloth to form some kind of 'body'. In this Kentish custom, it is known as a 'hooden horse', and it consists of a distinctive wooden head emerging from an arched, cloth-covered carapace that forms the body, beneath which a person walks bent over, clacking the horse's wooden teeth with a cord or short stick as they go. The hooden horse usually appeared in short plays, widespread in the nineteenth century, that were performed from house to house to raise funds at Christmas, and which, alongside the hooden horse, featured several standard characters, including a mischievous 'boy' and a 'moll' with a broom. Handbells were often rung at the horse's appearance, and money was given at its departure. The exact difference between a 'hooden' horse and other hobby-horses is a point of debate, but the hooden-horse tradition was particularly strong in east Kent before dying out in the early twentieth century.

In 1956, however, the Swan pub in Wickhambreaux near Canterbury was renamed the Hooden Horse, a transformation that was celebrated with a revival of the Hoodening custom, with handbell ringing and the possibly newer addition of Morris dancing. In subsequent years, the amalgamation of the custom with a thanksgiving celebration of the hop harvest has brought these two aspects of Kentish popular tradition together, and this now forms part of the autumn calendar of Canterbury Cathedral, as well as of the city. But beware: hooden horses with wild staring eyes and clacking jaws can turn up at any Kentish celebration where Morris dancers perform. The custom, now firmly re-established, has become a treasured, if slightly unnerving, part of life in the Garden of England.

REBECCA WARREN

Assize of Bread and Ale

York

LATE SEPTEMBER

There can be few more pleasant civic duties undertaken by the Sheriff of York than carrying out the city's annual Assize of Ale. On a Saturday afternoon, usually in August, the sheriff, dressed in a scarlet robe with a brown fur collar, and sporting the gold chain of office over a lacy cravat, stands on the steps of the rather grand Mansion House to proclaim the commencement of the assize. After the proclamation, the city's 'sergeants', wearing quasi-medieval costumes, head off in procession to visit a selection of inns and pubs, where they sample the beer. Assuming the quality is deemed up to standard – and it always is – the publican receives a certificate of satisfaction. Not surprisingly, the ceremony is carried out with considerable enthusiasm all round. Moreover, in the last few years, the custom has been extended to include an 'Assize of Bread', for which local bakeries offer up a selection of products for 'judgement'. It's a far cry from the reality of the historical assizes of bread and ale, which were an altogether more serious undertaking.

Bread and ale used to be staples of the British diet. Before the seventeenth century, bread was eaten in some form at every meal. Made of wheat, barley or oats, it filled hungry stomachs relatively cheaply and was an essential source of nutrition. It also played an important role as a thickener for puddings, pottages and sauces. Although other carbohydrates were available, none were as ubiquitous as bread; homegrown peas and beans required long cooking, which used up a lot of fuel, while rice, although imported increasingly from the fifteenth century onwards, remained relatively expensive. Potatoes and pasta entered Britain in the sixteenth century, but potatoes only began to be widely eaten at the end of the eighteenth century, and pasta remained a niche food. It was bread that fuelled the country, and when the cereals grown for bread weren't being baked, they were used to produce ale.

Ale, made from any or all of the three major cereals, was brewed and drunk widely. In part, this reflected a sensible precaution about drinking water, which was easily contaminated, but ale also provided a significant portion of the necessary daily intake of calories and vitamins, which was especially important for the poor. Indeed, in the nineteenth century, the success of the temperance movement, which replaced ale with water or tea, resulted in an alarming rise in malnourishment among this sector of society. Ale and beer, therefore, have long been as critical to the national diet as bread, and for this reason, governments, even in the medieval period, were keen to ensure that they were easily accessible for all citizens. And the only means of doing this was by controlling the quality and price of both.

In 1266, the government of Henry III passed a statute establishing the *Assisa Panis et Cervisie* or Assize of Bread and Ale. It was widely recognised that standard weights and measures were critical for a well-functioning economy, and the assize laws formed part of the drive to achieve this, by ensuring that the cost of a loaf of bread or gallon of ale remained constant. Of course, the price of wheat itself necessarily fluctuated, depending on how good or bad the annual harvest had been. This meant that although the government decreed that loaves must cost either a halfpenny or a farthing (a quarter of a penny), it accepted that the *weight* of those loaves would vary, reflecting the cost of the wheat used to produce them. In other words, a halfpenny loaf might weigh twelve ounces one year but ten ounces the following year, because wheat had become more expensive. Similarly, the price that brewers could charge for their ale, which was also made from cereals, was also fixed to the variable price of wheat.

Enforcement of the assize originally came from the Crown, undertaken primarily through peripatetic officers known as clerks of the market. They were also empowered to punish those traders who failed to adhere to the necessary standards, as well as those who tried to subvert the regulations by buying up goods before they reached the market, in order to sell them on at an inflated price. Gradually the task of enforcing the assize overwhelmed the Crown's administrative capacity, and by the fourteenth century, some of the responsibility was devolving to the county sheriffs, who passed it down to town mayors, bailiffs and aldermen or, in the case of ale, to a designated ale-taster or 'ale-conner'. In later years, the price was set by the local justices of the peace.

In a way that would astonish the medieval assize clerks and ale-conners, many towns still retain a ceremonial and light-hearted Assize of Bread and/or Ale even today. There is one, for example, at Holsworthy in Devon, where the Pretty Maid ceremony takes place. Nowadays, the serious matter of controlling the quality of these staples is governed by national legislation covering food standards and trades descriptions, so these assize ceremonies are devoted purely to celebrating the still-vital role of local pubs and bakeries in our communities.

REBECCA WARREN

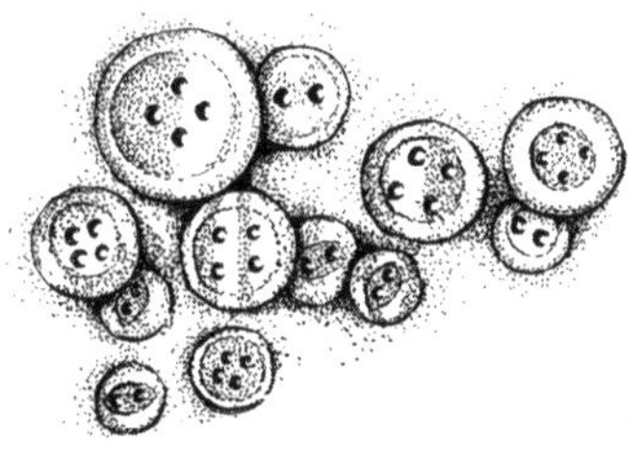

Pearly Kings and Queens Harvest Festival

London

LAST SUNDAY OF SEPTEMBER

Steve Jobs, the co-founder of technology giant Apple Inc., was koumpounophobic: he had an aversion to buttons. He famously wore turtlenecks to avoid them, and the lift in Apple's Tokyo store routinely stopped at every single floor rather than having a panel of the usual circular push controls. And, of course, the Apple iPhone, introduced in 2007, also banished them, replacing a rubberised keypad with a sleek touchscreen.

At the opposite end of the spectrum to Steve Jobs are the pearly kings and queens of London. Based in the East End of the city, they wear black clothes resplendent with hundreds, if not thousands, of white mother-of-pearl buttons. The visual effect is the antithesis of an unembellished turtleneck: elaborate patterns and motifs abound, with the fabric of the underlying clothes sagging under the weight of this excess of decoration.

How did this singular sartorial tradition develop? London street traders, formerly called 'costermongers', used to wear trousers with a line of pearlescent buttons along the outer seam, running from the ankle to the knee. In the 1870s, a street sweeper named Henry Croft was fascinated by the look, and decided to take it to an extreme, adding buttons to every inch of his suit. An early photo of him shows a slight figure posing awkwardly for the camera, his tightly clenched fists a sharp contrast to his attention-grabbing clothes. He wears a 'skeleton suit', in which the black fabric background is decorated with white button motifs. A much later picture shows him posing more confidently, this time in a three-piece suit so smothered with fish-scale buttons that the underlying black fabric is invisible. Though he may not always have enjoyed being photographed, Croft was remarkably successful at using his eye-catching threads to create a new identity as the 'pearly king'. His purpose was philanthropic: he collected money to help fund local causes, notably hospitals, which often needed money in an era before NHS-style state funding.

Croft could so easily have been an eccentric one-off, but somehow his outlandish dress and charitable purpose took off, spreading out from the East End to become a distinctive London subculture. By the early twentieth century, every London borough had its own pearly king and queen, and the tradition continues today, with titles passed down through families.

Each autumn, the pearly kings and queens come together for not one but two harvest festivals. The first happens on the last Sunday in September, when families gather at Guildhall Yard, in the heart of the square mile that is known as 'the City', and parade to St Mary-le-Bow, whose famous bells make Cockneys of all those who are born within earshot. The second is more central, held traditionally at the church of St Martin-in-the-Fields near Trafalgar Square, and takes place in early October. A Pathé news reel from 1963 shows the pearlies proudly displaying traditional wheatsheaf loaves embellished with buttons. The voiceover comments ironically on the urban use of this agrarian imagery: 'The Stoke Newington wheat crop, apparently, wasn't below the average.' Today, it is charitable giving, rather than food, that is prioritised, with blue plastic buckets passed around for public contributions.

It would be easy to read the pearlies as a relic of an old white working-class London replete with pie and mash shops, local boozers and cheeky banter with a dose of rhyming slang. Louis Dunford's song 'The Angel (North London Forever)', which has become the anthem for the north London football club Arsenal, has adopted and modernised this narrative for an era of gentrification, contrasting the naked bricks and knobbly cobbles of childhood memories with the gleaming architecture of contemporary global capitalism that now dominates the area. The chorus, however, insists on the continuity of the local community, despite efforts to displace it. There is perhaps something comforting in this celebration of the resilience of the old East End, but it also presents only a partial view of the area and its inhabitants. Dunford's video, after all, depicts an almost entirely white community that is hardly representative of modern north London. As Georgie Wemyss has written, the idea of an unchanging Cockney culture can be used to obscure the long history of the East End's wider global connections, which have made it home to generations of black and Asian families.

There is another version of the pearlies' story, however, that connects its origins with the wider world. Some of Henry Croft's suits were completely covered in buttons, but how did a poor street sweeper, who was born in a workhouse, afford such a glinting array of relatively expensive decorations? One theory tells of a Japanese ship that foundered in one of London's notorious pea-souper fogs, subsequently sinking in the Thames. Its cargo of pearl-shell buttons apparently then washed up on the shores of the river, where they were gathered by the locals. There is no official evidence of a shipwreck of this kind, but it circulates as a kind of urban legend among the mudlarks who pick through the sediment of the Thames to find buried historical artefacts. If it were true, then Henry Croft's generously bedecked suit, and the wider pearly tradition, would only exist because of a global trade network that extends thousands of miles beyond any local manor in London.

I like this version of the story. My family are from the East End. My dad grew up in the slums of Hackney after the war, later moving to a council house in the same area, and I feel like I have a small but personal stake in the continuation of Cockney customs. But – at least to me – there's no conflict between the idea that the white working-class East End produced a distinctive culture that is important and worthy of preservation and the view that this has always been a diverse, outward-looking area that has welcomed people from across the globe who have brought their own distinctive customs with them.

A similar conviction underpins the work of Andy Green and Saif Osmani, co-founders of 'The Modern Cockney

Festival'. Their definition of the Cockney is class-based, celebrating 'non-posh Londoners' of all races and creeds. Sure, they recognise a threat from slick gentrification, and campaign against a vision of England (or 'Engbland' as they call it) that fails to recognise the significance of regional diversity and working-class identity. But their view of that identity is plural, and includes the cultures of black and Asian communities, who become the inheritors of the Cockney future. At the heart of Saif and Andy's collaboration is a conversation-starting piece of clothing made of black cloth and emblazoned with the words 'Pearly Power' in shimmering mother-of-pearl buttons. Instead of a masculine suit, though, this iconic sartorial symbol of the modern East End is distinctly feminine and definitely racialised. It's a burka.

KIERA CHAPMAN

OCTOBER

Corn Dolly Festival

Siddington, Cheshire

OCTOBER

Every October since 1990, All Saints Church in Siddington, Cheshire, has been filled with a thousand corn dollies made by local dairy farmer and artisan Raymond Rush. Known as the Corn Dolly Man, Rush made corn dollies for over fifty-five years, holding workshops and selling his work to visitors, as well as collecting over three thousand historic farming artefacts. He died in 2021, but the Corn Dolly Festival continues, preserving this traditional craft and his beautiful work.

Rush's handiwork adorns almost every surface of the fifteenth-century half-timbered church, with a vast array of designs and shapes, including 'maidens', plaited hearts, 'favours' and spirals. Corn dollies cover the window frames, beams, light fittings and organ pipes, creating a stunning display. He was part of a long line of agricultural workers who kept this highly skilled craft alive. The custom is said to be rooted in an ancient harvest ritual practised around the world to mark the end of the harvest and bring good luck for the following year's crops. Straw from the last sheaf to be cut was knotted and plaited into a 'dolly' (from 'idol') in which it was believed Ceres, the spirit of the corn, lived. The dolly was safely sheltered over winter and then its grains were planted in the spring to ensure a good harvest.

As is also evident in September's 'Crying the Neck' custom, before the advent of large-scale agriculture and global food transport, the harvest was a matter of life and death, so these fertility rituals were important to rural communities around the world. Some believe that without the understanding of seed germination we have today, communities placed their faith in spiritual beliefs. From Japan (with its *shimenawa* and Anatolia (with its wheat spike amulets) to North Africa and Zapotec Mexico, corn dollies were central elements in harvest rituals.

Yet the pagan roots of these customs may be overstated. It is highly possible that, instead of reflecting a deep belief in a dying-and-reviving deity, people created corn dollies to mark part of the agrarian seasonal cycle and to strengthen community cohesion. The forms corn dollies take depend on the maker's individual creative expression as well as on regional distinctions in designs, such as the Cambridgeshire bell, the Suffolk horseshoe, the Norfolk lantern and the Kentish ivy girl.

While the plaits and twists have a simple beauty, there is something sinister about the 'maiden' designs, which portray a female figure wearing a gown, with straw hands and a great burst of straw for a head. This effigy-like creepiness adds to a wider sense of the uncanny connected to corn fields and human forms created from organic matter. If you grew up in the 1970s you may remember the terrifying children's TV character Worzel Gummidge, a scarecrow who came to life and could unscrew his own head. Scarecrows were not made with the same artistry as other straw crafts and were there to serve a purpose, but they engender the same cognitive dissonance as corn dolly maidens. Worzel Gummidge's magical qualities reflected a broader perception of rural traditions and folklore as being innately malevolent, which may be rooted in Christian attempts to stamp out or assimilate pagan customs.

The mid-twentieth century also saw the emergence of 'folk horror' films, such as *The Wicker Man* and *Children of the Corn*, that embraced the supernatural in place of the old Gothic tropes. These films play on the sense of isolation and disorientation of cornfields. Although the American corn that features in films like *Dark Harvest* is what we call maize and is not the same as the rye, millet or wheat crops used to make corn dollies, there is a familiar quiet dread and ominousness about these inescapable, featureless fields.

Painterly representations of harvest time have tended towards the bucolic rather than the satanic. George Stubbs's 1785 *Harvest* depicts a line of workers all performing different tasks. They are wearing clean clothes and there is a sense of calm and order – some of them are looking up at a well-dressed man on horseback, reinforcing the social hierarchy. A church steeple in the background adds to the idyllic feel.

The nineteenth-century French artist Jean-François Millet took a more realistic approach in his 1857 oil painting *The Gleaners*, a depiction of the back-breaking work of the poorest peasant women collecting leftover grains after harvest. He shows them bent over, knuckles swollen and muddy. Such harsh realities of rural life make the artistry of corn dolly-making even more impressive. When conceptual artist Agnes Denes created *Wheatfield – A Confrontation* in 1982, growing wheat on a 2.2-acre Manhattan landfill site, she wanted to highlight issues of poverty and hunger by distributing the harvest to people in need around the world. This was agrarian art as a living act.

In Siddington, Raymond Rush was continuing a traditional craft that had nearly died out by the mid-twentieth century. Although making straw hats was traditionally women's work, making corn dollies was usually a male pastime. The seasonal ritual gradually became a more decorative craft, with a pair of two-metre-high corn dollies of a lion and a unicorn, made by Fred Mizen, featuring in the Festival of Britain in 1951. Small straw knots and favours were also decorated with ribbons and given as love tokens.

The Museum of English Rural Life in Reading houses a fascinating collection of corn dollies from around the world and features the work of Alec Coker, a skilled maker who discovered the craft after working on a 1930s BBC production of *Lorna Doone*. The museum also has an impressive collection of basketwork and a large straw sculpture of King Alfred, complete with moustache and crown, made by Jesse Maycock in 1961. Maycock was a thatcher by trade, but his sculpture of Alfred was another example of the way craftspeople turned practical skills into art.

Today's corn dolly crafts continue this artistic trend. It is harder to find the right kind of straw these days, as modern farming methods favour shorter, stubbier crops; but specialist growers supply the burgeoning ranks of keen corn dolly-makers around Britain with Maris Widgeon or Squareheads Master wheat. Vintage books offer instructions on tempering the straw so it doesn't get mildewed, handling the straw so you can turn as you plait, and 'feeding' the connecting hollow straws, as well as showing different designs. With YouTube tutorials, workshops, the Guild of Straw Craftsmen and Instagram influencers to teach us how to make corn dollies, you can try a Clove Hitch or a Surgeon's Knot, a Cambridge Umbrella or a Kern Baby, as this ritual evolves once more from harvest-time custom to artisanal hobby.

Such folk expressions are not fixed relics but are continually shaped by lived reality. They can be expressions of local identity too. Corn-dolly making is still enjoyed by cultures around the world (Ukraine, in particular, is famed for its straw work), incorporating local traditions and materials as well as region-specific patterns and techniques, and contributing to a form of cultural identity and collective memory. The appeal of corn dollies is partly their ornamental beauty, but also the tenacious allure of supposedly pagan customs.

LULAH ELLENDER

The Mop Fair

Tewkesbury, Gloucestershire

OLD MICHAELMAS DAY
(AROUND 10 OCTOBER)

If we were to make a league table of the organisms that have wreaked swift and lethal havoc on human society, the bacterium *Yersinia pestis* would be up there in the top five. Under an electron microscope, it looks surprisingly benign, like a tiny, immobile rice krispie. Yet inside its outer shell are small circles of DNA called plasmids, one of which allows it to survive inside the gut of a tiny flea. It colonises the flea's whole digestive tract, eventually blocking the valve between its oesophagus and gut. Now unable to eat, the starving flea finds a host and, in vain, keeps biting them, trying again and again to drink their blood but succeeding only in regurgitating *Yersinia pestis* into their bloodstream. If that host happens to be human, one of three things happens. First, the bacteria can proliferate in the lymph system, causing painful sores known as 'buboes'; second, it can multiply in the bloodstream, where it causes sepsis; or third, it can move to the lungs, resulting in pneumonia, which releases droplets containing the bacterium into the air. These can then transmit the bacterium directly from person to person, removing the need for the flea.

The disease that *Yersinia pestis* causes is commonly known as plague, and from 1347 to 1353, it devastated Europe in a pandemic that we now call the Black Death. Rats have long been blamed as the primary vector responsible for carrying plague from their own species of rat flea (*Xenopsylla cheopis*) to humans, but new evidence suggests that they may have been unfairly scapegoated. Scientists now think that the pandemic that decimated Europe jumped from a disease reservoir in ground-burrowing mammals, especially marmots, to human fleas (*Pulex irritans*) and lice, whence it spread through the population, perhaps assisted by person-to-person droplet transmission.

The first known case in the UK was a sailor who arrived in Weymouth from Gascony in June 1348. By autumn, people in London were infected, and a wave of sickness then engulfed the whole country. Sufferers experienced fever and flu-like symptoms, often followed by those telltale bubonic sores in the groin, neck and armpits, which turned from red to black as gangrene set in.

The Black Death was a human disaster on an unimaginable scale. In the UK, the population at the time was between 4.5 and 6 million people, of whom between 45 and 60 per cent died. Aside from the sheer scale of human loss, the pandemic's social and economic effects were far-reaching. One brutally logical consequence was a labour shortage: by 1349, so many people had succumbed that there were serious concerns about whether the harvest could be brought in, meaning that those who had survived were at very real risk of starvation.

The elites of the day quickly became concerned that workers would use the scarcity of labour to demand higher wages and lower rents. In 1349, as plague raged, King Edward III rushed through the Ordinance of Labourers, followed in 1351 by the still harsher Statute of Labourers. This set day rates for a wide range of work at pre-plague levels, forced able-bodied people under the age of sixty to work, and forbade labourers from moving around to get better rates of pay. It also gave employers greater security, prioritising annual employment contracts formed in a public forum over more casual day-rate arrangements. Those who broke the rules were usually fined, but imprisonment or a session in the stocks were also possible penalties. Though the use of law to regulate labour had occurred for some time, and enforcement was patchy at best, these Acts tightened the screws on workers. As historian Mark Ormrod comments, in moving to control waged labour, 'the state demonstrated its readiness to subordinate the interests of the many to preserving the advantages of the few'.

Mop fairs were a response to these new labour laws. Now that a larger proportion of agricultural workers were hired on an annual basis, rather than by day, week or task, the fairs acted as a kind of general employment exchange: alongside drinking, games and feasting, employers met new employees and negotiated terms and conditions for the coming year. The timing of this custom varied considerably depending on its location: mop fairs originally took place around Michaelmas Day in the south and east of England, on Martinmas in the north, and on May Day in the Fens and to the west. To enable an easy match to be struck between employee and employer, workers would wear a 'tassel', or token of their trade: shepherds might place wool in their buttonholes, carters would display whipcord, and farmers would put straw in their hatband. The tassel became known as a 'mop', which led to the term 'mop fair', though some maidservants also carried mops and brooms to denote their profession.

Prospective employees and employers clearly eyed one another up keenly. An 1846 article in the *Preston Guardian* describes the bargaining as 'on the same principle as you see in a cattle market', suggesting that both buyers and sellers were looking for a wide range of attractive qualities in a potential hire:

> One man, boasting to a neighbour how well he had succeeded, observed, 'Ay! She is a fine lass – I ken the breed of her.' The girls showed great freedom in asking the applicants numerous questions: 'Where is your house? How many kye [cows] do you keep? What is there to do?' One man thought he would secure his end; and, in answer to the last question said, 'Oh, we have nothing to do.' 'Then I'll not hire with you,' was the reply . . . 'Are you a milker?' cried a strapping farmer to a young woman: 'my wife is on her last legs, and I'll take you for good.' 'Aw can milk nin – an' ye're auld enough to be my grandfather. I am not gawn to hire for life just noo,' replied the buxom wench.

Those looking for work could therefore exercise a degree of agency in refusing undesirable places, though the above exchange also reveals something about the sexual as well as economic precarity experienced by many female employees on short contracts. Once an agreement had been reached, the new employer would pay the worker a shilling, and the worker would replace the tassel of their trade with ribbons. Feasting, drinking and games were the natural result of people spending the first instalment of their wages, secure in the knowledge that they had an income for the next year.

By the mid-nineteenth century, however, the spectacle of an itinerant rural workforce at mop fairs roused fears of working-class disorder. A Mr Wyatt, who worked as an agent for the Duke of Bedford in Monmouthshire, considered mop fairs 'one of the greatest evils of the county' in his part of Wales. Those who attended, he thought, were 'generally worse characters than the people who keep steadily to one place; they never seem to get attached to one locality. They do a deal of harm in the town; each public-house has its fiddler, and a dance generally takes place; they are almost all unmarried.' Moral, rather than literal, contagion was now the primary concern for some observers.

The connection between mop fairs and rural employment dwindled before the Second World War, as the practice of hiring servants declined. However, the events themselves survived, particularly in the West Country, morphing into more straightforward funfairs. The Tewkesbury Mop Fair is now one of the largest in the country. Since 1989 it has been organised by a partnership between the Tewkesbury Fair Society and the Showmen's Guild of Great Britain, an organisation that looks after the interests of travelling fairground businesses. Like many other customs in this book, it was cancelled during the COVID-19 pandemic, as local councils up and down the country temporarily refused funfair licenses in order to prevent coronavirus being spread at mass gatherings. The restrictions hit many showmen hard: since fairground operators do not always work from fixed premises, they did not qualify for the government grants that supported other hospitality and leisure-sector businesses. The survival of a custom that was a response to labour regulation during one epidemic was thus threatened by a ban on certain types of work associated with another, some 700 years later. Fortunately, the Tewkesbury Mop Fair survived – and though you might not be able to get a job there these days, you can still enjoy plenty of fairground fun.

KIERA CHAPMAN

Punkie Night

Hinton St George, Somerset

LAST THURSDAY IN OCTOBER

Once upon a tangled time there was a blacksmith known as Stingy Jack. The townsfolk knew that he was the meanest skinflint that ever set foot to soil, and cunning as a new-edged razor. He dearly loved a drink, did Stingy Jack, but every publican in the town knew not to give him a penny of credit. Though he would beg for it with a silver tongue, when the time came to pay, it was harder to coax a gold coin out of his pocket than to fashion a filigree tiara with a hammer and anvil.

Tighter than a vice was Stingy Jack, and wicked devious. He'd fasten a horse's shoe with a single nail if he could, and charge the rider a second time when it rung off on the road. And word went around so that the Devil himself heard of him, and grew green jealous as copper in a flame. He decided to meet Stingy Jack and bring him to hell, showing who was master of the fiery realms.

So the Devil lay in wait on the road one night, and Stingy Jack, swaying with liquor, stumbled over him in the darkness. 'Oh ho!' says the Devil, making a horrible grimace. And at the sound of the Devil's voice, which was like rusted iron, Stingy Jack was spitting with fear like the water in a quenching bucket, for he knew that his end had come. But his wits stayed as close to him as iron to a magnet. 'Oh, so ye are here for me, Devil,' he says, 'to drag off my soul at last. Fair play to ye. But before we go, I would like to get to know ye better, for ye are the master of trickery and I am but your humble pupil. Won't ye come to slake your thirst before we descend to that hot place you call home?' And the Devil's vanity made him malleable, so he agreed.

So the Devil and Jack went to the local inn, the Bearded Brothers, which served ales of formidable strength. On their entry, the two hirsute landlords went pale as ash, for Stingy Jack was long banned for his unpaid bills and for the time he took a horse piss up the wall which took the brothers a whole morning to clean up. Of course, Stingy Jack knew the price of all the beers, especially the ones that are heady as wine and cost a whole handful of coins. And since his thirst was prodigious, he ordered the best in the house, and he drank and caroused and drank again, until the cask ran dry. And the Devil grinned and looked on, feeling that any moment now, he would have Stingy Jack's soul locked away behind the clanking padlocked gates of the underworld. The bearded brothers meanwhile shuffled their feet, nervous as stallions waiting to be shod, but the Devil's terrible gurning, not to mention his sulphurous smell, kept them from complaining.

Eventually, the bell for last orders sounded, and one of the brothers sidled cautiously up to the pair, telling them the damage. And Stingy Jack, tight as a pair of tongs, looked at the Devil. And the Devil looked at Stingy Jack. And there was a pause as long as the wait for a cold rod to glow in the fire. And Stingy Jack said, 'The tab is for ye, mate, for I am giving ye me soul. And what's more, me wallet is at home.' At this, the Devil was taken aback, for he never touches money, since the bargaining he does is of another kind altogether. 'Stingy Jack,' he said, in a voice of steel, 'I do not possess a wallet.'

Another pause. 'Fear ye not,' said Stingy Jack, 'for I have a plan, and I swear it will cost us nothing, Devil. Now I have heard of your tremendous powers to change your shape to fool the unwary,' he said, bending the Devil over the horn of his own vanity once more. 'So I will distract the brothers, and ye can transform yeself into a silver coin, which I will offer them in payment. When their backs are turned, we can extract ye from the cashbox like metal smelted from ore, and we will have this ale for nothing.'

The Devil was impressed by the way Stingy Jack stayed true to his principles even to the last. So he changed himself, in the flash of an eye, into a shining silver coin. Stingy Jack picked him up, and faster than you could get hot metal into a clamp, the Devil was in his wallet, which had been in his pocket all along. And since he also carried a crucifix, the Prince of Darkness was trapped by the power of heaven, and unable to change back into his fiendish form. 'Oh ho, Devil!' says Stingy Jack. 'A coin is for exchanging, but if you want to circulate in the world once more, then you will need to strike a bargain with me.' And in this way, Stingy Jack forced the Devil to let him walk free for another ten years as the price of his release.

Now the Devil was furious as a red forge at this, but a promise is a promise and he had to bide his time. On the instant that ten years had passed, though, he seized Stingy Jack again, on the same road as before. 'Ach, fair play to ye,' says Stingy Jack, 'my time on earth is up and now I think on it, I do have sore regrets for the part I have played.' And he began to cry so pitifully that even the Devil was moved to ask if there was something he could do to ease Stingy Jack's passage to hell. And Stingy Jack eyed an old apple tree close by, and said, 'I am famished, Devil, and have no wish to spend eternity in hunger as well as in hellfire, so won't you fetch me an apple from the tree?'

So the Devil sighed like a bellows, but climbed the tree to fetch an apple. Quick as a spark, Stingy Jack arranged sticks in crosses all around the trunk, and the Devil was trapped in the apple branches by the power of all that is holy. 'Oh ho, Devil!' says Stingy Jack. 'If ye want to come down, you will have to strike another bargain. Only this time it will be a harder deal than before.' And the Devil's fury was white hot as a molten crucible, but there was nothing he could do. And so Stingy Jack drove the hardest bargain of his life, titan of tightwads that he was, and got the Devil to agree never to take his soul to hell in exchange for letting him down from the apple tree.

And that is how Stingy Jack hammered the Prince of Darkness himself into shape. But Stingy Jack's life was wicked, and stories cannot end with the triumph of the bad. So, when he died, full of liquor and rolling in sin,

Stingy Jack ascended to heaven. But one of the bearded brothers had got there before him and told God all about the bargain with the Devil. So God spoke to Stingy Jack in a voice that sounded like the sweetest chiming bells and told him St Peter's gates would remain welded shut against him.

So Stingy Jack, of his own volition, went down to hell, and at the infernal gates he met the Devil for a third time. 'The angels have forbidden me the bar in the higher place,' said Stingy Jack, 'so I've come here to cool my thirst.' But the Devil grinned a smile broad as a swinging sledgehammer and reminded Stingy Jack of the bargain he had made.

So Stingy Jack found himself banned from the Bearded Brothers, from heaven, and from hell. And he was raw dismayed at his plight, for those who wander forever between the worlds are stricken by a loneliness as black and dry as charcoal. 'But how will I see my way?' he asked. And the Devil laughed like a roaring hearth and threw him a glowing ember of eternal hellfire. Now Stingy Jack would have dearly loved a never-ending flame when he was a blacksmith, for it would have saved him a packet on coal, but now that he was forbidden from plying his earthly trade, he was perplexed as to how to keep it alight. As he climbed back up to earth, however, he saw a field of mangelwurzels, and his wits, still sharp as a new scythe, went to work. He found a large root, hollowed it out, and put the burning brand inside to light his way.

And that is how Stingy Jack came to be known as Jack-o'-Lantern. If you are alone on a dark night and you see a will-o-the-wisp of flame hovering above the ground, or what learned folks call the *ignis fatuus*, then you have seen the soul of Stingy Jack with his hellfire light. And it's best to hurry home, for they say the Devil still keeps a close eye on him, and that he lures folk to those marshland pools where the door to hell is opened just a fraction more than in other places on earth. And on Halloween, when the barrier between worlds thins to a knife point and you can hear the rustling of devilish wings on a dark night, it's wise to make your own lantern and keep it burning at your threshold to fend off evil.

Punkie Night in Hinton St George, Somerset is full of glowing jack-o'-lanterns. On the last Thursday in October, children walk in costume around the streets with a carved lantern, or 'punkie'. It can be made from a turnip or a mangelwurzel (a type of beet used to feed cattle), though pumpkins are now also common. The vegetable is hollowed out and a design is cut into the surface, which is then illuminated with a candle placed inside. Some are very basic faces, while others are more detailed, showing words or even animals. A handle, fashioned from rope or wire that has been looped through the flesh of the vegetable, enables it to be held securely in the hand and carried from place to place.

There is a special song for the occasion, which begs for candles and other treats, much like Stingy Jack did with the Devil in the old eighteenth-century folktale:

> It's Punkie Night tonight,
> It's Punkie Night tonight,
> Give me a candle, give me a light,
> If you don't, you'll get a fright!

As the lyrics make clear, there is a 'trick or treat' element to this ritual, which is another point of connection to modern Halloween traditions, though nowadays many participants choose to collect for local charities instead.

There are other stories behind this custom, besides the legend of Stingy Jack. One local legend tells that the custom originated when wives created mangelwurzel lights to go and find their husbands who had been out drinking at Chiselborough Fair a few miles away. Others relate Punkie Night to the pixie lore of southwestern England, with Jack-o'-Lantern being these notorious pranksters' mischief-working leader. Perhaps the truth is that all of these things have melded together somehow, so that the burning ember inside this ritual pumpkin has many different sources fanning its flames. But as you burn your own punkie light this autumn, do remember that you should always pay the publican. For there's no knowing what will happen if you don't.

KIERA CHAPMAN

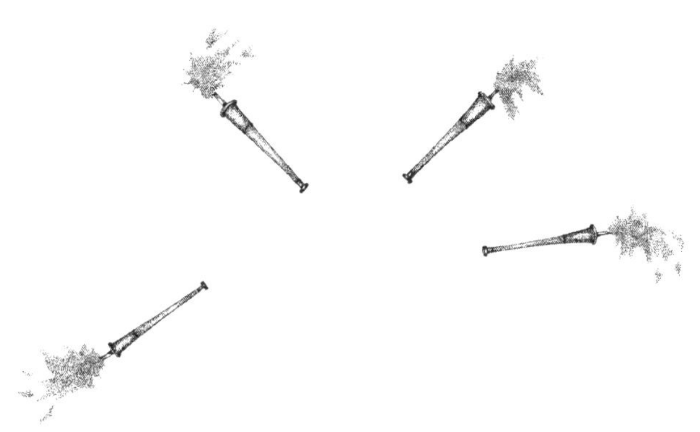

Samhuinn Fire Festival

Edinburgh

31 OCTOBER OR 1 NOVEMBER

Samhuinn, or Samhain, marks the end of the harvest season and the start of winter. It is associated with fire, spirits and the thinning of the veil between the spirit and physical worlds – a liminal time for mischief and mayhem before the stillness of the darker months. It is celebrated on 31 October or 1 November – and, while there is no Iron Age evidence for a Celtic festival precisely on this date, early-medieval Irish literature and later folklore clearly identify Samhain occurring then, as one of the four major seasonal festivals, the others being Imbolc, Beltane and Lughnasadh.

We find mentions of Samhain in the tenth-to-twelfth-century Irish saga *Tochmarc Emire* and in the twelfth-century *Acallam na Senórach*, as well as references in folklore traditions and customs across Britain. Edinburgh's Samhuinn Fire Festival reinvents this ancient celebration with a Halloween spectacle of fire, music, pageantry and street performance in Holyrood Park. After dark, performers painted in Celtic-inspired patterns and costumes form a torchlit procession to tell the story of the battle between the Summer and Winter Kings (or Queens) that's overseen by the Cailleach (a crone who embodies winter). In the story, the winter court triumphs over the jaded summer court, forcing it to make way for a new season. The performers enact this battle with flaming swords surrounded by spinning fire fans and human pyramids, as drummers accelerate the intensity with their rhythm.

Unlike other British folk customs where older women are either comic or peripheral characters in stories that focus on youthful fertility or male strength, the Cailleach represents a different kind of power. She personifies the forces of nature (particularly winter) and rules the dark half of the year, confronted by, and ceding to, Bríde in spring. She is a protector of the land – what author Sharon Blackie describes as 'the original ecofeminist in our ancestral traditions'.

While the Cailleach is a well-known figure in Celtic culture, the Samhuinn Fire Festival is less about historical accuracy and more about evoking ancient myth through immersive experience. Take the body paint worn by performers. We have Julius Caesar's account of the Britons painting themselves with woad 'which produces a blue colour and gives them a wild appearance in battle', and some Celtic coins show faces with swirls on, so the Samhuinn performers seem justified in using paints to create a *sense* of ancient traditions, regardless of the historical facts.

The atmosphere at the festival is strange and charged, with crowds of onlookers jostling for a view of the different performances around the park. Until recently, it took place at Calton Hill, but the local council forced the volunteer-run Beltane Fire Society, which organises the festival, to relocate it. In order to meet regulations, the society has to sell tickets and call it an 'event', which some locals have found disappointing. They say it is harder to see the action now, and that there are long queues to get into the park, while others complain about tourists pushing them out of the way. This reveals a tension at the heart of the more recent folk customs that can't draw on a long history of community support and entrenched ways of doing things. For Samhuinn to remain viable, it needs to attract big crowds, but that can dilute the experience for the audience.

This is an evolving custom, shifting from the parade and performance of twenty years ago to today's organised, more physically constrained event. And it is this evolution that also allows it to change focus and give performers the chance to interpret its stories in fresh ways. Recent performances have incorporated climate change into the conflict narrative, widening the battle from seasonal courts to global warming versus activism. Creativity is central to this festival, enabling it to find a balance between the demand for 'authentic', legitimate ancientness and a more dynamic interpretation. It draws on myths and symbolism as a generative impulse, not as its definition.

Scotland has a long history of outdoor performances like this, aimed at ordinary people. Mummers, guisers and processionals were common centuries ago, with costumed performers wearing masks and enacting tales in towns and rural fairs. Many of these were suppressed during the Scottish Reformation of the 1560s before being revived in the eighteenth and nineteenth centuries, with street ballad-singers, pedlars, travelling showmen and puppeteers putting on shows, or 'geggies' (pop-up theatre performances). Today's Edinburgh Festival Fringe continues the open-air theatre tradition, and the Beltane Fire Society is keen to promote street performance as a living art form. Fire-juggling is also an old practice, first recorded in Talmudic writings in the first century, and found in Māori fire poi practices (swinging burning balls), Indian Aarti dances, European fire-eaters of the Middle Ages, and Aztec, Balinese and Jamaican fire dances. In the Samhuinn festival, fire is not just symbolic, it is part of the performance itself.

While it doubtless faces logistical challenges, the celebration of Samhuinn is an inspiring example of reinvention and reconstructed paganism. It serves performers, audiences and neo-pagan or Wicca spiritual groups alike, putting aside the heated debates in archaeology and folklore studies and instead answering Ronald Hutton's call that historians should be 'prepared to stand back and let the public dream its own dreams'. So, this Halloween, let's dream of fire, acrobats, hags and drums.

LULAH ELLENDER

Quit Rents Ceremony

London

BETWEEN 11 OCTOBER AND 11 NOVEMBER

A quit rent is not, as it might sound, the final payment of a reluctantly departing tenant. In fact, the term has more obscure roots which reach back into the Middle Ages, when many people owed services to those above them in the social hierarchy. For example, a man might occupy a house and land owned by his local lord of the manor, in return for which he owed the lord three days of his own labour, without payment, on the manor lands. This meant three days of lost time, when our man could neither earn an income nor work on his own land. Alternatively, he might have to make himself available with a weapon to fight for his lord when called upon. But what happened if the lord of the manor no longer needed him to work on his land or fight in his army? In these circumstances, they might agree to a 'quit rent', which was a sum of money or some other 'payment' to recompense the lord for *not* demanding three days' work from him, or for his service under arms. In other words, it was a payment that meant our man was 'quit' of his former feudal service obligation.

Not many of us are required to work for free on someone else's land nowadays, and even fewer of us have to turn up with a sword when our landlord demands us to do so. Nevertheless, the custom of paying quit rents still survives, albeit now in purely ceremonial form. Perhaps the most famous example of this is the Quit Rents Ceremony that takes place in the Royal Courts of Justice in central London, sometime between old St Michael's Day on 11 October and St Martin's Day on 11 November. The custom was carried out for over 700 years before ceasing in 1958. Seventeen years later, however, the custom was revived, and it has been undertaken annually ever since.

The ceremony is carried out with the kind of red and gold pageantry that you might expect, given the involvement of the Corporation of the City of London, yet the event itself is, at heart, simple, focusing on the making of two payments by the Corporation to the Crown for the 'rent' of two pieces of land. There, however, the simplicity ends. For a start, the precise location of the two pieces of land is no longer known. One of the payments is for a site believed to have been either on the Strand or just to the south of that, on Tweezers Alley. Here, in about 1235, a blacksmith, Walter Le Brun, rented a spot from the Crown to set up a forge, perhaps to service the horses of the Knights Templars, whose headquarters and jousting grounds lay adjacent. Many years later, however, the City of London took over the land that had once been rented by

Walter from the monarch, yet it has continued to pay a quit rent to the Crown for this privilege ever since.

The other payment is for a piece of land called 'The Moors' somewhere near the village of Eardington in Shropshire, once tenanted by a man called Nicholas de Morrs. A medieval roll for Shropshire records that in 1211 a 'Richard the Meddler' held a virgate (20–30 acres) of land in this area, for which he paid 'two knives', and this may be the progenitor of the quit rent now paid for the unidentified land now known as 'The Moors', although it is unclear how Nicholas and Richard related to each other, if at all. Either way, the knives were, at one point, changed to a billhook and a small hatchet, before the custom returned to the use of knives.

The quit rents custom is full of delicious historical detail. The payments are made to the King's Remembrancer, a position established in 1154, and now the oldest British judicial office still in existence. Before the habitual use of pen and parchment for recording the debts owed to the Crown, the Remembrancer's role was, quite literally, to 'remember' these debts. In reality, they were usually recorded in some more physical form upon which he could rely. To receive the quit rents today, he sits at a desk covered with a black-and-white-chequered cloth, similar to that which in medieval times gave the governmental department of the 'Exchequer' its name. The quit rent for Walter's forge is not paid with money, however, but with six large horseshoes and sixty-one horseshoe nails, each one of which is held up in turn and counted out loud. When the count is completed, the Remembrancer calls out, 'Good number.'

The custom of handing over the horseshoes and nails is recorded as far back as the thirteenth century, when the City also had to pay an additional eighteen pence. Extraordinarily, the horseshoes and nails still used in the ceremony today were made in 1361 and have been lent back to the City ever since, to be re-presented to the Crown the following year. And in case you are wondering, each horseshoe only needs ten nails; the extra one is included as a spare! Somewhere along the line, however, the eighteen pence have been abandoned.

The payment of the quit rent for the land in Shropshire is more entertaining still. The Remembrancer is provided with a wooden board, two knives and a thin rod of hazel. Although the knives currently used are handmade in Herefordshire and of excellent quality, one of them is deliberately blunt so that when the Remembrancer bends the hazel rod over it, it does not cut into the wood. When he tries the same action using the sharp knife, the rod is, of course, cut straight through. It is thought that this peculiar ritual originated in the ancient use of tally sticks for recording debts and payments, on which notches were made equating to sums of money. Perhaps Richard the Meddler's payment of two knives was specifically intended for the making of such tallies? For a period in the later twentieth century, however, the knives were changed to a billhook, a hatchet and a small but neatly tied bundle of twigs. The Remembrancer sought to cut through the bundle of twigs with the blunted billhook but failed. The much sharper hatchet was then used, and with a loud crash, the sticks were severed, twigs flying off at all angles. Once the hazel rod has been cut, or the sticks have been chopped, the Remembrancer calls out, 'Good service,' and there's a polite round of applause.

Bizarre though this ceremony may sound, it is by no

means the only one that involves a peculiar form of payment. Records from the sixteenth century, for example, reveal the payments of numerous strange quit rents, such as the sum of four pounds and 'one couple of hounds' claimed by Francis Cockes and his son Walter, from the manor of Horwood in Staffordshire in 1589. Or the thirty shillings and seven pence along with 'two capons, one cockerel, nineteen hens and 190 eggs' paid to the manor of Kingsdown in 1603. The vast majority of these arrangements have since died out, of course, but there is something pleasing about the continuance of the London Quit Rents Ceremony, with its strange rituals and unknown locations – not to mention its history as the second oldest still-practised legal ceremony in the country. The oldest? Well, that's the coronation, of course.

REBECCA WARREN

Mischief Night

Yorkshire

30 OCTOBER TO 4 NOVEMBER

I first came across Mischief Night while staying in Philadelphia. In the run-up to my first experience of an American Halloween, I was delighted by beautiful autumnal displays of pumpkins, sweetcorn and wheat, amused by whole front yards strewn with plastic witches, ghosts and gigantic spiders, and awestruck by the humungous bins of sweets on sale in supermarkets to appease hungry bands of trick-or-treaters. What I did not expect, however, was that something strange would start to happen before we had even reached 31 October. In the middle of the preceding night, there were whoops and yells outside my flat, and I awoke to find that a neighbouring business had been spray-painted, while street trees were now festooned with toilet paper. It turned out that 30 October was Mischief

Night, and it involved high jinks and pranks, sometimes with a distinct sense of menace.

When I returned to the UK, I learned that Mischief Night is also commemorated here. However, what was once a widespread tradition across much of the north of England has dwindled in the last few decades, though Yorkshire remains a stronghold. Nineteenth-century accounts suggest that some places originally celebrated it on 30 April, the eve of May Day, but it subsequently migrated through the calendar to an October/November date, possibly as late as the twentieth century. Today, it is one of those customs that seems to be dying out. One explanation is that Halloween is becoming a larger and more commercial festival, drawing the energy out of other events that happen at around the same time. In Philadelphia, however, the two comfortably coexist, pouring cold water on this theory. Another possibility is that Mischief Night does not have a clear date: different places in the north of England celebrated it on different days, from about 30 October to 4 November, which perhaps dilutes the celebration somewhat. But the most plausible hypothesis is that perceptions of this custom have gradually changed, meaning that the naughtiness it involves has been reframed as a form of 'anti-social behaviour', drawing forth calls for punishment rather than amused tolerance.

This is not an entirely recent shift. In 1984, one Mr Woodall, a former headteacher, wrote an article in the *Police Journal* in which he complained that too many parents of errant pupils were using the custom to turn a blind eye to misbehaviour. 'If by luck I had become aware of some mindless bit of stupidity done by a youngster,' he railed, 'I asked the parents to visit the school. Inevitably,

I got the tale: "What's all the fuss about? I did worse, when I was young. Why be a spoil sport?"' You can almost see the schoolmasterly eye-roll at the idea that the usual laws governing behaviour had been suspended for a night. However, when the BBC ran a social media poll on Mischief Night in 2009, a good number of those who responded voiced similarly negative, censorious attitudes. While some people clearly found the antics amusing, or fondly recalled the high jinks of their youth, many others described the pranks in a language of criminality, thuggishness and vandalism. It is possible that the tricks played had become more serious in the intervening time, but perhaps we are also witnessing a change of attitudes here: the evaporation of the tolerance exhibited by Mr Woodall's pupils' parents, and its replacement by a new, harsher condemnation of misrule.

One particularly elaborate prank practised in northern England was the removal of house gates. Woodall recalls:

> One busy man I know to whom time is money was determined that no one was having his gates off. He had his front lights on and sat in his front room watching. He even had extra lighting fixed up to illuminate his front gates. Inevitably the phone went. He was out of the room for only about a minute, as it turned out to be a wrong number. When he looked out, his gates had gone. They were not in the vicinity of the house. They were finally found beside a main road about half a mile from his home. After that he decided to do without front gates and kept them in his garage.

Smearing doorhandles with treacle (or worse!), switching shop signs, covering trees with toilet paper, and throwing eggs and flour were other classic japes.

As the celebration of Mischief Night dwindles, some people will be glad not to have to sit guarding their gates all evening. But this is a custom that also highlights another kind of gatekeeping, around the way that the 'intangible cultural heritage' of folk customs is defined. Most of the rituals that we have covered in this book are officially organised: people prepare for weeks in advance, then come together on a certain prearranged date, at a set time, to do something collective. Even if that 'something' is completely bonkers, the weirdness is planned, and rarely involves anything but symbolic disorder. Mischief Night, by contrast, is a reminder that a certain date can hold the door open for more impromptu, unlicensed celebrations, creating space for the disruptive and subversive elements that would formerly have been a feature of many more of these events.

Rising discomfort around the mischief unleashed by these customs, then, raises questions about what we value in traditions. Is it just the visually spectacular, artistic elements, those that are repeated in relatively safe and sanitised ways, that count? Or are wilder, more disruptive rituals also an important form of heritage, and therefore also worthy of preservation? While some may not mourn the passing of an evening of mayhem, there may also be a certain loss in a world without these impish pranks.

KIERA CHAPMAN

NOVEMBER

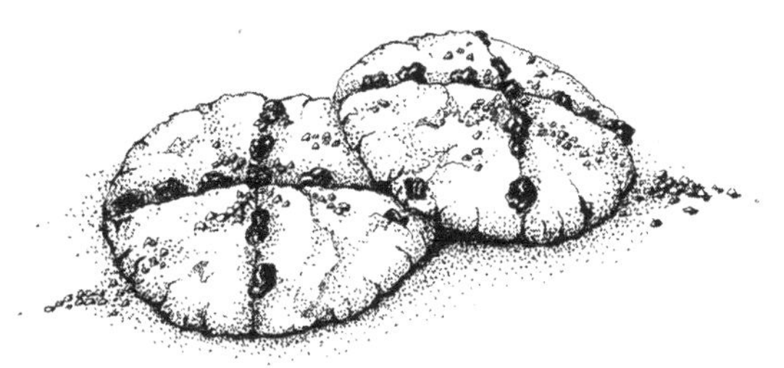

Soul-caking

Antrobus, Cheshire

2 NOVEMBER

All Souls' Day comes immediately after All Saints' Day, which is celebrated on 1 November. In the medieval Christian Church, both days were popular festivals that honoured and remembered the dead, for whom the church bells were tolled and special prayers were offered. Some parishes seem also to have baked 'soule-mass' cakes to give to the poor as an act of Christian charity. At the Protestant Reformation, the prayers and bells were banned, but the desire to remember the dead remained. The result was that, as with the candles of Candlemas, the sharing of soul-cakes moved from the religious into the domestic sphere. There is firm evidence from the seventeenth century of soul-cakes being given both to the poor and to visitors in many of the western counties of Britain. Moreover, in 1686, the antiquarian John Aubrey recorded that the taking of a soul-cake was expected to be accompanied by the spoken response, 'A soule cake, a soule cake, Have mercy on all Christen soules for a soule cake.'

At some point, the custom of offering soul-cakes to visitors evolved into one where children would beg for soul-cakes from householders in return for a short prayer or rhyme for the dead. As with the pace-egging custom in West Yorkshire, in some communities this loose tradition gradually coalesced into the more formal entertainment of a short mumming play, presumably to encourage further generosity. These plays were widely practised during the eighteenth and nineteenth centuries, until all but disappearing during the First World War.

In the Cheshire village of Antrobus, however, the words of the local 'souling' play were saved, and the custom began again in the late 1920s, since when the tradition has been maintained. Featuring a typical cast of mumming characters, including King George, the Black Prince and the Doctor, the most unique feature of the Antrobus play is the 'Wild Horse' called 'Dicky Tatton'. The head of the Wild Horse is a black-painted horse's skull that is able to clack its teeth together, and in the play, it is introduced with the lines:

> In comes Dick and all his men,
> He's come to see you once again.
> He was once alive but now he's dead,
> He's nothing but a poor old horse's head.
> Stand round, Dick, and show yourself.

Clacking horse teeth and painted skulls may seem a long way from the soule-mass cakes of the sixteenth century, but should you want to make your own soul-cakes to commemorate the dead more traditionally, there are numerous recipes in circulation. Here's a typical version, making about twenty-six biscuits, to which you can add a handful of currants if you wish:

- Beat 170g of butter and 170g of sugar together, then add in one egg and 2 teaspoons of white wine vinegar, along with 340g of plain flour and half a teaspoon each of cinnamon, mixed spice and ground nutmeg. Mix until you have a stiff dough, adding a little more flour if necessary.
- While the dough is resting for 15 minutes, heat the oven to 180 degrees/gas mark 4.
- Roll out the dough to about 4mm thick, cut it into rounds and transfer them on to a baking tray.
- Gently incise a cross on the top of each biscuit with a knife and bake for about 15–20 minutes, until slightly coloured. Alternatively, press currants into a cross shape on the surface of the biscuits before cooking.
- Cool on a wire rack.

Enjoy!

REBECCA WARREN

Lewes Bonfire

Lewes, East Sussex

5 NOVEMBER

If you visit the East Sussex town of Lewes sometime before 4 p.m. on 5 November, you would be forgiven for thinking the place was under attack. The scene – boarded-up shops, police barriers, loud volleys of firecrackers and people dragging flaming metal barrels through the streets – might seem dystopian. But it is just the preparations for the annual Lewes Bonfire celebrations.

The town is famous for its radical roots (revolutionary thinker Tom Paine composed his first political pamphlet while living there), and Lewes Bonfire, or 'the Fifth', as it's known locally, is part of its defiant history. In 1264, the town was the scene of the Battle of Lewes, after which

King Henry III was forced to cede some of his powers; until August 2025, Lewes had its own currency, the Lewes pound; when the council introduced new parking restrictions in 2004, some residents responded by blowing up the parking meters; and its independent spirit is summed up in the Sussex dialect phrase 'We wun't be druv.' There are stories of witches who protect the town, and in the 2021 census, twenty seven people marked their religion as 'Wicca' and six as 'Witchcraft'. Secret tunnels, a ruined priory, the old castle and the flint-walled lanes known as 'twittens' add to the slight air of spookiness that surrounds the town.

Although connected to the national Bonfire Night celebrations in November marking the failed Gunpowder Plot in 1605, the Fifth is nothing like the usual firework displays and baked potatoes you may be accustomed to. Instead, as night falls, hundreds of costumed townsfolk process through the streets bearing flaming torches and burning crosses, and pulling rattling barrels of fire and huge effigies past rowdy crowds. It is wild and noisy, the air filled with kerosene and bangers and drums. While other Sussex towns hold similar parades, there's nothing quite like the scale, noise and mayhem of Lewes on the Fifth.

The first records of this distinctive ritual date back to 1679, when, in addition to celebrating the defeat of the Catholic-led Gunpower Plot, people commemorated the seventeen Protestant martyrs who were burned at the stake in the centre of the town in the 1550s as part of Queen Mary's religious persecutions. Lewes's annual Fifth of November celebrations grew increasingly unruly, and in 1829 they turned into a riot when a magistrate tried – unsuccessfully – to prevent the Bonfire Boys from processing. After more riots in 1847, local people decided to form 'Bonfire societies' in an attempt to organise the chaos and ensure they were still able to march. There are now seven of these societies, each marching their own routes through the town, creating rivers of fire with their burning torches and displaying their effigies, known as 'tableaux'. They join together in the Grand Parade at the end of the night before marching to their separate bonfire sites, from where they launch incredible firework displays, throw bangers at men dressed as bishops, and burn their remaining torches on enormous pyres.

Each society has a band of 'smugglers' (reflecting the region's maritime history), who wear striped guernseys in the society's colours, while others are dressed in a confusingly wide array of costumes. You will see women in elaborate Tudor dresses, First World War soldiers, buccaneers, monks and kilt-wearing bagpipers, among many others. Lewes Bonfire has run into controversy not just for the uncomfortable imagery of burning crosses and the anti-Catholic origins of the celebrations, but also for some of these costumes, with accusations of cultural appropriation and racism being levelled at those who dress as Native Americans and Zulus, or who 'black up'. In response, the celebrations have had to adapt and adjust as times change, though this hasn't been without heated debate. The challenge for these rituals is to maintain their connections to the past while also acknowledging the sensitivities of the present.

Whatever you think of the ethics of the Fifth, it is an impressive spectacle and an important, much-cherished part of the town's unique story. After the failed Gunpowder Plot, the practice of burning effigies of Guy Fawkes spread across the British colonies, and it reflects a wider global history of this form of political protest that reaches back to at least 1328, when a straw puppet of Pope John XXII was burned. Judas is burned in Spain, Latin America and the Philippines; the Indian and Pakistani tradition of burning effigies of Ravana also appears in Scotland, Trinidad and England; and effigies were an important part of the Arab Spring protests of 2011.

The tableaux paraded through Lewes are part of this long tradition of satire and ridicule rather than an incitement to violence. You might see a giant Donald Trump astride a nuclear warhead, or an unpopular Home Secretary who has morphed into an octopus. They are ingenious, funny and compelling symbols of protest, drawing on an ancient custom that extends way beyond Britain. We are united, it seems, by an attraction to the power of fire.

LULAH ELLENDER

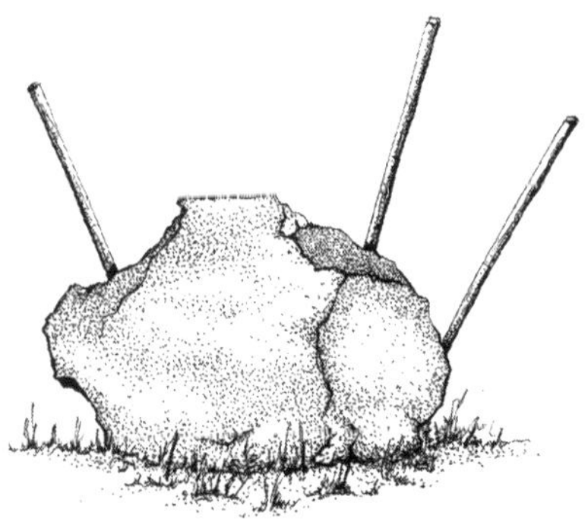

Turning the Devil's Stone

Shebbear, Devon

5 NOVEMBER

Story is what makes us human. Narrative binds us, offers hope, explains the impossible and unbearable, and gives us a sense of agency where we otherwise have none. So, here's a story for the fifth of November – and it has nothing to do with fire.

After being defeated in a battle for supremacy with God, the Devil fled from heaven, intent on creating hell on earth. The angel St Michael guessed the Devil's plan and threw a stone that knocked him to the ground and crushed him beneath it. The stone happened to fall in the Devon village of Shebbear.

In order to prevent bad things from befalling the village, so the story goes, the stone must be turned every year on 5 November. So while the usual fireworks and bonfires blaze across the rest of the country, in Shebbear things look and sound very different. At around 8 p.m., the bell-ringers sound a chaotic peal of bells and villagers gather around the six-foot-long stone, listening as the parish vicar recounts the story of St Michael and the Devil, and watching as the bell-ringers, armed with crowbars, slowly lever the stone up and tip it over. The crowd chants, 'Turn the stone! Turn the stone!' The bell-ringers strain, the stone teeters, and finally it reaches the tipping point. Cheers and applause erupt as the stone slaps back down. Disaster has been averted for another year.

The origins of this custom aren't clear, and the stone isn't local, which only adds to the mystery. With no scientific, historical or rational explanation for how it appeared in the village, the tale has emerged to account for why it's there. And like the rock, the story endures.

LULAH ELLENDER

Wroth Silver Ceremony

Knightlow Cross,
Ryton-on-Dunsmore, Warwickshire

11 NOVEMBER

Some folk customs are born from anarchy and resistance. In contrast, the Wroth Silver Ceremony represents continuity and fealty. The first documented record of the ceremony dates to ad 1170, and apart from the years 1800–15 and an official cancellation during the COVID-19 pandemic, it has been practised every year since, making it one of Britain's oldest continuous ceremonies.

A low-key event compared with some of our more flamboyant customs, but a significant and meaningful one for local people, the ceremony starts at dawn on 11 November at the Wroth Stone, an ancient stone cross base on Knightlow Cross in Warwickshire. There, representatives from twenty-five parishes in the Knightlow Hundred ('hundreds' were an administrative district established after the

Norman Conquest) gather to pay a symbolic tax, amounting to forty-six pence, to the lord of the manor, currently the 10th Duke of Buccleuch and Queensbury. A steward representing the duke reads the Charter of Assembly, and each representative steps forward saying, 'Wroth silver!' as they place their coins in a hollow in the cross stone. After the ceremony, the attendees have breakfast and rum with hot milk at a local pub, and then listen to speeches while smoking churchwarden pipes (a type of long-stemmed tobacco pipe).

The tax is thought to have originally been a feudal obligation to pay 'ward money' in lieu of providing military service, and similar ceremonies would have been held across the different hundreds. Failure to pay would have incurred fines or penalties, with one notable example being the forfeiture of a white bull with a red nose and ears (possibly a whimsy conjured up in the early eighteenth century by the second Duke of Montagu, who was known to be a prankster).

The fact that some regions were able to pay dues instead of giving military support shows the flexibility of the feudal system, but this custom also highlights the enduring impact of social hierarchies and structures. Although the ceremony is now entirely voluntary and celebrates community tradition, it also offers an intriguing glimpse into how echoes of historical power dynamics can still be seen in modern cultural practices.

LULAH ELLENDER

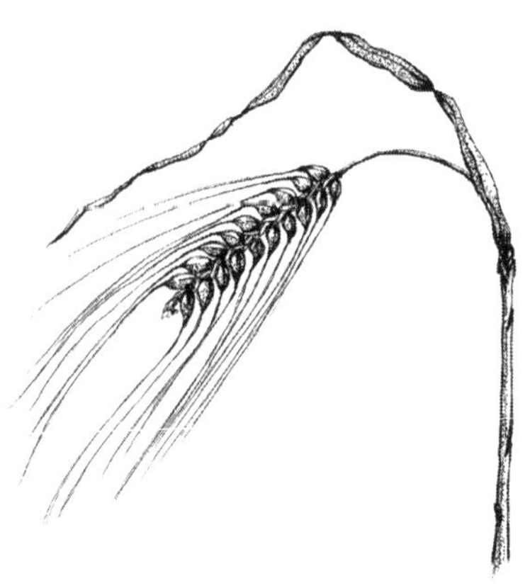

Jury Day

Laxton, Nottinghamshire

LAST THURSDAY IN NOVEMBER

If, like me, your knowledge of crop rotation extends little further than a distant history lesson about barley, then the Laxton Jury Day custom may be instructional as well as interesting.

On the last Thursday in November every year, twelve farmers from the Nottinghamshire village of Laxton gather for Jury Day, a practice that dates back to medieval times. Laxton is the last remaining village in England to have a working open-field system of agriculture, resisting the forced enclosures of the eighteenth and nineteenth centuries and retaining the ancient strips of land cultivated by tenant farmers to this day. The Enclosure Acts had a devastating impact on farming communities, as common land was parcelled into large private farms. Villagers could no longer graze animals or grow crops, and many migrated to the growing towns in search of new livelihoods. This was a transformation that disrupted and permanently changed the ancient fabric of rural England.

As with the closing of the coal mines in Wales and northern England during the 1980s, communities were torn apart, with declining populations, few prospects for young people, and the dismantling of employment. This is not to romanticise the life of a medieval peasant, or to pretend that mining is anything other than brutal, desperately hard labour and bad for the planet. But the work and way of life held communities together, and Laxton is an example of how these old systems can survive and adapt, if only people are given the means.

The land parcels in Laxton are the same today as those portrayed on a map held by the Bodleian Library in Oxford, painted in 1635 on sheep hides and showing three large open fields divided into multiple strips. The fields are shared fairly between local farmers, who rotate each strip between a wheat crop, a cereal crop and a fallow season. Unlike recent intensive farming practices, this prevents the soil from becoming depleted and builds resistance to pests and disease. These strips have never been treated with chemicals or fertilisers, and some are designated SSSIs (Sites of Special Scientific Interest) due to their biodiversity.

The land is organised by a Court Leet, a group of farmers tasked with making sure no one impinges on anyone else's strip or ploughs too far into the baulks (pathways) that separate the strips. Each year the court selects a jury of twelve people (usually, it seems, men), who are sworn in by kissing a Bible – the one currently used dating back to 1798. On the last Thursday in November they pile into a tractor trailer, carrying stakes and mallets, and drive up to the open fields to assess the situation. Historically, they would have been summoned at dawn by a horn. A bailiff, a foreman and a steward accompany them, and they proceed to knock stakes into the ground to mark the correct boundaries and inspect the sykes (areas of grassland between groups of strips).

A week later, the Court Leet convenes to discuss the jury's findings and fine those who have failed to stick within their strips. Fines are applied for improper boundaries and for missing the court hearing, but in the past they extended to things such as 'not ringing her swine' or 'scolding a disturbance to the neighbours'. It could be a heated affair, with arguments about encroachments or unfair fines, but after airing their grievances, the farmers settled things and celebrated. Until recently, these hearings took place at the local pub, but during the COVID-19 pandemic they moved to the village hall, where they have stayed. This may have altered the traditional celebrations of drinking ale and smoking long-stemmed clay pipes.

While this is a very particular and localised custom, it is fascinating for its focus on community and cooperation. The Court Leet has legal powers to impose its penalties, but the whole system is based around mutualism and respect. It only works because for years farmers have put aside personal gain and instead worked together to tend and maintain the land that has provided food for the village for centuries. Similar practices can be found in Alpine pasture communities, the Scandinavian *allmänning*, Japanese paddy-field irrigation associations, Native American tribal councils and Andean *ayllu* land-management systems. Yet Laxton Jury Day remains distinctly rooted in the feudal agricultural, socioeconomic and judicial structures.

There is no spectacle or pomp here. This is not a custom that brings great crowds from far-flung places. It is a reminder that communities need meaningful ways to stay connected, and that quietly determined cooperation can sometimes outlast the pursuit of individual gain.

LULAH ELLENDER

DECEMBER

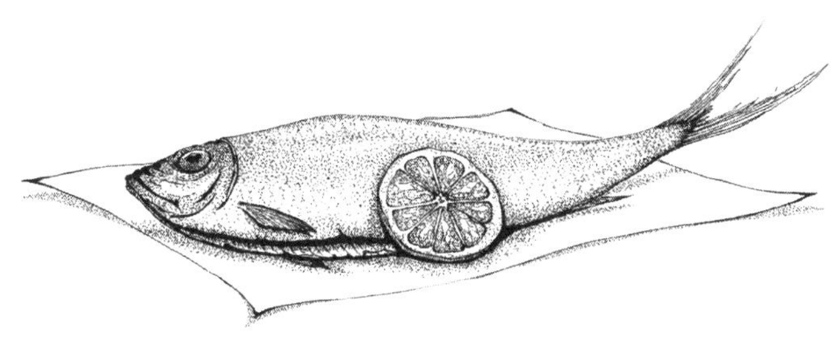

Election of the Deputy of the Cinque Port Liberty of Brightlingsea

Brightlingsea, Essex

EARLY DECEMBER

Here's a custom that proudly traces its roots back to the Middle Ages, involving the defence of the realm and the provisioning of this island country, with its strongly maritime nature. On the Monday after St Andrew's Day (30 November), the 'Deputy of the Cinque Port Liberty of Brightlingsea' is elected at a ceremony held in All Saints' Church in the town. After the election, the gathered local dignitaries and freemen watch a second ceremony, known as the 'Recognition of New Inhabitants', during which anyone who has been living in the town for a year and a day or more, or has married a Brightlingsea resident, can formally become a 'freeman' (or freewoman). Incomers must hand over eleven pennies (in pre-decimalisation currency) to the town's treasurer for the privilege of their new status, and while money is changing hands, the newly elected

Deputy and his six assistants must also pay the treasurer 'four shillings'.

Seven months later, the Deputy, accompanied again by a group of assistants and freemen, hires a bus to take them all south, across the Thames and down to Sandwich on the east Kent coast. Here, they meet the Mayor of Sandwich and swear an oath of loyalty. He then confirms the Deputy in his or her position. The Deputy hands over the princely sum of 'ten shillings' as Brightlingsea's 'ship money' contribution and, the formalities over, the event is celebrated in time-honoured fashion with tea and cake.

Of course, if you know anything about the Cinque Ports, the elements of this annual custom will make some kind of sense, but if you don't, it will certainly require some deconstructing. So here goes.

The Cinque Ports were originally a medieval confederation formed for military and trade purposes, and consisting of five coastal towns – Sandwich, Dover, Hythe, New Romney and Hastings – which, as a result of their reliance on trading and fishing, had ready access to seagoing ships and their crews at fairly short notice. Situated at key points along the south-east coast of Kent and Sussex, the towns were able to guard the narrowest part of the English Channel and control the most likely points of entry into the country.

The date of the earliest establishment of the Cinque Ports confederation is lost in time, but there is good evidence that by 1066 and the Norman conquest, some of these coastal towns were already providing ships and sailors for use by the English monarch if required, in return for financial and political advantage. In the 1150s King Henry II formalised this arrangement with a charter which bound several of the ports into a contract with the Crown: they would provide a certain number of ships and crew for about two weeks a year when the king demanded, and in return they would receive considerable rights and privileges, including freedoms from certain taxes and enhanced rights to self-governance. Over time, however, the burden of providing both ships and men became increasingly onerous, and to ease the financial impact of the agreement, the five original Head Ports roped in a number of nearby towns to help out. These 'limb' ports would share some of the legal and financial benefits of Cinque Port status in return for providing 'ship money' to help fund the sailors and their boats, whenever they were required by the Crown.

All of the limb ports were in Sussex or Kent except for one: Brightlingsea. Situated on the northern shore of the Thames estuary, this little Essex town provided a useful refuge for fishing vessels from Kent, as they followed the enormous shoals of herring into the North Sea and headed up with their catches to the annual Herring Fair at Yarmouth. As Yarmouth grew in size and importance during the thirteenth and fourteenth centuries, however, so did the rivalry between the Kentish and Yarmouth fishermen. The Crown sought to control an increasingly violent situation through a series of royal awards and agreements, which finally confirmed the Cinque Ports' right to manage the Yarmouth Herring Fair. The ports now controlled much of the fishing industry around the east coast of Britain, and in order to protect this hard-won privilege, they developed closer corporate ties with each other.

Brightlingsea, although a geographical outlier, remained an important part of the confederation's holdings, but this was not without its problems. As it was a limb of Sandwich, it was the Mayor of Sandwich who had authority over the town's activities, but it took an average of two days to travel between the two ports. Much of the day-to-day running of Brightlingsea's affairs was therefore handed over to the Mayor's Deputy, elected from and living among the local townsmen. To this day, the Deputy remains an important civic position in Brightlingsea, celebrated with the pomp and pageantry usually associated with a mayoralty – but at the price of a trip down to Sandwich every year to acknowledge his or her ultimate allegiance.

REBECCA WARREN

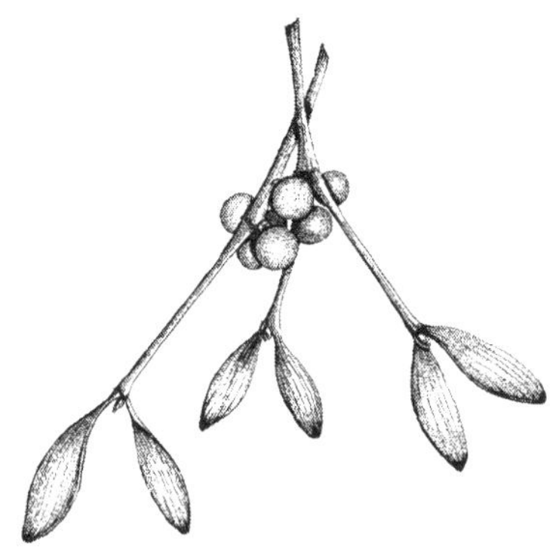

Sheffield Carols

Sheffield, Yorkshire

MID-NOVEMBER TO DECEMBER

I have never been a great singer. I vividly remember carol services at primary school: one dreary afternoon close to Christmas, we would walk in crocodile formation from our cabbage-scented assembly hall to the draughty flat-roofed church next door. There, we would be poked and prodded into rows next to a threadbare plastic Christmas tree that looked like it had fallen victim to acid rain. Duly filed, we droned through miserable renditions of classic carols. Not even Miss Fortune's enthusiastic piano playing could save our version of 'Away in a Manger' from dragging on, slower and ever slower, until it gave up the ghost and died miserably in a corner. It took an adoring parent indeed to enjoy the service. But it was inconceivable that it could happen anywhere other than a church.

Nothing could be further from this childhood experience than the Sheffield carols. For a start, they happen in the distinctly secular atmosphere of a pub, with most of those taking part warmed by a pint or two. This is not a concert, and there is no proscenium arch, literal or imaginary, between spectators and performers. Instead, there is a genuine, if understated, sense of coming together for an inclusive purpose: to sing special songs for another year.

Earlier generations of folklorists did not always consider the Sheffield carols to be 'folk music'. In the early twentieth century, the folk music collector Cecil Sharp defined the folk song narrowly: it had to be passed down by a continuous oral tradition that supposedly represented the 'authentic' rural culture of the country. This was a definition that ignored more than it included: new urban traditions, the haphazard ways that music gets transmitted, and the constant reinvention of material to make new songs. It also tended to divorce music and lyrics from their context, as an artefact for scholars to pore over, rather than as a living, breathing social practice. Many of Sheffield's singers today don't see themselves as part of a 'folk scene' and just consider this annual ritual as a performance of local songs.

The Sheffield carols start early, in November, the week after Armistice Sunday. They have a distinctive geography because, to this day, Sheffield is a city that is decentred: many cultural events happen on the outskirts, where there is an enduring sense of neighbourhoods with distinct identities. To the west and north, where the housing brick of the southern city gives way to Pennine stone, areas like Dungworth, Worrall, Stannington, Oughtibridge and

Wharncliffe Side still retain something of the feel of the old villages that preceded industrialisation. It is here that the carol singing finds an anchor in the taprooms of local pubs. There are also enclaves in north Derbyshire, to the south of Sheffield, in places like Hathersage, Grindleford and Eyam.

Pub singing in Sheffield used to be a year-round phenomenon: most pubs had a piano, and by the 1970s, the repertoire of non-seasonal popular songs was twice the size of the Christmas one. Yet only the carols really remain today. Many of them date back to the early nineteenth century: the subsequent rise of a Victorian hymn-singing culture and the teaching of 'approved' folk songs in schools made these earlier songs, with their contrapuntal, fugal elements, seem dated and old-fashioned by comparison.

Sometimes the tunes are similar to more famous Christmas carols, but the words are different; sometimes the words are the same, but the music is new; other times, the whole song is likely to be entirely novel to many listeners, including 'The Mistletoe Bough', the spooky nineteenth-century tale of a bride who playfully hides from her wedding party in a large chest, only to find herself trapped inside. It is only years later that a mouldering skeleton is discovered inside the box. Carols can be sung unaccompanied, but often there is a piano, an organ, or even the occasional string quartet or brass band backing the singers. There are lots of local variants, with unexpected twists and turns of melody, perhaps testament to the way in which folk songs tended to be carried hither and thither across the country by navvies, Gypsies, ballad singers and travelling people of all kinds.

*

One evening in early December, I meet Fay Hield, folk singer and academic, and ask her about the significance of song to folk customs. 'It brings a lot,' she explains, 'but it also creates a lot of problems, because people are terrified of singing. When we are kids, we love singing and dancing, but as we get older, we become self-conscious and afraid.' At their heart, she argues, the Sheffield carols are not about watching music being made, but about participating. My heart sinks, and I point out that she might well change her mind about the joys of collective music-making once she's heard me try to hold a tune. 'You don't have to be a brilliant singer,' Fay reassures me, 'it's all about the sense of connection for people, with themselves and with the music. And people let themselves sing at Christmas in a way that they might not let themselves sing at other times of year.'

This secular kind of carolling is, however, vulnerable to change. In the 1970s, the increasing affordability of cars meant that new city-dwellers unfamiliar with the local carols were suddenly visiting peripheral local pubs. This sometimes resulted in hostilities between the local musicians and this new audience, who could be condescending towards, or even irritated by, the performance. Even more devastating were the effects of a wave of pub renovations: a revamp of The Sportsman at Lodge Moor removed the small rooms where working people felt comfortable performing music in front of local friends. Instead, a plush, open interior placed anyone who wanted to sing on display in front of the whole pub.

Today, the demographic of those giving voice to the old songs has changed. While a lot of the long-established locals still turn out in force, many singers are not originally from the area, but are Sheffielders by adoption – people like me who see value, and perhaps even comfort, in this gathering together to build community via music. Others travel quite a distance to take part. As the demographics of the city, along with the interiors of pubs, have changed, the singing, too, has adjusted.

A few evenings later, I am standing in a local pub, clutching my copy of the lyrics, known locally as 'the Blue Book'. One deep breath, and I throw caution to the wind, launching into my first, shaky attempt at one of the very many versions of 'While Shepherds Watched' that circulate in this part of the world. Somewhat to my surprise, no one winces or backs away in horror at the sound I am making. In the wider room, too, none of the individual voices sound in any way trained, but the overall result is very far from a drunken pub karaoke dirge: it's wholesome, even rousing. Being a newcomer can be bewildering: there are carols with many parts, in rounds that interweave and resolve, with separate lines for male and female voices, and moments of surprisingly intricate harmony. But the atmosphere of the night is welcoming. Giving voice feels oddly freeing and very communal – and the perfect way to lay to rest the ghosts of carol services past.

KIERA CHAPMAN

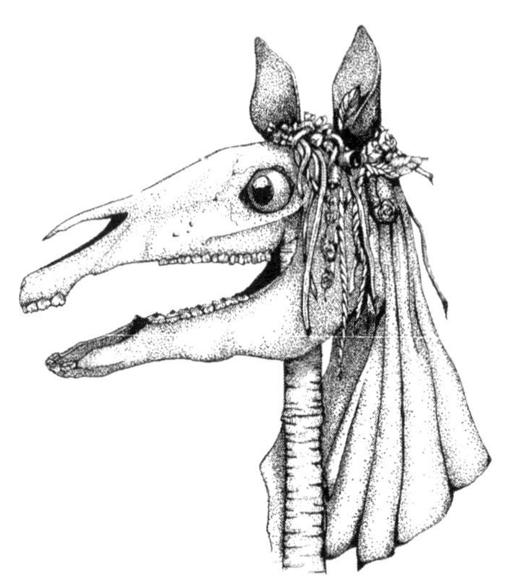

The Mari Lwyd

South Wales

1 NOVEMBER TO MID-JANUARY

A light rain falls. The barrier between air and rain has long dissolved, haloing the streetlights but coagulating the atmosphere outside their reach into a uniform thick murk. As I turn a corner, a sudden unearthly movement snatches at the edge of my attention. Whirling around, I find myself face to face with a grinning skull. Its leering eye socket looms down at me, while its jaw snaps in my face. More frightening than the white-boned face is the creature's body, which is hunched, yet also bent upwards at a sickening, unnatural angle. Behind this devilish beast stands a human figure, trying in vain to restrain it with a set of reins.

Only after the initial shock do I notice that the skull has a mane of ropes and horsehair, decorated with cheerfully coloured ribbons, and that behind its sheeted body stands a band of laughing revellers. Relief trickles over me, and I laugh out loud as I belatedly realise that this is the very thing I have come to see: the Mari Lwyd (pronounced 'marr-y loo-id').

The Mari Lwyd is celebrated mainly in south Wales, usually in ex-mining areas that have a distinctly urban and industrial history. It goes by many names: in Llandybïe it is simply *Y Warsel* (The Wassail); in the Rhymney area it is *Y Fari Lwyd Lawen* (The Merry Mari Lwyd), and in the Vale of Neath it is *Pen Ceffyl* (Horse's Head). Historically, the date of its celebration also varies: customs are recorded from 1 November through Christmas, and well into the new year.

In some places, the skull at the centre of this custom used to be buried in lime to keep it safe, and to ensure that the bones remained white. The eyes were fashioned from the bottoms of broken bottles, or from pieces of glistening coal. The jaw can be articulated, and the whole head is mounted on a pole decorated with rope and ribbons for a mane. The horse is a distinctly mischievous presence, running rings around the Leader, sometimes called 'Ostler Smart', who holds her reins, and occasionally requiring restraining interventions from her surrounding guard. They are a varied cast, but usually comprise a Sergeant, a Corporal, a Merryman, and sometimes Pwnsh and Siwan, a Welsh Punch and Judy, who disrupt proceedings further with their havoc-wreaking fights. The procession is so eerily eye-catching that videos of the custom have captured a fascinated worldwide audience on the internet. Yet in person, and in Welsh-language verses about the custom, the Mari Lwyd is often described as a beautiful, enlightening, even cheerful presence. Rhiannon Ifans, a specialist in Welsh-language literature, has translated some of those verses into English in her wonderful book on wassailing:

Ma'r Feri Lwyd yma
'N llawn sers a rybana,
Ma' i'n werth i roi gola [x3]
'R nos heno.

Ei chefan a'i chynffon
A'i dou lygad gleision
A'i thrimins yn gochion [x3]
Nos heno.

Mari Lwyd is here
Full of stars and ribbons,
It is worth bringing light [x3]
Tonight.

Her back and her tail
And her two bright eyes
And her red trimmings [x3]
Tonight.

The Mari Lwyd tradition is rooted in songs of call and response, often with as many as six different kinds of vocalisation. Families would often hide on the initial approach of the Mari Lwyd band, locking their doors against her, with the women indoors singing a 'waiting' stanza. This was followed by a sung petition for admittance from Mari and her followers. Not everyone was overjoyed at their approach. In a letter published in *Country Life* on 11 April 1968, one 'F David' of Swansea described his or her terror as a child at this visitation: 'a ghastly dirge would begin outside the front door, and with the bells rattling and the skull's teeth being made to champ, it was time for me to get under the kitchen table or retreat to the bottom of my bed and wait for its departure. In either case it meant an almost sleepless night.'

However, Mari's entry to the household was not to be granted too easily: the right to cross the threshold had instead to be won via an exchange of competitive verses in which each party insulted the other in song – a bantering ritual called *pwnco*:

Mari Lwyd: *Nawr grynda'r gŵr digri,*
Ma'th anal di'n drewi
Trwy ddwylath o dderi'r [x3]
Nos (h)eno.

Answer: *Ma'r tecill a'r ffrimpan*
Yn tampo (a)r y pentan
Wrth glywad shwd glerian [x3]
Y Nos (h)eno.

Mari Lwyd: Now listen, you crazy man,
Your breath stinks
Through two yards of oak [x3]
Tonight.

Answer: The kettle and the frying pan
Are bouncing on the hearthstone
On hearing such low-quality rhyming [x3]
Tonight.

Usually those in the household would lose the challenge, and the Mari party would sing a concluding verse in triumph at having won their way indoors. In some places, Pwnsh and Siwan would take this opportunity to cause chaos in the household – for example, by extinguishing the domestic fire. A further song would mark the party's departure, heaping blessings on the hospitable households who had offered the party food, drink and a donation, and being rather less than polite about those who had not.

There is considerable debate over the age of the Mari Lwyd. Its spectacular skeletal visuals have an ancient feel to them, and many folklorists link it to older customs, including 'hobby-horse' rituals, the French medieval Feast of the Ass on 14 January, forms of Marian devotion and mumming plays. Alternatively, the word *Llwyd* has been associated with 'grey' and is believed to connect to folklore about a monstrous 'grey mare', or even the grey death of the year. Others, however, register impatience at what they see as speculation, pointing out that there is no evidence that the ritual is any more than about 250 years old.

Contemporary artist Ben Edge's painting of the Mari Lwyd is filled with starlight, but this is no romanticised scene filled with light and shadow: it has something of the matter-of-fact flatness of contemporary LED street lighting about it. It shows Mari, looking cheerful rather than fearsome, and her Leader in Victorian-era costume, yet unmistakably a contemporary figure. They stand outside a titanic grey Chepstow castle, and at first sight the combination of Mari, the top-hatted figure and the Norman architecture looks like a statement about ancient survival, about the unchanging solidity of the past. Yet, look more closely and you see that the keep's walls are softened by greenery, making this a scene of ruin. Continuity and renewal are both present here, but it is the latter, the contemporary unfolding of the custom, that is the focus.

'It's important for it to look like what it really is,' Ben tells me, 'and that is a part of today.' For him, customs are not the dutiful repetition of some ancient tradition that is important because it is venerable, but a way for people to come together now, in the present moment. Belief in the supernatural elements of customs, which might be difficult for some to muster in our era of disenchanted modernity, isn't necessary for them to work either. 'It's a kind of secular magic,' he explains. 'I compare it to a placebo effect. People take pills without knowing that they don't have any medication in them, but they feel better all the same. There's something in the mind that has an ability to create that magic on its own.'

If this is right, then perhaps it doesn't really matter whether the Mari Lwyd is a thousand or only a couple of hundred years old, or if we believe individually in a folkloric grey mare, or in the supernatural power of wassail. All that matters in this and other customs is that they hold open a communal, interactive and creative space. Inside their enchanted ring, the ritual does the believing for us.

KIERA CHAPMAN

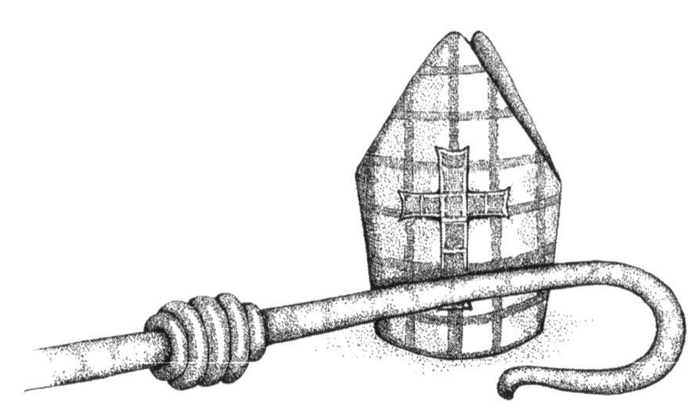

St Nicholas Night

Alcester, Warwickshire

6 DECEMBER

Held every year on 6 December, the St Nicholas Night celebrations in Alcester have all the trappings of a modern Christmastide event – food stalls, a brass band, Morris dancers, fireworks, fairground rides and candyfloss. But there is one element that stretches back much further in time: it starts with a parade led by children dressed as angels and a boy dressed as a bishop, part of the symbolic role-reversal ritual of this custom. A man dressed as Father Christmas (our modern version of St Nicholas) follows at the back. Harking back to medieval times, the anointing of a temporary 'Boy Bishop' in parishes across England represented a subversion of social hierarchies and a statement of humility on the part of church leaders. Traditionally, the Boy Bishop, dressed in gold and white robes and a mitre, would lead processions and deliver sermons between

St Nicholas' Day (6 December) and Holy Innocents' Day (28 December).

In the past, the custom often became rowdy, with many taking the suspension of authority as an invitation to disorder. Henry VIII banned this creation of temporary boy bishops, though Mary I reinstated it, but it was then banned again by Elizabeth I. It was also popular in parts of Europe, such as Spain and Germany, where it continued up to the end of the eighteenth century. It has recently been revived in several parishes and cathedrals across England, with boys nominated or elected by their choir or clergy. In order to be inclusive, girls have also been appointed as girl bishops, and some churches refer to them as 'child bishops' to avoid specifying their gender.

This subversion of normal rules is a key part of the feast of St Nicholas, the protector of children. While for us today he embodies generosity and kindness as Father Christmas, there are few documented records of the original St Nicholas. He is thought to have been born at the end of the third century ad in a region that was then Greek and that is now Turkish. Orphaned at a young age, Nicholas is said to have donated his inheritance to help the sick and poor. After his death, a liquid substance with healing powers, known as 'manna', was said to have appeared on his grave. This was taken to be a sign of Nicholas's holiness. There are tales of him rescuing kidnapped children, pacifying stormy seas and providing food for the starving. As the stories and legends swirled, so reverence for the saint grew.

In Alcester's parade, St Nicholas joins the Boy Bishop and onlookers for prayers and readings at the church. A countdown signals the switching-on of the Christmas tree lights, and the evening ends with a carol service and fireworks. While the adults enjoy mulled wine, hot mince pies and a bit of present shopping, for the children of Alcester, it is the day when one of their own takes charge – a reminder that Christmas is all about them, after all.

LULAH ELLENDER

The Tin Can Band

Broughton, Northamptonshire

FIRST SUNDAY AFTER 11 DECEMBER

At the opposite end of the musical spectrum to the Sheffield and Plygain carols described elsewhere in this book are the raucous tin can bands of Broughton. As midnight strikes and a mid-December Sunday turns into Monday, this tranquil Northamptonshire village witnesses a resounding performance from an orchestra composed of anything made of metal that lies to hand. Old tin baths, dustbin lids, baking trays, dented pots and pans, and more traditional brass instruments all blend together in an improvised cacophony that clatters its way around the streets for an hour, to the chagrin of some residents, and the delight of others.

Broughton's tin can band could be the relic of *charivari*, or 'rough music', a tradition of ritual hostility that provided a means of channelling a collective reaction to transgressions of social norms. Some contemporary writers describe this custom as a noisy way of excluding either Gypsies or more supernatural devilish forces from the local community. But historian David Hopkin suggests an alternative explanation – namely, that the tin can band is part of a larger, richer Midlands custom of 'Tandering', the name given to the celebration of St Andrew's Day. In the old calendar (see Introduction), this fell on 11 December, and Broughton's custom is still celebrated today on the first Sunday after that date. Thomas Sternberg's 1851 account of Tandering describes a day of 'unbridled licence', in which many different folkloric elements came together, from cross-dressing to mumming:

> Towards evening the sober villagers appear to have become suddenly smitten with a violent taste for masquerading. Women may be seen walking about in male attire, while men and boys have donned the female dress, and visit each other's cottages, drinking hot 'eldern wine,' the staple beverage of the season. Then commences the *Mumming*, too often described to need mention here, save to note that in the rude drama performed in the Northamptonshire villages, St George has given place to George III, and the dragon, formerly the greatest attraction of the piece, been supplanted by Napoleon, who is annually killed on this night in personal encounter with the aforesaid monarch, to the intense delight and edification of the loyal audience.

If we place the tin can band in the context of these wider festivities, the hour of metallic din that survives today appears as the remaining fragment of a much larger and more extended celebration.

Yet Sternberg's view that the custom was a harmless demonstration of a patriotic allegiance to king and country was not shared by members of the Broughton Parish Council of the late 1920s, who tried to ban the tin can band as a nuisance. The result was particularly raucous disobedience in December 1929, when an army of villagers crashed and banged their way around the village in an atmosphere of stubborn revelry. 'Where there were 29 tin can beaters last year, there were over 100 this morning,' reported the *Leicester Daily Mercury*, 'and a crowd of fully 400 looked on.' They paid particular attention to the home of local Conservative Mr William Sculthorpe, Chairman of the Parish Council, and one of the chief objectors to the custom, who lived in a large villa on School Hill. His pleas to the villagers to go home fell on deaf ears, though they did hush the noise around the home of Mrs Botterill, a characterful local centenarian who also opposed the custom. There was true music too: the crowd sang carols as they moved, and ended the night with the national anthem and 'Auld Lang Syne'.

Nevertheless, four policemen were also in attendance, and fifty-four people were consequently summoned to appear in court, creating a day of considerable local theatre. Villagers stood outside on their doorsteps, cheering and, according to one local paper, generally giving their neighbours a send-off 'as hearty as any reception ever accorded to a cup-winning football team'. Many went by bus, hooting their way through the streets, since the driver himself had been required to put in an appearance for playing the concertina. He showed his contempt for the summons by putting it through the bell push that was used to punch passenger tickets. Another protester later framed theirs to show their pride in this resistance. The atmosphere at court was jovial and full of banter, with the defendants bolstered by the knowledge that a local referendum had shown 545 in favour of the tin can custom and only twelve against, with twelve people staying neutral. The authorities proved unsympathetic, however, and the accused were bound over for two years and fined for their participation. The village stepped in to help defray the costs, raising the princely sum of £31, 14 shillings and 1½ pence. Of this, £10 and 15 shillings was spent on fines, £2 and 16 shillings on recompensing people for lost time, £5 and 5 shillings on legal help, and 7 shillings on printing. The surplus – the not inconsiderable amount of £11 – was put towards a tea for a hundred local elderly people.

For some time afterwards, parish council business was disrupted by this issue, with Broughton divided into three factions: the unofficial 'village committee', who wanted the custom reinstated; the parish council, who had banned it; and the 'League of Progress', led by one Councillor Baker, who supported the continued suppression of the custom. In February 1930, the village committee demanded that Sculthorpe should resign as chairman, and when he didn't, the next parish council meeting was so overcrowded with protesters that people had to wait outside, eventually bursting through the doors in their enthusiasm to make their feelings heard. Throughout the proceedings, the villagers in the hall shouted, sang and beat their metal instruments, creating 'a perfect Babel' that made it extremely difficult to get anything done. Councillor Baker was accused of calling the tin-canners 'scroof', an allegation that hints at a wider class politics between the factions, and he was howled down when he tried to speak. The press proved to be a quieter place for the censorious to vent their spleen: 'St Andrew will not object if the people of Broughton choose some less uncivilised way of honouring him,' opined an anonymous local writer.

'Civilisation' is a word often used to belittle and reduce, to paint the masses as ignorant and prone to disorder. But we can read this condemnation against the grain: there was clearly something about the tin can band so meaningful to many of the residents of Broughton that they were willing to risk getting into trouble with the law and local government to celebrate it.

The following year, 1930, saw the custom continue, and though the stygian blackness of the night made it difficult to estimate the size of the crowd, estimates in the press suggested that up to 1,000 people attended. More than a dozen were arrested, including a fourteen-year-old-girl, though the charges against her were later dropped. The policing of the event seems to have had a dampening effect on subsequent celebrations, which were much less well attended.

Interestingly, this popular protest didn't translate directly into political action. The Broughton Parish Council election of 1931 saw the anti-tin-canners victorious, suggesting that the relationship between the custom and the wider electoral issues of the area was not a straightforward one. This may indicate the power dynamics in play in 'official' local elections: perhaps workers and tenants felt unable to campaign openly against employers and landlords, who tended to take a prominent role in parish bodies.

But if we listen carefully to today's metallic clanging, we may hear the echoes of a working-class past. Its beat draws attention to a collective refusal to conform to the quiet demanded by the wealthy, and to a defiance of those in positions of local authority. Hidden inside the cacophony is a trace of the voices and actions of generations of past villagers, who couldn't necessarily express themselves in the local press or even in local elections, and who have left little trace in the written record – yet who nonetheless deserve to be heard.

KIERA CHAPMAN

Plygain Carol Singing

North Wales

AROUND 25 DECEMBER

Carol singing is as much part of the Christmas season as mince pies and presents. Walk through any town in December and you're likely to meet a festive-jumper-clad choir belting out some traditional tunes or remixing modern Christmas Number One hit singles. In my family, Christmas proper always began with *Carols from King's* on the radio, the exquisite solo chorister singing 'Once in Royal David's City' and my mum crying at its beauty. I was always fascinated by the way the music affected her, although the rest of the service felt more formal. The magic was in that one voice, that first moment. In parts of Wales you might be lucky enough to find a similarly stirring but altogether different carolling tradition.

In December and January, in forty to fifty churches and chapels across mainly north Wales (especially Montgomeryshire), congregations gather for the plygain carol service. Unlike Sheffield's pub-based carol singing, plygain is a church service, and although it may have medieval origins, it is most clearly documented from the seventeenth century onwards. As religious practices changed, so did the service, evolving from Catholic tradition to Protestant and Nonconformist styles, while preserving its distinct carol-singing focus. The service had nearly died out by the end of the nineteenth century, but work by St Fagan's National Museum of History (particularly folklorists Meredydd Evans and Phyllis Kinney) to collect and preserve the plygain carols in the 1960s led to a revival that continues today.

The name 'plygain' comes from the Latin *pulli cantus* (song of the cockerel), because the service was traditionally held between 3 and 6 a.m. on Christmas morning. The festivities, however, began the night before. In the evening and long into the night, people would gather in nearby farmhouses making treacle toffee and decorating the house, or tipping out into the streets, dancing and singing. In the darkness of the early morning they would make their way to the candlelit church or chapel. After a short reading, a prayer and a congregational hymn, the rest of the service was all about song. Today, many of these services are held on different evenings, to make them more accessible to those who like their sleep before the big day. But the format is the same.

Once the formalities are over, groups of singers come forward to share their carols; there is no order of service, no planning, and no restrictions other than that the carols must not be repeated, and they should be sung in Welsh. For around two hours people sing unaccompanied, often using carol books passed down through their families for generations. Usually, groups of three or four will sing harmonies. Sometimes they will set the pitch with a tuning fork, but otherwise they sing entirely *a cappella*. The plygain ends with the *Carol y Swper* (the 'Supper Carol'), sung by all the men in the congregation with vigour, resonance and pride. If the sound doesn't move you, I don't know what will.

The plygain tradition has weathered centuries of change, and it continues to adapt as new collections are published, including a *Carol y Swper* written specifically for women's voices. It taps into the powerful role song has played in Welsh culture and identity – it is known as the 'Land of Song', and Welsh male voice choirs are renowned for their stirring sound and energy. These choirs often originated in mining communities as a means of creating solidarity and pride, but people have always sung in chapels, pubs and schools across the country. Nonconformists saw singing as inherently democratic – everyone's voice counts. The *eisteddfod* tradition of musical and literary competitions and performance is a long-standing and popular celebration of Welsh-language culture. It has roots in the ancient bardic traditions and song at its core. Now an annual national event, the Eisteddfod is one of Europe's largest cultural festivals, and a powerful expression of Welsh national identity.

But where *eisteddfod* began as a competitive secular

tradition, plygain is a Christian devotional ritual, albeit with strong folk roots. If you can't get to north Wales in December, I invite you to find a clip of a plygain service on YouTube. Turn the volume up loud. Close your eyes. Imagine yourself in a small, cold, candlelit chapel. Let the song wash over you as snow falls on the wet, black mountains outside. Be transported by sound.

LULAH ELLENDER

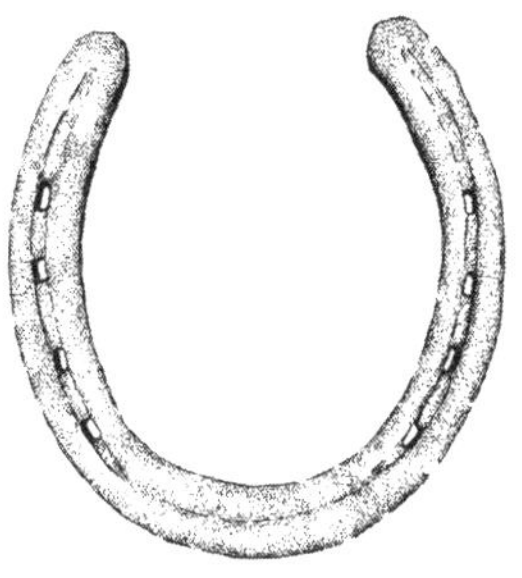

Christmas Horse Pub Crossing

Bucks Green, West Sussex

25 DECEMBER

Everyone knows that animals are an important, if secondary, part of the Christmas story: the donkey who bears the pregnant Mary to the inn; the ox and the ass kneeling by the manger, providing coveted roles for small children in school nativity plays; the plodding camels bringing the three wise men across the desert to the stable; the sheep watched over by their shepherds in the hills above Bethlehem. And what would the season be without a robin or two scattered cheerfully across cards and wrapping paper? But horses? Well, no, horses not so much.

Except, that is, at the Fox Inn at Bucks Green in West Sussex, where, on Christmas Day, just before lunch is served, a horse is led straight through the bar, sometimes pausing along the way for a carrot or a sneaky mouthful of crisps, before emerging from the back door into the pub garden. Horses being rather fond of beer, there may or may not on occasion be a little liquid refreshment waiting for him out there too.

Given the name of the pub, one might think that this was a tradition related to the now-illegal sport of fox hunting – after all, it was customary across the country for hunts to meet on Boxing Day – but in fact the given explanation is something quite different. The current building dates from the seventeenth century and is thought in the past to have consisted of two separate properties, divided by a public bridleway. After the two buildings were amalgamated into one, the old path – for reasons that are now obscure, and which was by then surfaced in brick – was maintained in practice, if not in any legal sense, by the simple expedient of exercising the right of public access through the building once a year by horse.

It's an intriguing story and a charming custom, and maybe there is some truth hidden behind it. A public footpath still runs from north to south there, although now it skirts the end of the building rather than passing through it. Perhaps some local dispute over access remains enshrined in this curious Christmas custom – who knows? One thing's for sure though: once the horse has walked through the pub, tradition has been observed and, at last, lunch can be served.

REBECCA WARREN

Hunting the Wren

Middleton, Suffolk

26 DECEMBER TO 5 JANUARY

One of the strangest customs of the year, the hunting of the wren, is also one of the oldest. It is celebrated right across Britain and parts of Europe, mostly between St Stephen's Day (26 December) and Twelfth Night (5 January). Contemporary festivals survive in Ireland, Wales and the Isle of Man, but also in rural Suffolk, in a small village close to the sea called Middleton. Nowadays, Middletonians celebrate wren hunting on Boxing Day, but there are some historical accounts that suggest it used to occur on Valentine's Day, perhaps reflecting an old medieval link between wrens and love that has since been lost.

Formerly, groups of men and boys would go out beating the hedgerows to uncover, hunt and kill one of these small birds, before parading the tiny carcass through the streets in a decorated cage. Thankfully most contemporary versions of the custom make use of a less bloody alternative to a dead bird, such as a stuffed fabric wren or a carved wooden version, so the hunting element of the ritual has declined. The structure in which the replica wren is placed varies from place to place: in some of the Welsh locations, it is held in a small house decorated with ribbons. On the Isle of Man, it is displayed in an open hoop or sphere, generously decorated with glossy evergreen foliage. In Middleton, the ceremony centres on a staff that erupts into a densely woven ball of holly and ivy, inside which a small wooden bird is hidden.

Many folk stories about the wren have become tangled together in this custom. One element that is at least as old as Aristotle is the idea that it was the king of all the birds, having cunningly won the title by perching on top of the back of a soaring eagle to fly higher than all other winged creatures. Another relates the wren to the winter solstice, connecting it to the fading sun, which imparts the symbolic role of renewal to its hunting. Another story, from the Isle of Man, concerns a wicked fairy woman who enchanted all the men of the island, eventually leading them to their deaths in a swift-running local river. When the community banded together to hunt her down, she transformed into a wren, cocking her tail in defiance and darting out of their eager hands and into nearby bushes – turning this custom into a tale of revenge.

Since the custom's revival in the 1970s, the Middleton version of the ritual has become one of the more elaborate takes on it. It begins at the village hall, where the local Morris troupe gather in green-faced makeup under rather harsh electric lights. The dancers are all men, the musicians largely women, and the latter wear hats festooned with evergreen foliage. After a little music to set the scene, and a request to those watching to turn off their phones, dancers and observers move outside, into the darkness, where dozens of jam jars, each holding a lit candle, await. Each person takes one and lines up quietly in the car park outside. Anticipation builds as the dancers light large torches. Then, in a silence broken only by the deep beat of a drum, and lit only by the flaring flames, the procession sets off down the narrow unlit road.

The scene is striking, mysterious and undeniably atmospheric. The first walking figure is a man in Victorian agricultural costume, who sweeps the street with a broom. Behind him follow a lord and cross-dressed 'lady', in finer clothes. Then comes the 'cutty wren' ('cutty' meaning 'small') on its staff, carried by a group of men in trousers and hobnail boots, who are followed by the musicians and a man holding a box for donations. It is only when the troupe arrives at the local pub that the silence is broken: a figure steps forward to introduce the dancers as the Old Glory Morris troupe, though at this time of year, they are 'Molly dancers', reflecting an activity that agricultural workers took on in the lean winter months, when they needed to busk to have any income (for more on this, see the 'Whittlesea Straw Bear' entry). The dancing is rough and weighty, with plenty of stomping and a spirit of slight menace.

As the night wears on, however, the forbidding elements of the performance gradually wear away, and the dancers begin to welcome the participation of spectators. The ceremony ends with everyone joining hands to dance in a huge rotating circle that covers the whole of the considerable area outside the pub. Once the music and laughter have finally died away, many of the company and spectators adjourn indoors, where a well-earned Boxing Day pint and furthcr music awail.

KIERA CHAPMAN

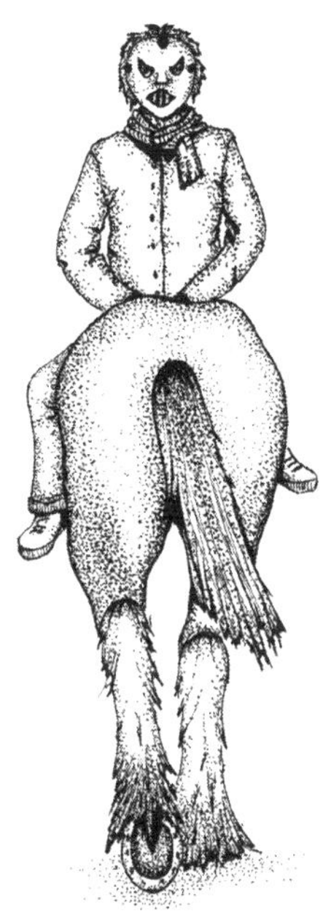

Year's End Oddfellows Parade

Newburgh, Fife

31 DECEMBER

Newburgh's Oddfellows Parade is not for the faint-hearted or easily 'frit'. Held every year on 31 December, this torch-lit procession features officer bearers, a silver band, men dressed as creepy clowns, monkeys in hi-viz suits, camouflaged soldiers and devilish rabbits. The procession is led by a masked man sitting backwards on a Clydesdale draught horse, to add to the eerie spectacle. The parade is part of Scotland's Hogmanay traditions but has a unique feel – part horror show, part charity fundraiser.

It was established by the Newburgh Caledonian Lodge of Oddfellows and is the oldest surviving Oddfellows parade in Scotland. The friendly society known as the Oddfellows was set up in 1827 to support working men, before trade unions and the welfare state offered a more formalised safety net. Many similar fraternal societies, like the Freemasons and Foresters, spread across Britain in the eighteenth and nineteenth centuries in response to increasing industrialisation and urban migration, and some claim they have roots as far back as medieval times. As traditional guilds (associations of craftsmen and merchants) declined, the Oddfellows (so named because of the variety of trades that made up its ranks) offered friendship, financial help and moral guidance. Many of these organisations disappeared after the introduction of basic financial assistance via the 1911 National Insurance Act rendered them less necessary, but the Newburgh Oddfellows are still going strong. Their emphasis on community service and charity is still evident in today's parade, where participants shake collection buckets for local good causes.

Although women are now admitted into the Oddfellows fraternity, originally these groups were exclusionary and patriarchal, modelled in part on the male-only hierarchical structure of medieval brotherhoods. The 'undeserving' poor and racial minorities were also banned from joining. Left-wing historian E. P. Thompson saw these societies as 'instruments of social control' – ritualistic, undemocratic and moralistic. But today's good-natured parade feels more like a fun custom that brings the community together to raise money and celebrate the turn of the year.

Hogmanay has a long history of disguise and subversion, a sense that something uncanny and sacred is happening as the year tips. Frightening masks are also part of folkloric traditions around the world, serving to ward off evil. What is especially interesting about the Oddfellows Parade is the apprentice Oddfellow riding backwards. Like the Earl of Rone whom we met in May, the apprentice wears a Janus-faced mask, but this time he is looking back on the year that's ending and forward to the coming year. Similar representations of thresholds, duality and all-seeing wisdom are found in the dual-faced helmet masks of Cameroon's Fang and Ekoi peoples, Vanuatu's Nalawan rituals featuring Janus headdresses, and Northern Ireland's Boa Island statues with two faces.

The night before January, the month named after Janus, the Roman god of gateways, is an important hinge moment as we are reborn into a new calendar year and midwinter starts to transition towards spring. Now is a good moment to raise a glass of Newburgh's whisky from its renowned Lindores Abbey distillery, and toast to protection from evil and the promise of a fresh new year.

LULAH ELLENDER

Notes

HAXEY HOOD GAME, 6 JANUARY

'the boggans had nearly suffocated a fool . . .': Mabel Peacock, *The Hood-Game at Haxey, Lincolnshire*, read at Meeting 19 May 1896, published in *Folklore 1896*, babel.hathitrust.org (accessed 26 April 2025).

James George Frazer, *The Golden Bough*. London: Macmillan and Co., 1890.

Venetia Newall: cited in Catriona M. Parratt, 'Of place and men and women: Gender and topophilia in "Haxey Hood"', *Journal of Sport History*, 27(2) (Summer 2000), pp. 229–45, University of Illinois Press.

Catriona Parratt: ibid.

singing is a fast way to create social bonds: Eiluned Pearce, Jacques Launay and Robin I. M. Dunbar, 'The ice-breaker effect: Singing mediates fast social bonding', *Royal Society Open Science*, 2(10) (October 2015), https://doi.org/10.1098/rsos.150221 (accessed 24 April 2025); Daniel Weinstein, Jacques Launay, Eiluned Pearce, Robin I. M. Dunbar and Lauren Stewart, 'Singing and social bonding: Changes in connectivity and pain threshold as a function of group size, *Evolution and Human Behaviour*, 35(2) (March 2016), https://obi.org/10.1016/j.evolhumbehav.2015.10.002 (accessed 24 April 2025).

HINCKLEY PLOUGH BULLOCKERS, PLOUGH MONDAY

Good Master and Good Mistress, you sit around the fire: The Full English: English Folk Dance and Song Society Project, *Plough Monday play script from Morton near Bourne* (2014), p. 10.

WHITTLESEA STRAW BEAR, FIRST SATURDAY AFTER PLOUGH MONDAY

a shared early language may have emerged: for more information, see the Indo-European Lexicon project at the University of Texas, https://lrc.la.utexas.edu/lex (accessed 12 December 2025).

***rktho*:** A. Irving Halliwell, 'Bear ceremonialism in the northern hemisphere', *American Anthropologist*, 28(1) (1926), pp. 1–175. See also Oliver Grimm (ed.), *Bear and Human: Facets of a Multi-layered Relationship from Past to Recent Times, with Emphasis on Northern Europe*. Turnhout: Brepols, 2023.

Roslyn Frank: 'Recovering European ritual bear hunts: A comparative study of Basque and Sardinian ursine carnival performances', *Insula*-3 (2008), pp. 41–97; see also Frank's 'Hunting the European sky bears: German 'straw-bears' and their relatives as transformers', in Michael and Barbara Rappenglück (eds.), *Symbole der Wandlung – Wandel der Symbole*. Munich: *Proceedings of the Gesellschaft für wissenschaftliche Symbolforschung*, 21–23 May 2004, pp. 141–66.

'Molly' sides: see Elaine Bradtke, 'Molly dancing: A study of discontinuity and change', in *Step Change: New Views on Traditional Dance*. London: Francis Boutie, 2001, pp. 61–86; Joseph Needham and Arthur Peck, 'Molly dancing in East Anglia', *Journal of the English Folk Dance and Song Society*, 1(2) (1933), pp. 79–85; R. Humphries, *For a Little Bit of Sport: Molly Dancing and Plough Monday in East Anglia*. Linton: R. & K. Humphries, 1986. Cecil Sharp saw Molly dancing as too ordinary and too simple to be worthy of note. He wrote that it was the 'everyday dance of the country-folk, performed not merely on festal days, but whenever opportunity offered and the spirit of merrymaking was abroad'. The steps, he claimed, were 'simple and easily learned, so that anyone of ordinary intelligence and of average physique can without difficulty qualify as a competent performer', in *The Country Dance Book Part I: Containing a Description of Eighteen Traditional Dances Collected in Country Villages*, reprint. Surrey: H. Styles, 1985, p. 12.

One 1851 account: *The Cambridge Chronicle*, 18 January 1851, quoted in Tony Forster, *Molly Dancing into the Twenty-first Century*. Morris Federation, 2002.

Sometimes they would sit on one another's Laps: Rictor Norton, *Mother Clap's Molly House: The Gay Subculture in England 1700–1830*. Stroud: The Chalford Press, 2006, p. 88.

'Moorish' and 'Morisco': see David Matless, *England's Green: Nature and Culture since the 1960s*. London: Reaktion, 2024.

Pig Dyke Molly: for images, see the gallery at https://pigdyke.co.uk (accessed 12 December 2025).

BURNS NIGHT, 25 JANUARY

Craig Ferguson: *The Ross Kaminsky Show*, 'Interview with Craig Ferguson at Comedy Works', 1 October 2024, transcript at https://www.spreaker.com/episode/10-1-24-interview-craig-ferguson-at-comedy-works-this-weekend--62182045 (accessed 12 December 2025).

Reverend Hamilton Paul: for a detailed history of Burns Night, see Clark McGinn, *The Burns Supper: A Comprehensive History*. Edinburgh: Luath Press, 2019.

University of Glasgow keeps a global map: Paul Malgrati and Brian Aitken, 'Interactive World Map of Burns Suppers', Centre for Robert Burns Studies, https://burnsc21.glasgow.ac.uk/supper-map/ (accessed 12 December 2025).

nine million people: at the time, whisky company Famous Grouse mapped celebrations on a special website at www.burnssupper2009.com. See Paul Malgrati, 'Geography and typology of contemporary Burns Suppers', *Burns Chronicle*, 130(2) (2021), pp. 127–48.

'Auld Lang Syne': The tune changed in the 1790s from a rather melancholy melody to a more upbeat one. See Kirsteen McCue, 'How Auld Lang Syne switched tunes en route to world domination', *The Conversation*, 31 December 2015.

Hugh MacDiarmid: *A Drunk Man Looks at the Thistle*. Edinburgh: W. Blackwood, 1926. For a Chinese translation and a description of MacDiarmid's reception in China, including an able dismissal of the argument that it is the poet's narrator, not the poet himself, who expresses racism, see Li Li and Lia Aihua, 'From Scots to Mandarin: The Translation and Reception of Hugh MacDiarmid's Poetry in China', *Translation and Literature*, 31(3) (2022), pp. 341–57.

Clark McGinn: ibid.

surprisingly promiscuous in his political associations: see Kenneth Simpson, *The Protean Scot: The Crisis of Identity in Eighteenth Century Scottish Literature*. Aberdeen: Aberdeen University Press, 1988; and Christopher A. Whatley, *Immortal Memory: Burns and the Scottish People*. Edinburgh: John Donald, 2016.

celebrated in politically contradictory ways: for an excellent discussion of the changing politics of Burns Night, see Paul Magrati, *Robert Burns and Scottish Cultural Politics: The Bard of Contention 1914–2014*. Cambridge: Cambridge University Press, 2023; and Graeme Morton, *Unionist-Nationalism: Governing Urban Scotland, 1830–1860*. East Linton: Tuckwell Press, 1999.

Theresa May: Steerpile, 'Theresa May's Burns Night faux pas', *The Spectator*, 23 January 2018. https://www.spectator.co.uk/article/theresa-may-s-burns-night-faux-pas/ (accessed 12 December 2025).

Glasgow Afghan United: see their website at https://glasgowafghanunited.co.uk/ (accessed 12 December 2025).

CANDLEMAS AND THE BLESSING OF THE THROATS, 2 AND 3 FEBRUARY

lasted in some areas until the late eighteenth century: R. Hutton, *Stations of the Sun: A History of the Ritual Year in Britain*, Oxford: Oxford University Press, 2001, p. 143.

BLIDWORTH CRADLE ROCKING, SUNDAY NEAREST CANDLEMAS

Candlemas: Niall Edworthy, *The Curious World of Christmas*. London: Penguin, 2008.

newsreel from 1952: *BBC News*, 'Blidworth Cradle Rocking Ceremony', 10 February 1952, BBC Archive, https://www.facebook.com/watch/?v=524461107926924 (accessed 12 December 2025).

Thomas Leake: for the tale, see William Andrews, *Curious Epitaphs, Collected and Edited with Notes*. London: William Andrews, 1899.

Preaching in 1935: an account of the sermon is given in 'Blidworth Rocking', *Nottingham Evening Post*, 4 February 1935, p. 3, col. 3.

LUNAR NEW YEAR IN SOHO, SECOND NEW MOON AFTER THE WINTER SOLSTICE

There has been a Chinese community in London since the eighteenth century: Gregor Benton, *Chinese Migrants and Internationalism: Forgotten Histories, 1917–1945*. London: Routledge, 2007.

Limehouse: for a brilliant history, see Yat Ming Loo, '"Mixed race", Chinese identity, and intercultural place: Decolonizing urban memories of Limehouse Chinatown in London', *Journal of Race, Ethnicity and the City*, 3(1), 2022, 23–41; and John Seed, 'Limehouse blues: Looking for Chinatown in the London docks, 1900–40', *History Workshop Journal*, 62(1) (2006), pp. 58–85.

a 'Yellow Peril': Vanessa Künnemann and Ruth Mayer, *Chinatowns in a Transnational World: Myths and Realities of an Urban Phenomenon*. London: Routledge, 2011.

Gerrard Street area: Venetia Newall, 'A note on the Chinese New Year celebration in London and its socio-economic background', *Western Folklore*, 48(1) (1989), pp. 61–6.

Roy and Monica Vickery: 'Chinese New Year Celebrations in London 1971–1973', Folklore, 85(1) (1974), pp. 43–5, this quotation pp. 43–4.

fend off the planners: for two nuanced spatial accounts of the relationship between planning and migrant communities, see Wun Fung Chan, *Chinese Identities: Official Representations and New Ethnicities*, PhD, University of Birmingham; and Yasminah Beebeejaun, 'What's in a nation? Constructing ethnicity in the British planning system', *Planning Theory & Practice*, 5(4) (2004), pp. 437–51. For an illuminating video that discusses the significance of Chinese Lunar New Year in Soho as a statement about place, see Thames TV's report 'Chinese New Year', available at https://www.youtube.com/watch?v=JZ9c65G99IM (accessed 12 December 2025).

Critics of this version of the Lunar New Year: Kay J. Anderson, 'The idea of Chinatown: The power of place and institutional practice in the making of a racial category', *Annuals of the Association of American Geographies*, 77(4) (1987), pp. 580–98; and Shannon Case, 'Lilied tongues and yellow claws: The invention of London's Chinatown 1915–45', in S. Deen (ed.), *Challenging Modernism: New Readings in Literature and Culture, 1914–45*. London: Ashgate, 2002, pp. 17–34.

But another group disagrees: C. Wang, 'Negotiating diasporic identities in glocal heritage discourses: The case of the Chinese New Year celebration in London', in C. Wang and T. Lamb (eds.), *Negotiating Identities, Language and Migration in Global London: Bridging Borders, Creating Spaces*. Bristol: Multilingual Matters, 2024, pp. 144–69.

Shaftesbury Capital: for an excellent discussion, see Q.-D. Dang, 'The practice of neoliberal multiculturalism in urban management in British cities: A case study from London's Chinatown', *Mémoire(s), identité(s), marginalité(s) dans le monde occidental contemporain*, 31, 2025.

its politics have also shifted: Y. Ren, 'Traditional Chinese New Year is changing – and the UK needs to catch up', *The Guardian*, 16 February 2018.

Chinese government: Liu Hui, 'China's soft power and its Lunar New Year's culture', *Modern Diplomacy*, 18 February 2018.

PENNY LOAF DAY, SUNDAY NEAREST 11 MARCH

they may lay on eternal life: National Archives, PROB 11/234/142.

ST CUTHBERT'S DAY, 20 MARCH

disagreement was over the way they calculated the dates for Easter: David Ewing Duncan, *Calendar: Humanity's Epic Struggle to Determine a True and Accurate Year*, 1st ed. London: Avon Books, 1998.

'like five tiny birds riding on the waves': Bede, 'Life of St Cuthbert', in Bertram Colgrave (ed.), *Two Lives of Saint Cuthbert*. New York: Greenwood Press, 1969, p. 163.

'Let no man pray for them': Bede, ibid., p. 165.

A literary tradition of tales sprang up: for an in-depth discussion of these stories, see Dominic Alexander, *Saints and Animals in the Middle Ages*. Woodbridge: Boydell Press, 2008.

Reginald of Durham: Antone Minard, 'The mystery of St Cuthbert's ducks: An adventure in hagiography', *Folklore*, 127(3) (2016), pp. 325–43.

modern conservation movement: John Jenkins, 'St Cuthbert's ducks', 29 October 2015, at https://www.pilgrimageandcathedrals.ac.uk/blog/st-cuthbert%E2%80%99s-ducks-1446120484 (accessed 12 December 2025).

CARLIN SUNDAY, FIFTH SUNDAY OF LENT

'sundry other sorts and varieties which were endlesse to recite': J. Parkinson, *Theatrum Botanicum: The Theater of Plants* (1640), p. 1058.

PACE-EGGING PLAYS, GOOD FRIDAY

a study by Eddie Cass: E. Cass, 'Pace egg', in *Northern Earth*, 105 (2006), pp. 7–12.

CHULKHURST DOLE, EASTER MONDAY

the sisters' surname was Preston: E. Hasted, *The History and Topographical Survey of the County of Kent*, vol. 7 (1797), p. 138.

MARSDEN CUCKOO FESTIVAL, LAST WEEKEND IN APRIL

early natural historians such as Pliny: Cynthia Chris, *Cuckoo*. London: Reaktion, 2024.

an impressive feat of biological forgery: Nick Davies, *Cuckoo: Cheating by Nature*. London: Bloomsbury, 2015.

British Trust for Ornithology: see https://www.bto.org/cuckoos (accessed 12 December 2025).

Along the southern Chilterns: for this and other legends of cuckoo-penning, see John Field, *The Myth of the Pent Cuckoo*. London: Elliot Stock, 1913.

As a 1630 chapbook recounts: quoted in Field, ibid., p. 1.

presenting this apparent idiocy as a clever ruse: Robert Thoroton, *Thoroton's History of Nottinghamshire Republished, with Large Additions, by John Throsby*. London: B. and J. White, 1797.

Washington Irving: *Salmagundi; or The Whim-whams and Opinions of Launcelot Langstaff, Esq. & Others*. New York: Harper and Brothers, 1835, first series, vol. 1.

their numbers have dropped: C. Denerley et al., 'Breeding ground correlates of the distribution and decline of the Common Cuckoo *Cuculus canorus* at two spatial scales', *Ibis*, 161 (2019), pp. 346–58.

Climate change: Jacob Davies et al., 'Spring arrival of the common cuckoo at breeding grounds is strongly determined by environmental conditions in tropical Africa', *Proceedings of the Royal Society*, 2023, *B*.29020230580.

ADDERBURY MORRIS MEN DAY OF DANCE, LAST WEEKEND IN APRIL

Tim Plester: dir., *Way of the Morris*, 2011.

50.6 per cent of the UK's 13,000 dancers: 'Meet the maths teacher who's the first queen of the morris dancers', *The Times*, 27 April 2025.

'folk is not a museum piece': bossmorris.com/fff (accessed 28 June 2025).

TISSINGTON WELL DRESSING, ASCENSION DAY

floral garlands: R. Shirley, 'Festive landscapes: The contemporary practice of well-dressing in Tissington', *Landscape Research*, vol. 42 (6) (2017), 650–62.

CHEESE ROLLING, LATE MAY BANK HOLIDAY

'all rising fields of poppies': Valerie Grove 'Laurie Lee's rural myths', *New Statesman*, 18 December 2019.

'long shadows': Laurie Lee, *Cider with Rosie*. London: Vintage Classics, 2014, p. 34.

HUNTING OF THE EARL OF RONE, LATE MAY BANK HOLIDAY

Authenticity: I'm indebted to the brilliant discussion of this term by Regina Bendix in *In Search of Authenticity: The Formation of Folklore Studies*. ACLS Humanities e-book: Madison: University of Wisconsin Press, 1997.

folklorism: the literature on this is vast and long-running, but see Hans Moser, 'Vom Folklorismus in unserer Zeit', *Zeitschrift fur Volkskunde*, 58 (1962), pp. 177–209; Hermann Bausinger, *Volkskultur in der technischen Welt*, Stuttgart: W. Kohlhammer, 1961; Venetia Newall, 'The adaptation of folklore and tradition (folklorismus)', *Folklore*, 98(2) (1987), pp. 131–51.

Hugh O'Neill, the Earl of Tyrone: Hiram Morgan, 'The "Wild Man of the Woods" and "The Hunting of the Earl of Rone": Tyrone in English folk tradition', *History Ireland*, 15(4) (2007), pp. 9–11.

Tom Brown: *The Hunting of the Earl of Rone*, Combe Martin: S&A Projects, 2017; and 'The hunting of the Earl of Rone: The emergence of "new" folklore motifs: Individual creativity and group control', *Folklore*, 116(2) (2005), pp. 201–13.

APPLEBY HORSE FAIR, EARLY JUNE

Henry VIII tried to banish them: it is difficult to date when Gypsies first began to arrive in Britain, but they were certainly a presence by the early sixteenth century. See David Cressy, 'Trouble with Gypsies in early Modern England', *The Historical Journal*, 59(1) (2016), pp. 45–70.

Egyptians Acts: John Morgan, 'Counterfeit Egyptians': The construction and implementation of a criminal identity in early modern England', *Romani Studies*, 26(2) (2016), pp. 105–28.

northern India: G. F. Ena et al., 'Population genetics of the European Roma – a review', *Genes*, 13(11) (2022), 2068.

Romantic era: Sarah Houghton-Walker, *Representations of the Gypsy in the Romantic Period*. Oxford: Oxford University Press, 2014.

a hostile argument: Peter Widmann, 'The campaign against the restless: Criminal biology and the stigmatization of the Gypsies, 1890–1960', in R. Stauber and R. Vago (eds.), *The Roma.*

A Minority in Europe. Amsterdam: Central European University Press, 2007, pp. 19–29.

as many as 500,000 Gypsies were murdered: Barbara Warnock, 'Nazis murdered a quarter of Europe's Roma, but history still overlooks this genocide', *The Conversation*, 24 January 2020.

hidden forms of prejudice: for a series of discussions of this phenomenon, see *When Stereotype Meets Prejudice: Antiziganism in European Societies*, ed. Timofey Agarin. Stuttgart: Ibidem Press, 2014, pp. 143–69.

2018 report: *Developing a National Barometer of Prejudice and Discrimination in Britain*, Equality and Human Rights Commission, 2018.

***Daily Mail*:** Fred Kelly 'Appleby Ground Zero: Fighting in the street, urine through letter boxes and locals terrified into silence . . .', *Daily Mail*, 4 June 2024.

30,000 and 50,000 visitors: figures from the official Appleby Fair webpage, www.applebyfair.org (accessed 12 December 2025).

accusations of backwardness: see Sarah Holloway, 'Articulating otherness? White rural residents talk about Gypsy-Travellers', *Transactions of the Institute of British Geographers*, 30(3) (2005), pp. 351–67.

Police, Crime, Sentencing and Courts Act: at the time of writing, the future of this piece of legislation is uncertain. The High Court has ruled that it is incompatible with human rights provisions, and Parliament is currently reconsidering its provisions. See Garden Court Chambers blog 'High Court issues declaration of incompatibility finding that provisions in the Police Act unlawfully discriminate against Gypsies and Travellers', 14 May 2024, https://gardencourtchambers.co.uk/high-court-issues-declaration-of-incompatibility-finding-that-provisions-in-the-police-act-unlawfully-discriminate-against-gypsies-and-travellers/ (accessed 12 December 2025).

traditional stopping places: for an account of these, see Damian Le Bas, *The Stopping Places: A Journey Through Gypsy Britain*. London: Chatto and Windus, 2018.

KNOLLYS ROSE CEREMONY, EARLY JUNE

'height of 14 feet': 'The Parish of All Hallows, Barking', vol. II, in *Survey of London*, ed. G. H. Gater and W. H. Godfrey, vol. 15 (1934), pp. 16–17.

a royal grant or pension: https://watermenscompany.com/heritage/ (accessed 12 June 2025).

THE COMMON RIDING, MID-JUNE

'all Englishmen and Scottishmen': https://artsandculture.google.com/story/mAWBn3cfFYTLIA (accessed 19 August 2025).

SOLSTICE AT STONEHENGE, 21 JUNE

Mike Pitts, *How to Build Stonehenge*, London: Thames & Hudson, 2022.

BAWMING THE THORN, THIRD SATURDAY IN JUNE

1 May: Della Hooke, 'Holly and May: Cultural symbolism and reality', *Landscape History*, 45(1) (2024), pp. 119–27.

***Crataegus monogyna 'Biflora'*:** Carole Cusack, 'The Glastonbury Thorn in Vernacular Christianity and Popular Tradition', *Journal for the Study of Religion, Nature & Culture* 12(3) (2018), pp. 307–26.

ceremonially cut and then sent to Buckingham Palace: for an account of this separate calendar custom, see Marion Bowman, 'The Holy Thorn ceremony: Revival, rivalry and civil religion in Glastonbury: Presidential address given to the Folklore Society', *Folklore*, 117(2) (2006), pp. 123–40.

sought to increase the prestige of their abbey: Richard Hayman, *Holy Grail and Holy Thorn: Glastonbury in the English Imagination*. Croydon: Fonthill Media, 2014; Robin Croft, Trevor Hartland and Heather Skinner, 'And did those feet? Getting medieval England "on-message"', *Journal of Communication Management*, 12(4) (2008), pp. 294–304.

William of Malmesbury: *The Early History of Glastonbury: An Edition, Translation, and Study of William of Malmesbury's* De antiquitate Glastonie ecclesie, tr. John Scott. Rochester, NY: Boydell Press, 2001.

when his manuscript was copied in 1247: Deborah Crawford, 'St. Joseph in Britain: Reconsidering the legends, Part I', *Folklore*, 104(2) (1993), pp. 86–98.

cult of pilgrimage around Joseph: Alexandra Walsham, 'The Holy Thorn of Glastonbury: The evolution of a legend in post-Reformation England', *Parergon*, 21(2) (2004), pp. 1–25.

Richard Pynson: W. Skeat, *Joseph of Arimathie*. London: Early English Text Society, 1871 contains an edited version of Pynson's *Lyfe of Joseph of Armathia*. Quotes here are from the digitised version of Skeat's book at https://www.otago.ac.nz/english-linguistics/tudor/ioseph_armathia14807 (accessed 12 December 2025).

It was revived in 1971: the village website keeps a set of videos of the ceremony, at https://appletonthorn.org.uk/bawming-day/ (accessed 12 December 2025).

Irish bypass: Gordon Deegan, 'Fairy bush survives the motorway planners', *The Irish Times*, 29 May 1999, https://www.irishtimes.com/news/fairy-bush-survives-the-motorway-planners-1.190053 (accessed 12 December 2025).

BLESSING OF THE FISHERIES, LAST SUNDAY IN JUNE

100,000 fishing-related deaths every year: Pew Research, https://www.pew.org/en/about/news-room/press-releases-and-statements/2022/11/03/more-than-100000-people-die-annually-across-global-fishing-sector-new-research-shows#:~:text=WASHINGTON%20–%20More%20than%20100%2C000%20fishing,by%20The%20Pew%20Charitable%20Trusts (accessed 15 June 2025).

'all who go down to the sea in ships': Psalm 107:23.

HOLSWORTHY PRETTY MAID, EARLY JULY

Thomas Meyrick wrote his will: National Archives, PROB 11/1947/265.

SWAN UPPING, JULY

Six percent of swan deaths: Kevin Wood, 'Mute Swans and lead poisoning' in BOU blog https://bou.org.uk/blog-wood-mute-swan-lead-poisoning/, (accessed 15 April 2025)

BRADFORD MELA, MID-JULY

international media storm: for an account, see Jed Fazakarley, *Muslim Communities in England 1962–90: Multiculturalism and Political Identity*. London: Palgrave, 2017.

Bradford was now its epicentre: for a detailed account of Bradford's local politics in the 1980s, see Philip Lewis, *Islamic Britain: Religion, Politics and Identity among British Muslims*. London: I.B. Tauris, 1994; also, Kieran Connell, 'The Rushdie affair and the politics of multicultural Britain', *The Historical Journal*, 67(5) (2024), pp. 1066–88.

tamasha: Chris Newbold and Rakesh Kaushai, *Mela in the UK: A 'Travelled' and 'Habituated' Festival*. Leicester: De Montford, 2014.

a tricky and politically sensitive task: for more information, see the beautiful and authoritative account of mela by Thomas Hodgson, *Journeys of Love: Kashmiris, Music and the Poetics of Migration*. Chicago: University of Chicago Press, 2025; also, T. Hodgson, 'Multicultural harmony? Pakistani Muslims and music in Bradford', in *Music, Culture and Identity in the Muslim World*, ed. Kamal Salhi. London: Routledge, 2016, pp. 200–29.

strident plastic horns: Thomas Hodgson, 'Le mela de Bradford', *Cahiers d'ethnomusicologie. Anciennement Cahiers de musiques traditionnelles*, 27 (2014), pp. 243–60.

what image of 'the community' the mela organisers seek to convey: Elizabeth Carnegie and Melanie Smith, 'Mobility, diaspora and the hybridisation of festivity: The case of the Edinburgh Mela', in *Festivals, Tourism and Social Change: Remaking Worlds*, ed. D. Pickard and M. Robinson. Bristol: Channel View Publications, 2006, pp. 255–68.

TAMIL PILGRIMAGE TO WALSINGHAM, MAY–AUGUST

But this is a simplification of a more complicated history: see Dee Dyas, *The Dynamics of Pilgrimage: Christianity, Holy Places, and Sensory Experience*. London: Routledge, 2020.

Richard Pynson: to read the short Pynson ballad in its entirety, visit https://www.walsinghamanglicanmedieval.org.uk/pynson.htm (accessed 12 December 2025).

historians – those terrible sticklers for facts!: J. C. Dickinson, *The Shrine of Our Lady of Walsingham*. Cambridge: Cambridge University Press, 1956.

from overseas too: J. C. Dickinson, *Monastic Life in Medieval England*. Connecticut: Greenwood Press: 1961.

William Langland: *The Vision of Piers Plowman*. London and New York: J. M. Dent and E. P. Dutton, 1978, pp. 53–4.

Father Hope Patten: see P. Severn, 'A history of Christian pilgrimage', *International Journal for the Study of the Christian Church*, 19(4) (2019), pp. 323–39.

European colonialism in the region: Nira Wickramasinghe, *Slave in a Palanquin: Colonial Servitude and Resistance in Sri Lanka*. New York: Columbia University Press, 2020.

Mariyamman: Patrizia Granziera, 'Catholic and Tamil divine mothers: Mary and the village goddess', *International Journal of Asian Christianity*, 6 (2023), pp. 229–49.

the idea of a powerful female divinity: Selva J. Raj, 'Being Catholic the Tamil way: Assimilation and differentiation', *Journal of Hindu-Christian Studies*, 21(12) (2008), pp. 1–8.

accommodated the new Catholicism into these older, more established Hindu beliefs: religious patronage enabled colonial authorities to build alliances with existing groups, such as the pearl-fishing Paravas, by distributing prestige and social standing that they were denied under the Hindu caste system, though always with the ultimate aim of extracting value from their community. See Kenneth Ballhatchet, *Caste, Class and Catholicism in India 1789-1914*. London: Routledge, 1998.

Tuticorin festival: Arockiaraj Johnbosco 'Tamil Nadu: The legend of Our Lady of Sorrows', *The Times of India*, 11 August 2023. https://timesofindia.indiatimes.com/city/chennai/the-legend-of-our-lady-of-snows/articleshow/102634515.cms (accessed 12 December 2025).

EBERNOE HORN FAIR, 25 JULY

widely known for its debauchery: Anon, *A Frolick to Horn-Fair with a Walk from Cuckold's Point thro' Deptford and Greenwich* (1700); Anon, *Hey for Horn Fair: The General Market of England or Room for Cuckolds . . .* (1674).

'Cures for crack'd maiden-heads . . .': Anon, *Mercurius verax or The prisoners prognostications for the year 1675 . . .* (1675), p. 53.

'at last likely to be discontinued': Anon, 'Discontinuance of Charlton Pleasure Fair', *Morning Post*, 29 June 1869.

'If you would see Horn Fair you must walk on your way': S. Godman, 'Horn Fair', *Journal of the English Folk Dance and Song Society*, 8(2) (1957), pp. 105–08.

BONSALL HEN RACES, FIRST SATURDAY IN AUGUST

records of hen racing: John Dugdale Astley recalls racing chicks in Chichester as a young man in his late-nineteenth-century memoir, *Fifty Years of My Life in the World of Sport at Home and Abroad*. London: Hurst and Blackett, 1895.

THE BURRY MAN, SECOND FRIDAY IN AUGUST

Queen Margaret's visit: Isabel A. Dickson, 'The Burry-Man', *Folklore*, 19(4) (1908), pp. 379–87.

a scapegoat: Carole M. Cusack, 'The Burry Man Festival, South Queensferry: Warding off evil spirits, connecting with nature, and celebrating local identity', *Scottish Labour History Society*, 13 (2010), pp. 37–53.

to raise the herring: Charlotte Burne, 'The Burry-Man', *Folklore*, 20(2) (1909), p. 227; R. C. McLagan, 'The Burry-Man', *Folklore*, 20(1) (1909), p. 91.

BOYS' PLOUGHING MATCH, MID-AUGUST

pigs, goats and sheep: C. Wickham-Jones, *Orkney: A Historical Guide* (2015), p. 24.

RAS BECA, MID-AUGUST

the Rebecca Riots: Pat Molloy, *And They Blessed Rebecca: Account of the Welsh Toll Gate Riots, 1839-44*. Llandysul: Gomer Press, 1983.

newspapers across Britain: *The Northern Star*, 1 July 1843, p.6; *The Leicestershire Mercury*, 24 June 1843, p. 2; *The Ipswich Journal*, 24 June 1843, n.p.

NOTTING HILL CARNIVAL, AUGUST BANK HOLIDAY

It is 1948: I have drawn on a wide range of sources to write this opening, including: Samuel Selvon, *The Lonely Londoners*. London: Penguin, 1956, repr. 2006; George Lamming, *The Emigrants*. Ann Arbor: University of Michigan Press, 1954, repr. 1994; Colin Grant, *Homecoming: Voices of the Windrush Generation*. London: Jonathan Cape, 2019; Beryl Gilroy, *Black Teacher*. London: Faber and Faber, 2021; Stuart Hall, *Familiar Stranger: A Life Between Two Islands*. Durham, NC: Duke University Press, 2017.

Britain needs a workforce after the war: for the often cruel contradictions of British immigration policy, see Kathleen Paul, *Whitewashing Britain: Race and Citizenship in the Post-war Era*. Ithaca: Cornell University Press, 1997; Paul Gilroy, *There Ain't No Black in the Union Jack: The Cultural Politics of Race and Nation*. London: Hutchinson, 1997.

pamphlets circulated by the government: for example, H. Carberry and Dudley Thompson, 'A West Indian in England'. London: Central Office of Information, 1950.

buildings blackened by smoke: for a history of air pollution at this time that discusses accounts of London by recent immigrants, see Kiera Chapman, 'An aerial slum': Race, air pollution and the affective atmospheres of urban modernity', *Environment and Planning D*, 43(5) (2025), pp. 748–69.

You need to find a place to live: for accounts of immigrants' struggles to find housing, see D. Phillips and M. Harrison, 'Constructing an integrated society: Historical lessons for tackling black and minority ethnic housing segregation in Britain', *Housing Studies*, 25(2) (2010), pp. 221–35; J. Rhodes and L. Brown, 'The rise and fall of the "inner city": Race, space and urban policy in postwar England', *Journal of Ethnic and Migration Studies*, 45(17) (2019), pp. 3243–59.

landlords have subdivided the old Victorian blocks: for an account of Perec 'Peter' Rachman, one of the worst London landlords of this era, see Shirley Green. *Rachman*. London: Michael Joseph, 1979; and J. Davis, 'Rents and race in 1960s London: New light on Rachmanism', *Twentieth Century British History*, 12(1) (2001), pp. 69–92.

Oswald Mosley: Christopher Hilliard, 'Mapping the Notting Hill riots: Racism and the streets of post-war Britain', *History Workshop Journal*, 93(1) (2022), pp. 47–68.

a Mardi Gras ball: For a history of carnival in Trinidad, see Patrick Murphy, 'Canboulay and the negre jardin: Combat, carnival, and the city in nineteenth-century Trinidad', *Journal of Festive Studies*, 6(1) (2024), pp. 318–39; also M. Riggio (ed.), *Carnival: Culture in Action – The Trinidad Experience*. London: Routledge, 2004.

Claudia Jones: For a history of the Notting Hill Carnival, see N. Ferdinand and N. Williams, 'The making of the London Notting Hill Carnival festivalscape: Politics and power and the Notting Hill Carnival', *Tourism Management Perspectives*, 27 (2018), pp. 33–46; also D. Forbes-Erickson, 'The imperative of "human happiness"', *Angles*, 19 (2025), https://doi.org/10.4000/130fs (accessed 11 December 2025); C. Schofield and B. Jones, '"Whatever community is, this is not it": Notting Hill and the reconstruction of "race" in Britain after 1958', *Journal of British Studies*, 58(1) (2019), pp. 142–73.

Rhaune Laslett: Ernest Taylor and Moya Kneafsey, 'The place of urban cultural heritage festivals: The case of London's Notting Hill Carnival', in K. J. Borowiecki et al. (eds.), *Cultural Heritage in a Changing World*. London: Springer Nature, 2016, pp. 181–96; Margaret Busby, 'The Notting Hill Carnival has an unsung hero – Rhaune Laslett', *The Guardian*, 24 August 2014.

Costumed masquerade, or 'mas': P. Alleyne-Dettmers, 'Ancestral voices: Trevini – a case study of meta-masking in the Notting Hill Carnival', *Journal of Material Culture*, 3(2) (1998), pp. 201–21.

pretty mas: B. Alleyne, '"Peoples War": Cultural activism in the Notting Hill Carnival', *Cambridge Journal of Anthropology*, 20(1/2), 1998, pp. 111–35; P. Franco, 'The invention of traditional mas and the politics of gender', in G. Green and P. Scher (eds.), *Trinidad Carnival: The Cultural Politics of a Transnational Festival*. Bloomington: Indiana University Press, 2007, pp. 25–47.

inherently spatial: Lesley Ferris, 'Incremental art: Negotiating the route of London's Notting Hill Carnival', *Social Identities*, 16(4) (2010), pp. 519–36; G. P. Martin, 'Narratives great and small: Neighbourhood change, place and identity in Notting Hill', *International Journal of Urban and Regional Research*, 29(1) (2005), pp. 67–88.

CRYING THE NECK, AUGUST–SEPTEMBER

Caribbean is three weeks away: Community Centred Knowledge workshop, 2017. https://communitycentredknowledge.org/food-justice/ (accessed 1 February 2025).

nine meals away from anarchy: Lord Cameron of Dillington, first head of the UK Countryside Agency, 2007.

James George Frazer: *The Golden Bough*. London: Macmillan and Co., 1890.

THE HORN DANCE, WAKES MONDAY, EARLY SEPTEMBER

Ohthere: 'English translation of King Alfred's version of the *History of Paulus Orosius*', in *The Life and Works of King Alfred*, tr. R. Pauli. London: George Bell, 1902.

the indigenous Sami paid him tribute: for a brilliant discussion of the complexities of Sami representation, see Solveig Marie Wang, *Decolonising Medieval Fennoscandia: An Interdisciplinary Study of Norse–Saami Relations in the Medieval Period*. Berlin: de Gruyter Brill, 2023.

In 2020, they finally won an important legal battle: Richard Orange, 'Indigenous reindeer herders win hunting rights battle in Sweden', *The Guardian*, 23 January 2020.

the international trade network that supplied materials for specialist crafts: S. P. Ashby, A. N. Coutu and S. M. Sindbæk, 'Urban networks and Arctic outlands: Craft specialists and reindeer antler in Viking towns', *European Journal of Archaeology*, 18(4) (2015), pp. 679–704.

radiocarbon dating: for the radiocarbon dating of the horns, see Theresa Buckland, 'The reindeer antlers of the Abbots Bromley Horn Dance: A reexamination', *Lore and Language*, 3(2A) (1980), pp. 1–8. The mean radiocarbon date was AD 1065, give or take eighty years.

Nor does it have the swagger of a hunting celebration: for an account of the multitude of ways in which deer can be used in ritual celebration, see Maxim Fomin, 'Hunting the deer in Celtic and Indo-European mythological contexts', in Emily Lyle (ed.), *Celtic Myth in the 21st Century: The Gods and their Stories in a Global Perspective*. Cardiff: University of Wales, 2018.

WHITWORTH RUSHCART, WAKES WEEK, EARLY SEPTEMBER

compacted earth underfoot: suspended timber floors were largely an eighteenth-century invention. See Historic England, *Energy Efficiency and Historic Buildings: Insulating Suspended Timber Floors*. London: English Heritage, 2012; also Paul Watts and Gillian Tesh, 'Traditional Solid Ground Floors'. https://www.buildingconservation.com/articles/solid-ground-floors/solid-ground-floors.htm (accessed 12 December 2025).

Native species: a large range of species seem to have been used, from *Juncus* species to common club-rush (*Schoenoplectus lacustris*). See Anne O'Dowd, 'Green rushes under your feet! Spreading rushes in folklore and history', *Béaloideas*, 79 (2011), pp. 82–112; see also Richard Mabey, *Flora Britannica*. London: Sinclair-Stevenson, 1996; Linda Fletcher, 'Strewings', *Folk Life*, 36(1), pp. 66–71.

***Acorus calamus*:** see entry in the Botanical Society of Britain and Ireland's *Plant Atlas 2020*. https://plantatlas2020.org/atlas/2cd4p9h.4xq (accessed 12 December 2025).

Cardinal Wolsey: Timothy J. Motley, 'The ethnobotany of sweet flag, *Acorus calamus* (Araceae)', *Economic Botany*, 48(4) (1994), pp. 397–412.

Erasmus: letter 1532 to John Francis, sent from Basel on 27 December 1524, in *The Correspondence of Erasmus*, tr. R. A. B.

Mynors and Alexander Dalzell. Toronto: University of Toronto Press, 1992, p. 471.

'the Wakes': see Susan Barton, *Working-class Organisations and Popular Tourism, 1840–1970*. Manchester: Manchester University Press, 2005; Robert Poole, *Wakes Holidays and Pleasure Fairs in the Lancashire Cotton District, c.1790–1890*. PhD thesis, University of Lancaster, 1985; Patrick Joyce, *Visions of the People: Industrial England and the Question of Class, 1848–1914*. Cambridge: Cambridge University Press, 1991.

'groups of rough, half-drunken, disorderly young men': 'Saddleworth Wakes', *Huddersfield Chronicle*, 28 August 1858, quoted in Daniel Theyer, 'The Saddleworth Rushcart Festival', *The Yorkshire Journal*, 201, pp. 22–33, this citation p. 26.

Rushes also became harder to find: John Walton and Robert Poole, 'The Lancashire Wakes in the nineteenth century', in *Popular Culture and Custom in Nineteenth-century England*, ed. Robert Storch. London: Croom Helm, 1982, pp. 100–24.

wider changes afoot in the way leisure time was spent: John Walton, 'The demand for working-class seaside holidays in Victorian England', *The Economic History Review*, 34(2) (1981), pp. 249–65.

HOP HOODENING, MID-SEPTEMBER

what of the Hop Hoodening? https://wantsum-morris.org.uk/hop-hoodening/hop-hoodening-east-kents-original-hop-festival/ (accessed 26 May 2025).

a point of debate: http://hoodening.org.uk/ (accessed 26 May 2025).

PEARLY KINGS AND QUEENS HARVEST FESTIVAL, LAST SUNDAY OF SEPTEMBER

Steve Jobs: Anne Jolis, 'Steve Jobs's button phobia has shaped the modern world', *The Spectator*, 22 November 2014.

Henry Croft: Philip Carter, 'Henry Croft', in *Oxford Dictionary of National Biography*. Oxford: Oxford University Press, 2012, rev. 2017.

Pathé news reel: 'Pearlies Harvest Festival', 10 October 1963,

1776.09. https://www.britishpathe.com/asset/87035/ (accessed 12 December 2025).

Louis Dunford's song: 'The Angel (North London Forever)', RCA records, 2022. https://www.youtube.com/watch?v=wjCJv4W4kvw (accessed 12 December 2025).

As Georgie Wemyss has written: Georgie Wemyss, *The Invisible Empire: White Discourse, Tolerance and Belonging*. London: Routledge, 2009.

a Japanese ship: see Nina Edwards, *On the Button: The Significance of an Ordinary Item*. London: I. B. Tauris, 2012; for examples of white buttons found in the Thames, see Malcolm Russell, *Mudlark'd: Hidden Histories from the River Thames*. Princeton and Oxford: Princeton University Press, 2022.

The Modern Cockney Festival: Saif Osmani and Andy Green, *The Modern Cockney Manifesto*. https://moderncockneyfestival.co.uk (accessed 12 December 2025).

THE MOP FAIR, OLD MICHAELMAS DAY (AROUND 10 OCTOBER)

small circles of DNA called plasmids: B. Joseph Hinnebusch et al., 'Role of *Yersinia murine* toxin in survival of *Yersinia pestis* in the midgut of the flea vector', *Science*, 296 (2002), pp. 733–5; Wyndham W. Lathem et al., 'A plasminogen-activating protease specifically controls the development of primary pneumonic plague', *Science*, 315 (2007), pp. 509–13; Frank M Snowden, *Epidemics and Society: From the Black Death to the Present*. New Haven, CT: Yale University Press, 2019.

marmots, to human fleas: M. Green, 'The four Black Deaths', *American Historical Review*, 125(5) (2020), pp. 1601–31; K. Dean et al., 'Human ectoparasites and the spread of plague in Europe during the Second Pandemic', *Proceedings of the National Academy of Sciences*, 115(6) (2018), pp. 1304–09.

4.5 and 6 million people: there is considerable debate among historians about both the size of the population before the Black Death and the level of mortality in England. Estimates of death rates vary considerably, from 20 per cent at the lower end, to as much as 60 per cent of the population at the upper end of the spectrum.

the use of law to regulate labour: Mark Bailey, 'The implementation of national labour legislation in England after the Black Death, 1349–1400', *Economic History Review*, 78 (2025), pp. 529–52.

Mark Ormrod: *Edward III*. New Haven, CT: Yale University Press, 2012, p. 362.

The timing of this custom varied considerably depending on its location: for a list of early mop fairs, see A. Kussmaul, *Servants in Husbandry in Early Modern England*. Cambridge: Cambridge University Press, 1981. The dates of Michaelmas Day and Martinmas Day changed with calendar reform in 1752 (see Introduction). Old Michaelmas Day was 29 September; new Michaelmas Day was 10 October. Old Martinmas Day was 11 November 11, and new Martinmas Day was 22 November.

'tassel': Caroline Foley, *Of Cabbages and Kings: The History of Allotments*. London: Quarto Publishing, 2014.

***Preston Guardian*:** Quoted in Henry Ellis and John Brand, *Observations on the Popular Antiquities of Great Britain: Chiefly Illustrating the Origin of Our Vulgar and Provincial Customs, Ceremonies and Superstitions*. 1869, vol. 2, p. 456.

Mr Wyatt: quoted in Hugh Seymour Tremenheere and Edward Carleton Tufnell, *Great Britain. Commission of Employment of Children, Young Persons and Women in Agriculture*. London: Eyre and Spottiswoode, 1867, p. 62.

do not always work from fixed premises: 'Coronavirus lockdowns "catastrophic" for funfair industry say Showmen', *Travellers' Times*, 8 April 2020. https://www.travellerstimes.org.uk/news/2020/04/coronavirus-lockdowns-catastrophic-funfair-industry-say-showmen (accessed 12 December 2025).

PUNKIE NIGHT, LAST THURSDAY IN OCTOBER

Stingy Jack: For an early written version of this tale, see 'Jack O'The Lantern', *Dublin Penny Journal*, 16 January 1836, pp. 229–32; also Blane Bachelor, 'The twisted transatlantic tale of Jack O'Lanterns', *National Geographic*, 27 October 2020.

pixie lore: Museum of Witchcraft and Magic, *A History of Halloween*. Boscastle: Museum of Witchcraft and Magic, nd.

Hinton St George: for local rivalries over the origin of the custom, see K. Palmer, 'Punkies', *Folklore*, 83(3) (1972), pp. 240–4.

SAMHUINN FIRE FESTIVAL, 31 OCTOBER OR 1 NOVEMBER

Sharon Blackie: Sharon Blackie, *Greening the Hag*, Substack.com (accessed 22 June 2025).

Julius Caesar's account: Julius Caesar, *Commentarii de Bello Gallico*, 58–49 bc.

Ronald Hutton's call: Ronald Hutton, *Pagan Britain*. New Haven, CT: Yale University Press, 2013.

QUIT RENTS CEREMONY, BETWEEN 11 OCTOBER AND 11 NOVEMBER

Horwood in Staffordshire: National Archives, SP12/229, f.61.

manor of Kingsdown: National Archives, SP12/288, f.56.

MISCHIEF NIGHT, 30 OCTOBER TO 4 NOVEMBER

Mr Woodall, a former headteacher: R. Woodall, 'Mischief Night – Should We Tolerate Deliberate Vandalism?', *The Police Journal: Theory, Practice, and Principles*, October–December 1984, p. 356.

when the BBC ran a social media poll: 'Mischief Night: your view', BBC York and North Yorkshire, 3 November 2009. http://news.bbc.co.uk/local/york/hi/people_and_places/newsid_8341000/8341241.stm (accessed 12 December 2025).

SOUL-CAKING, 2 NOVEMBER

'Have mercy on all Christen soules for a soule-cake': J. Aubrey, 'Remaines of Gentilisme and Judaisme, 1686–87', in *The Folklore Society for Collecting and Printing Relics of Popular Antiquities &c*, vol. 4, ed. J. Britten (1881), p. 23.

'In comes Dick and all his men': A. Helm, 'The Cheshire Soul-Caking Play', *Journal of the English Folk Dance and Song Society*, 6(2) (1950), p. 49.

SHEFFIELD CAROLS, MID-NOVEMBER TO DECEMBER

Cecil Sharp: David Schofield, 'Cecil Sharp and English folk song and dance before 1915', *Country Dance and Song Online*, vol. 1. https://cdss.org/publications/read/cds/cds-volume-1/cecil-sharp-and-english-folk-song-and-dance-before-1915/ (accessed 12 December 2025). See also Vic Gammon, 'Introduction: Cecil Sharp and English folk music', in *Still Growing: English Traditional Songs and Singers from the Cecil Sharp Collection*, Steve Roud, Eddie Upton and Malcolm Taylor (eds). London: English Folk Dance and Song Society in association with Folk South West, 2003, pp. 2–22.

the repertoire of non-seasonal popular songs was twice the size of the Christmas one: the best source by far on the Sheffield carols is the magnificently comprehensive PhD thesis by Ian Russell, *Traditional Singing in the West of Sheffield*. PhD thesis, University of Sheffield, 1977. https://villagecarols.org.uk/articles/traditional-singing-in-west-sheffield.html (accessed 12 December 2025).

Fay Hield: *English Folk Singing and the Construction of Community*. PhD thesis, University of Sheffield, 2010.

THE MARI LWYD, 1 NOVEMBER TO MID-JANUARY

It goes by many names: Rhiannon Ifans has written a wonderful book on Welsh wassailing customs, with a detailed section on Mari Lwyd, to which I am indebted throughout this entry. It is called *Stars and Ribbons: Winter Wassailing in Wales*. Cardiff: University of Wales Press, 2022.

the date of its celebration also varies: Iorwerth C. Peate, 'Mari Lwyd: A Suggested Explanation', *Man*, 43 (1943), pp. 53–8.

buried in lime: 'Mari Lwyd, a Welsh Christmas Tradition', Amgueddfa Cymru (National Museum of Wales) blog, 14 June 2014. https://museum.wales/articles/1187/Christmas-Traditions-The-Mari-Lwyd/ (accessed 12 December 2025).

Pwnsh and Siwan: 'Mari Lwyd: Make no bones about it, the tradition is just galloping away', *FolkWales Online Magazine*, 6 December 2015.

***Ma'r Feri Lwyd yma*:** cited in Rhiannon Ifans, *Stars and Ribbons*, pp. 108–09.

'F David' of Swansea: 'Childhood horrors of the Mari Lwyd', *Country Life*, 21 March 1968, p. 677.

***Nawr grynda'r gŵr digri*:** cited in Rhiannon Ifans, *Stars and Ribbons*, pp. 122–3.

debate over the age of the Mari Lwyd: Iorwerth C. Peate (in 'Mari Lwyd: A Suggested Explanation') considered the ceremony a pre-Christian ritual, but David R. Howell argues that we should really consider two different Mari Lwyds: a lost tradition that ended in the nineteenth century, and a modern revival, which is equally legitimate and authentic as a form of intangible cultural heritage. David Howell, 'Contemporising custom: The re-imagining of the Mari Lwyd', *International Journal of Intangible Heritage*, 13 (2018), pp. 66–79.

'hobby-horse' rituals: David Jones, 'The Mari Lwyd: A Twelfth Night custom', *Archaeologia Cambrensis*, 5 (1888), pp. 389–93. For the 'grey mare' view, see E. C. Cawte, *Ritual Animal Disguise: A Historical and Geographical Study of Animal Disguise in the British Isles*. Cambridge: D. S. Brewer, 1977.

Ben Edge: *Folklore Rising: An Artist's Journey through the British Ritual Year*. London: Watkins Publishing, 2024.

THE TIN CAN BAND, FIRST SUNDAY AFTER 11 DECEMBER

***charivari*:** for a vivid account of the custom that notices the local church's involvement, and the vicar's reading of the Collect for Advent to cast out evil at the beginning of the ceremony, see the 31 December 2104 blog by Pixyled Publications, 'Custom survived: Broughton Tin Can Band'. https://traditionalcustomsandceremonies.wordpress.com/2014/12/ (accessed 12 December 2025).

Tandering: David Hopkin, 'Saint Andrew and "Tanders", Midland lacemakers' other holiday', in 'By the poor, for the rich: Lacemaking in context' (blog), 29 November 2015 https://laceincontext.com/saint-andrew-and-tanders-midland-lacemakers-other-holiday/ (accessed 12 December 2025). See also D. Hopkin, *Voices of the People in Nineteenth-century*

France. Cambridge: Cambridge University Press, 2012, p. 6.

Thomas Sternberg's 1851 account: Thomas Sternberg, *The Dialect and Folk-Lore of Northamptonshire*. London & Northampton: John Russell Smith, 1851, pp. 183–4.

***Leicester Daily Mercury*:** 'Tin can "fusiliers" defy police', 16 December 1929, p. 12, col. 2.

local Conservative: Sculthorpe is listed as an attendee of a local Conservative Association dinner in March 1930; see 'Broughton Conservative Association', *Northampton Herald*, 7 March 1930, p. 1, col. 6.

a large villa on School Hill: the notice of sale is in 'Country Notes and District News', *Northampton Mercury*, 15 January 1926, p. 3, col. 1.

Mrs Botterill: she seems to have been a well-known local character and gave several interviews to the local press on and after her 100th birthday. 'Hard work and contentment' was her recipe for a long life, along with washing in cold water, and she strongly disliked short skirts: 'I have never seen them of course, but they wouldn't do for me. They are hardly decent. I wonder girls are allowed to go on like that.' 'A Centenarian's Warning', *Northampton Mercury*, Friday 13 September 1929, p. 8, col. 2. For her opposition to the custom, see 'Broughton's centenarian now 102', *Northampton Herald*, 15 August 1930, p. 8, col. 4: 'I call it a load of rubbish and childish' was her verdict.

cup-winning football team: 'Two busloads of "bandsmen"', *Market Harborough Advertiser and Midland Mail*, Friday 27 December 1929, p. 2, cols 6–7.

£31, 14 shillings and 1½ pence: 'Money for charity', *Northampton Mercury*, 24 January 1930, p. 2, col. 3.

February 1930: 'Uproar over "kettle" parade', *Northampton Herald*, 21 February 1930, p. 6, col. 6.

'a perfect Babel': for an account of the meeting, see 'Tin cans at parish meeting', *Northampton Herald*, 14 March 1930, p. 7, col. 3.

'some less uncivilised way of honouring him': 'Spectator', in 'Town and Country Notes', *Northampton Mercury*, 2 January 1931, p. 5, col. 2.

Broughton Parish Council election of 1931: 'Notes of the week', *Northampton Mercury*, 6 November 1931.

HUNTING THE WREN, 26 DECEMBER TO 5 JANUARY

Valentine's Day: Karl P. Wentersdorf, 'The folkloristic significance of the wren', *Journal of American Folklore*, 90 (1977), pp. 192–8.

Acknowledgements

We are extremely grateful to the wonderful team at Granta, and especially to Laura Barber for her encouragement and critical eye, and to Christine Lo for her helpful advice. We are also indebted to the meticulous eye for detail possessed by our copyeditor, Mandy Woods. And our agent, Jonathan Conway, also has our sincere thanks for his advice and support.

KIERA

As someone who is in no way an experienced folklorist, I'm extremely grateful to a number of key individuals who were extraordinarily generous with their time, attention and expertise as I navigated a new and unfamiliar area. They helped me to understand the wider context of customs and saved me from a number of embarrassing errors. Any remaining mistakes, however, are of course entirely my own.

Historian Susan Barton generously offered her time and expertise on shifts in leisure cultures, which changed my view of the Whitworth Rushcart. Georgie Wemyss assisted me with the Pearly Kings and Queens and the perils that surround the idea of a white Cockney culture. Solveig Marie Wang became a valued friend and an expert correspondent on Sami culture in relation to the Abbots Bromley Horn Dance. Mark Bailey offered me the kindest feedback on the medieval history of mop fairs, and saved me from my old-fashioned, rat-dominated concept of the plague with the latest science on the subject. David Hopkin, whose work I discuss in relation to the Broughton Tin Can Band, helped me understand its clanging cacophony, as well as offering comments on my piece on Mischief Night. Nicole Ferdinand developed my grasp of the intersectionalities of carnival and Notting Hill, forcing me to complicate my account of this custom. Regina Bendix, whose book on authenticity inspired much of my writing here, offered some wise comments on the Earl of Rone.

Academic and musician Fay Hield guided me through the Sheffield carols and even endured my attempts at singing. Musician and writer Thomas Hodgson encouraged me to develop a deeper, more complex account of mela, though my piece still falls short of his beautiful research on Kashmiri cultures in the UK. Roslyn Frank helped me with the pre-history of the Whittlesea straw bear and complicated my rather simplistic understanding of race and Morris dancing with enormous patience. Ryan Powell, an expert on Gypsy and Traveller culture, offered extensive feedback in response to my entry on the Appleby Horse Fair, pointing out the fair's importance as an event that connects these two marginalised communities. Yat Ming Loo inspired me on Lunar New Year customs.

Rhiannon Ifans, whose book on wassail in Wales is a must-read, kindly gave me permission to cite her wonderful translations of the Mari Lwyd verses and caught some mistakes in my piece that would otherwise have left me red-faced. Ben Edge spent an hour chatting with me about his fascinating art and his view of customs – if you enjoyed this book, you'll love his exhibitions!

Three friends offered particularly important advice and encouragement. David Higgins, whose friendship has been important in my life for so many decades, checked through my piece on Burns Night. Katie Murphy, who is an unfailing source of inspiration, advice and kindness, picked me up when I was feeling rather despondent and helped me to understand the modern theological complexities of the Tamil pilgrimage. Yasminah Beebeejaun offered invaluable solidarity and an astute and insightful critical eye on race at a moment when her advice was most needed.

My sections of the book are for my husband, Malcolm, who has woven memories with me at many of these customs, and for my mother, whose memory sadly unravelled during its gestation.

REBECCA

I would like to thank all those kind people who have offered me their thoughts and insights into various customs featured in this book. In particular, I am grateful to William Upton, KC., David Chalk, Nigel Pullman and Gregory Jones, KC., and to Andrew Jackson of the Company of Watermen and Lightermen, all of whom provided me with helpful information regarding the customs of the City of London. Geoffrey Forster was very generous with his time and research into the operation of the Pretty Maid ceremony and of the Speccotts Charity. And Sarah Mercer entertained and enlightened me with her knowledge of, and enthusiasm for, the folklore and customs of the Isle of Man, so to her also I offer my sincere thanks. And my grateful thanks, as ever, go to Paul Brown, KC, for his unfailing support.

LULAH

My heartfelt thanks to Philip Carr-Gomm for his insights on Druidry, to Emma Carlow for inspiration and wonderful old books on corn dollies, and to Owen Shiers for our conversation about plygain. The staff at the Museum of English Rural Life in Reading were helpful and enlightening in equal measure.

I'm grateful to our agent, Jonathan Conway, for steering the book from proposal to publication, and to the team at Granta for their hard work in bringing it to life. It is always a pleasure and privilege to be edited by Laura Barber, whose wisdom and expertise tightened up many a flabby sentence in my contributions.

I'd like to dedicate my parts of the book to my pa, who died while I was writing it.

Index

[allow index 10pp]]

INDEX

INDEX

INDEX

INDEX

INDEX

INDEX